Quality Quest in the Academic Process

Edited by

John W. Harris and J. Mark Baggett

Samford University
Birmingham, Alabama

This book was organized and compiled at Samford University through a subcontract of a Fund for Improvement of Post-Secondary Education (FIPSE) grant to the Center for Assessment Research and Development at the University of Tennessee, Knoxville. FIPSE funds provided for approximately 33% of the total costs for writing and publishing of this book which in turn was 7% of the total FIPSE grant.

Published by:

Samford University
800 Lakeshore Drive
Birmingham, Alabama   35229
Phone: 205-870-2011

and

GOAL/QPC
13 Branch Street
Methuen, MA 01844-1953
Phone: 508-685-3900
Fax: 508-685-6151

CONTENTS

Contents

Contents

Introduction

John W. Harris and J. Mark Baggett
Samford University
Birmingham, Alabama

This volume captures the emergence and potential of Quality Improvement in higher education. The authors are educators, not merely "academicians," who have a professional commitment to the "academic process" in which the larger goal of learning takes place. Their "quest" represents a genuine attempt to bring about demonstrable improvement in the work they do, both incremental improvement and more dramatic breakthroughs, by using the paradigm of Quality Improvement. Their research is important because they have not merely given lip service to the concept, but have applied the tools to their work. Our title suggests this process of exploration and discovery, but it clearly acknowledges a greater potential beyond the present efforts of integrating Quality Improvement techniques into academic settings.

Quality Improvement understood as continuous improvement of processes is, on one hand, new to higher education and, on the other, a deeply ingrained tradition. For the most part, American higher education in the 1900s has insisted that quality can be assured through providing resources, i.e., credentialled faculty, admission of high ability students, library holdings, along with individual teacher assessment of student performance. In a sense, higher education relied on process resources to assure quality. But it has not assessed results of processes to determine if they are properly orchestrated.

This "resource-individual-teacher-assessment model" of quality had a greater chance of assuring quality when only a limited number of relatively capable students went to college, and when there were still traces of implicit, commonly shared standards and curricula. Postsecondary education has now become so diverse in curricula and range of students' abilities that it can no longer rely on the accepted model to assure quality.

The common response to declining standards in elementary and secondary education has been to require tests of one kind or another to identify deficient students and prevent them from being passed through. As for assessment in higher education, more than two thirds of the states have also asked state colleges and universities to conduct some type of assessment. In a few cases, such as Florida, all students are required to take a comprehensive, general education test and to make a minimal score before they can advance to upper division status. Most other states requiring assessment ask their institutions to conduct some type of program evaluation by testing samples of students using external tests, not individual-teacher-designed-and-administered-tests.

Furthermore, accrediting agencies increasingly expect member institutions and programs to conduct some form of outcome assessment. That is, they must go beyond reporting on resources, structure, faculty credentials, and library holdings to assess the educational results in terms of student attainments.

The new assessment practices, for the most part, are rooted to the paradigm of accountability to outside agencies. Assessment has not been integrated into the curriculum approval, instructional development, and administrative processes of most colleges and universities. In Quality Improvement (QI), as classically advanced by Deming, Juran, Ishikawa, and others, assessment is one phase of the continuous improvement cycle: PLAN (administrative or instructional processes)-DO-CHECK (assess)-ACT (on the assessment and then continue to)-PLAN-DO-CHECK-ACT.

The deeper paradigmatic origins of QI come from the pragmatism of "form following function," the statistical thinking and techniques of process control, and the instrumentalist view that education should not be judged by its results (i.e., worth is weighed by consequence, not by assumed intrinsic value).

While the organizational origins of QI were in manufacturing, QI is now finding its way into service industries and education. We believe it is a paradigm capable of integrating several disparate higher education movements or emphases so that they can make their optimal contributions: (1) For example, higher education governance already depends heavily on committee work; QI team techniques offer ways to improve the effectiveness, efficiency, and credibility of committee work. (2) Institutional Research has established its presence in higher education administrative structures for over the last three decades; and Total Quality Management (TQM) is inevitably driven by data. (3) Planning and program budgeting become central in deploying QI throughout a college or university. (4) In TQM, assessment becomes more than accountability to appease external agencies; it becomes the fulcrum for "Acting" to improve processes.

Objective

Believing QI has much to offer colleges and universities, we write about its potential as we understand its theory and techniques. We cannot yet write about having done it; we have only begun our journey of increasing understanding and taken the first tentative steps of practicing it. Our individual papers will, therefore, reflect the part of the elephant we happen to touch. This writing effort did not begin with any attempt to outline every aspect of higher education that QI may affect. That will come later when our experience has led us to see the full landscape more clearly and completely. For now, we represent academics—teaching faculty, administrators, and specialist consultants—describing how we believe QI can contribute to our piece of higher education.

Chapter 1

Customers: You Can't Do Without Them

Thomas E. Corts
Samford University
Birmingham, Alabama

Every one of us *is* a customer.
Every one of us *serves* customers.

We are almost as ambidextrous in our customer roles as the fellow in the old vaudeville joke. He had horses, but nothing to feed them; so he traded the horses for some hay. Slowly, he realized his new quandary in having hay but no horses. To the rescue came the new horse owner, who kindly lent him the horses to eat his hay.

No college or university (or other eleemosynary institution) can exist without serving. It is the service they perform that makes charities valuable to the public and justifies the government's granting tax exempt status, tax-deductibility of contributions, and encourages donors to support them. Contributions are essential since non-profit charities cannot *charge* enough to recover what their service actually *costs*. Peter Drucker believes that this simple fact about the source of funds—that charities' funds come from voluntary contributions, whereas profit businesses' funds derive from customers' exchanges—is what most differentiates non-profit from profit-making units. (Peter Drucker, *Managing the Non-Profit Organization: Principles and Practices*). Fulfilling its mission as a servant organization is what makes an effective charitable entity: thus, a university serves students, a hospital cares for patients, an overnight shelter helps the homeless, a soup kitchen feeds the hungry, the Boy and Girl Scouts are servants of children, and so forth. In each case, the organization justifies its existence by shaping its mission, its reason-for-being, around *serving* someone in meaningful ways. Charitable organizations can be analyzed on the basis of location, price/cost, delivery, personnel, etc., just as any other business. But the justification for both non-profit and profit firms depends on an ample supply of customers to be served.

Therefore, for all enterprises, the customer, the recipient of the service provided, is paramount. The primacy of the customer is rooted in history and tradition. Drucker points out that even thousands of years ago, generals plotted military strategy by first considering the enemy and what it was likely to do, rather than their own troops. (Drucker, *Managing the Non-Profit Organization*). The Judeo-Christian tradition follows the *schema*: "You should love the Lord with all your heart, strength, soul and mind, and your neighbor as yourself." From that principle came "The Golden Rule," "Do unto others as you would have others do unto you." That ancient principle, incorporated in various forms into many of the world's religions, inspires us to attempt to grant to others the regard in which we hold ourselves—a beginning point for the customer-conscious.

Almost four centuries before Christ, Aristotle in his *Rhetoric* stated that "It is the hearer that determines a speech's end and object." His work emphasized the audience—i.e., the *recipients* of the message—as key determinant of the success of the speaker. Aristotle's observations laid the groundwork for today's trial lawyers, politicians, advertisers and other persuaders who have become so adept at audience analysis, psychological profiling, market research—identifying the interests and inclinations of the listener in order to persuade the listener.

Native Americans are said to have originated the ethical admonition: "Do not criticize a man until you have walked a mile in his moccasins," another graphic way of counseling consideration of others. Today, Better Business Bureaus, Chambers of Commerce, governmental offices of consumer affairs, and even laws that specify consumer rights, have helped the customer become aware of the ultimate power of the consumer: the freedom to do business with whatever vendor he or she may choose. As general educational levels have risen, persons planning to exchange money for goods and services have become more sophisticated, more inclined to compare prices, terms, and value before choosing—whether acquiring an automobile, a certificate of deposit, the services of an attorney, or a university education. Therefore, smart business persons have built their businesses upon the principle that the customer should be satisfied. This concept is so intense in the public consciousness that *Business Week* Magazine has called the 1990s "the decade of the customer."

The term "customer" may meet with some resistance in academic circles. Influenced by marketing principles, my article, "Colleges Should be Consumer-Minded," appeared in *The Chronicle of Higher Education* for May 14, 1973. In the article, I stated that the college was the "seller"; education was the "product"; and the student was the "consumer." Hence, it is obvious that the primacy of the student is not a new idea. (In truth, some other term, such as "client" or "constituent" may be substituted, though neither carries quite the connotation of responsiveness and service that could be desired.) Even though the sophists of the fifth century B.C. were among the first teachers to unabashedly accept compensation for their services (an innovation for which modern-day educators can be grateful), many contemporary academics feel the term "customer" is too crass a commercial term, denoting a cash exchange. However, the education community has increasingly been forced to consider its consumers and their rights in the manner of commercial enterprises. For example, colleges and universities sponsor advertising. They are required to meet minimal consumer standards concerning refunds, truth-in-advertising, and truth-in-lending.

So even higher educational institutions should ask: how shall we satisfy the customer? Philip Kotler suggests (*Marketing for Nonprofit Institutions*) that customers' wants might be satisfied by goods (objects), services (acts), or money. In truth, higher education may speak to all three in some measure. A student enrolls in a college/university to benefit from *services*—instruction. The student probably also desires an *object*—a transcript of credit hours, a credential such as a diploma or certificate, an ROTC commission, licensure, etc. It is not uncommon for a student to expect his or her tuition dollars to yield *money*—increased compensation upon completing a degree or level of study, and, ultimately, more lifetime income than is projected on-average for non-college-degree-holders.

By definition, a customer is: "(a) one who is served"; or, (b) "one who makes, or who has the potential to make, a voluntary exchange of values in order to meet some need or want, or to influence others to do so." In a normal commercial sense, (b) is probably a sufficient definition. The concept of exchange indicates that two parties are willing to trade something to the benefit of each. (One still occasionally hears senior citizens talk about "trading"—i.e., "doing business"—at a certain store.) The (a) definition, "one who is served," is necessary when speaking about charities and non-profits, because many charitable transactions are by nature one-sided. A soup kitchen in a depressed area may feed the needy, hungry and homeless, receiving almost nothing in exchange; perhaps, not even "thank you."

The *Oxford English Dictionary* cites two definitions of customer that seem pertinent: "One who frequents any place of sale for the purpose of purchasing; . . . a buyer, purchaser." A second definition is: "A person with whom one has dealings. . . . " Particularly, the latter definition should be acceptable to even the most traditional academic.

Every enterprise that involves more than one person has both internal and external customers. Peter Drucker says that "Practically everybody has more than one customer, if you define a customer as a person who can say no." (Drucker, *Managing the Non-Profit Organization*) Internal customers are those persons or units within the organization that interact, and depend upon another person or unit within the organization for some particular service. With a business, purchasing, shipping and receiving, payroll, marketing, are all interdependent; each interacts and is a customer of the other, the success of the whole relating in some measure to the success of the various parts. Similarly, a college/university's history department, admissions office, alumni office, housekeeping, trustees, faculty, for example, are all linked in various ways. Each is depended upon for some key function. Strength in one area can by cancelled out by shoddiness in another area. Each unit is a customer of the other in some manner.

All the internal customers know the institutional mission and work together to fulfill it to serve the external customers, those outside the organization who may potentially make a value exchange, or influence others to do so. For a college, external customers might include among others: current and prospective students, current and prospective donors, the media, high school counselors, parents, governmental and regulatory agencies, the business community, suppliers. A college or university probably has more than a thousand categories of customers.

Assuming that internal customers can work together, to stay in business an enterprise has to attract external customers who desire the goods or services offered. Customers want to make exchanges that benefit them. The enterprise wants to make exchanges from which it benefits. Obviously, the two would be at a perpetual standoff if some viable win/win, mutually advantageous exchange could not be arranged. The challenge then to the business enterprises, whether profit or non-profit, is to so structure its product of service to meet the customer's desires and to afford the customer satisfaction. Theodore Levitt of Harvard has written: "Customers don't buy things . . . they buy betterness. To create betterness requires knowing what customers believe betterness to be. This precedes all else in business." (Levitt, *The Marketing Imagination*). Customers' decisions about what to buy, when to buy, which product or service to buy, are often complex, giving rise to market research, customer satisfaction surveys, products focus groups, and product testing. We know a great deal about consumers, but predicting their behavior is a less-than-exact science. Among well-known attempts to catalog human requirements is Abraham Maslow's "Hierarchy of Human Needs," which Maslow posed in 1943. Some are physiological and some are social; some are probably innate and some learned. We are all a bundle of needs and wants, but also desires, lusts, demands, hopes, dreams, aspirations, and yearnings.

Since we all do not have the same preferences, needs and desires, the marketplace tends to develop multiple approaches, a variety of appeals. In theory, the consumer is well-served by a multiplicity of offerings from which selection can be made. Thus, a 30,000 student, urban university with almost open admissions, graduate and professional programs, a multicultural student body, low or no tuition, and little on-campus housing, will serve very different customers than a 1200 student, religious, small-town college without graduate or professional programs, admitting only high-SAT scoring students, charging very high tuition. Since each customer has a distinctive matrix of needs, wants, hopes, expectations, the customer is well-served by the ability to choose. If an institution listens to customers, it can incorporate into its mission and program those features its customers prefer.

Drucker states that "strategies begin with research and research and more research. They require organized attempts to find out who the customer is, what is of value to the customer, how the customer buys. You don't start out with your product but with the end, which is a satisfied customer." He concludes: "Non-profit people must respect their customers and their donors enough to listen to *their* values and understand *their* satisfactions." (Drucker, *Managing the Non-Profit Organization*).

The Cadillac Division of General Motors Corporation won the Malcolm Baldrige Award for Quality. In explaining some of its strategies for meeting customers' needs and preferences, an official of Cadillac explained that for years they built cars as management thought they should be built. Subsequently, they realized that their dealers, who sold and serviced the autos and supported the warranty, actually had a better sense of what their cars should be, so they initiated a process of meeting with representative dealers to determine how best to design their cars. But recently they realized: how better to know buyer wants, needs and preferences than to ask the customer? So, Cadillac developed an extensive process of surveying men and women buyers and potential buyers in order to build the car their customers desired.

In recent years, colleges and universities have been drawn to the issue of effectiveness, as legislatures and taxpayers, supporting denominations and foundations have asked, "What are we getting for our investment? How do we know whether what we are doing is making a difference? Are our institutions doing a quality job?" In the face of global competitiveness and troubling statistical evidence, colleges and universities (as well as K-12 institutions) have looked for ways to demonstrate their effectiveness. They have relied upon reputation, admission test scores, size of endowment, percentage of Ph.D.s on the faculty and other generalized information for support, even though those factors may be incidental to the central issue: How and how much and in what ways does our educational service benefit the student customer and society, as a secondary customer?

For many educators, this reality has been reluctantly confronted out of the insistence of accrediting bodies (of which the Commission on Colleges of the Southern Association of Colleges and Schools has been a strong leader) and state legislatures insisting that institutions demonstrate effectiveness and assessment of results. Still, many university administrators, along with other non-profits, have felt themselves insulated from a key component of modern management philosophy, as spoken by a corporate chief executive. "Quality is what the customer says it is—it is not what an engineer or marketeer or general manager says it is. If you want to find out about your quality, go out and ask your customer. He is the one most affected by your product's quality on a daily basis." (Armand V. Feigenbaum, "Better Than the Rest," *Chief Executive*, April 1992)

Higher education during the 1960s was violently made aware of the student's centrality in the higher education task. However, the torch of customer concern is being carried in the 1990s, not by revolutionary students, but by the business community. Six business chief executives challenged college and university leaders in the December 1991 *Harvard Business Review*, stating in an open letter: "We believe business and academia have a shared responsibility to learn, to teach, and to practice total quality management. If the United States expects to improve its global competitive performance, business and academic leaders must close ranks behind an agenda that stresses the importance and value of TQM." They went on to say that "widespread adoption of TQM is moving too slowly to meet the challenge."

Higher education has a remarkable opportunity to model for its customers high standards of responsiveness. In the "Decade of the Customer," do we really have an alternative?

Thomas Corts is President of Samford University.

Chapter 2

Key Concepts of
Quality Improvement for Higher Education

John W. Harris
Samford University
Birmingham, Alabama

Caveats

Someone should and I am sure will try to write a *summa—Continuous Quality Improvement in Higher Education*. This is not it! I am still trying to grasp the "key elements" of "quality control, assurance, and improvement," and at the same time also trying to apply it to the leading and managing of Samford University while I am still learning it. So don't expect too many answers or an integrated theoretical thesis with a complete and pilot-tested plan for infusing quality improvement into institutional planning and management, curriculum planning and evaluation, instructional improvement, and faculty development. Because quality improvement appears to require and thrive in collaborative environments where fear has been driven out or greatly diminished, I am recklessly going to assume collaboration is honored and fear is reduced here.

So I invite you to the collaborative quest of increasing our understanding of quality improvement and how it applies to higher education. At this point in my search, my understanding is fragmented. I'm sure some of the fragmentation is due to my own limitations, particularly in "statistical thinking." But the field of "quality" is itself fragmented; I suspect healthily so because it is dynamic and growing. While it includes, it is not *just* inspection, quality control, or even quality assurance. Even the "master" himself, W. Edwards Deming, at 91 wants to learn. A footnote on the first page of his presentation, "Foundation for Management of Quality in the Western World," given at the July 1989 meeting of the Institute of Management Sciences in Osaka, indicates he is still open: "Comments and help appreciated." In his seminars given through George Washington University's Continuing Engineering Education Division, Deming frequently asks specialists, such as psychologists, to present new approaches for some aspect of quality improvement.

Furthermore, Deming fascinatingly speaks of "profound knowledge" characterized by knowledge of variation, primacy of theory, and judging any information system by its ability to predict future occurrences (Deming 1989). His latest paper on "profound knowledge" of which I am aware treats the four interrelated parts of "profound knowledge": (1) Appreciation for a system, (2) Statistical theory (theory of variation), (3) Theory of knowledge, and (4) Psychology (Deming, 1990). And he champions education and self-improvement on every hand; for example, the thirteenth of his Fourteen Points for moving the U.S. out of its economic crisis is "Institute a vigorous program of education and self-improvement" (Deming 1986, p. 24).

Quality improvement rests on increased understanding and insight using all the powers of statistics and scientific knowledge and approaches. It is not an "instant pudding" solution as Deming is fond of saying. It is not another set of nifty cliches amenable to evangelistic presentations. It is a body of theory and techniques that rests on rational thought and empirical tools, subject itself to improvement through inquiry and analysis. So on its face, it should invite, not repulse academics.

"Quality improvement" stretches from statistical process control to philosophies of human nature to theories of leadership to corporate planning. At this point in its evolution, it seems too broad to be captured by and integrated into a unified theory and consistent collection of techniques.

Nevertheless, understanding that some of you will want a more systematic summary of where and how this "quality improvement" trend fits with assessment in higher education than I will provide you, I refer you to Daniel Seymour's "Beyond Assessment Managing Quality in Higher Education" which I have only as an unpublished paper. (See Seymour in References for an address.) Seymour's paper summarizes the evolution of industrial quality, the approaches taken by higher education to achieve quality assurance, and suggests generally how the academy can creatively use quality improvement concepts and techniques.

The following notes are only that. They represent my effort to outline the "key concepts" of quality improvement, as I understand them, as they may be related to colleges and universities.

Customer Orientation

Quality improvement and planning is driven by a deep understanding of and commitment to customer needs. For me, the characteristic that distinguishes "quality planning" from other planning approaches is its intense, empirical focus on customer needs.

Thomas E. Corts, Samford's President, named the Samford quality effort Student First Quality Quest. At my request, he has written and presented the paper "From One Customer to Another" in which he identified the following historic roots of "Customer orientation":

> Aristotle's *Rhetoric* "It is the hearer that determines a speech's end and object."

> American Indian saying "Do not criticize a man until you've walked a mile in his moccasins."

> Golden Rule "So in everything, do to others what you would have them do to you, for this sums up the Law and the Prophets." (Cited by Corts, 1990, pp. 1-2)

> The *Oxford English Dictionary* traces the word 'customer' to a person who hangs around a place expecting to make a purchase and, thus, getting accustomed to a place. So for us, a customer is one expecting to make an exchange of money for goods or services, an exchange the customer perceives as meeting some wants or needs. The vendor offers to convey ownership of a material object, or to perform some service. The vendor is free to manufacture, package, warrant and represent the goods or services in any manner that is legal. However, it is in his best interest to develop and present his goods or services in accordance with the buyer's preferences. The buyer holds ultimate power in the ability to buy or not to buy a particular object or service and to choose which vendor, if any. (Corts, 1990, p. 4)

A physician is not judged by how the superficial and surface desires of the patient are met; rather he or she is judged by how well the patient's needs are determined and met. Diagnosis of a malady means having a profound knowledge of many interacting variables and the predicted consequences of the malady if untreated and the consequences of various medications and treatments. Paul Batalden, a physician, writing about the knowledge health care providers should have of their customers, cites Barbara McClintock's biography: She said her work became meaningful when she learned to "think like corn." Her biographer described this as "a feeling for the organism." (Batalden, 1990, p. 8) University educators must enter the mindset of students and the world in which they will use their university knowledge and skills to understand their short- and long-term needs.

Curricula and teaching must be driven by students' needs rather than what professors want to teach without regard to the student needs. Analyses of student needs should include students' present interests as well as knowledge of late adolescent and young adult psychology. Furthermore, such analyses should also include the "professional," considered judgment of faculty, administration, and trustees of student long-term needs. Because educators are adding their experience and understanding of long-term needs to balance against possible short-term interests of students, they should strive to focus on true student needs rather than rationalizing needs that allow them to teach what they wish.

Who are the customers? How are they identified?

Juran: " [F]ollow the product to see whom it impacts. Anyone who is impacted is a customer." (Juran, 1988, p. 24)

Juran suggests using a flow chart to track to the customers and that they be divided as follows:

1. A relative few ('vital few'), each of whom is of great importance to us.
2. A relatively large number of customers, each of whom is only of modest importance to us (the 'useful many') (Juran, 1988, p. 26).

The "Useful Many and Vital Few" in business means a few customers account for a disproportionate number of sales dollars. Is this concept applicable to higher education? The way many institutions support athletes suggests to me that the concept is not foreign to us. Are Honors students the Vital Few? Who are the Useful Many? Do we actually treat all students the same? Each institution has its Vital Few and its Useful Many, given its mission, particular constituencies, and cultural ethos. Quality planning requires the identification of the Vital Few and Useful Many and of their needs and expectations in priority order.

Higher education will have several difficulties with a customer orientation. While students are prime customers of colleges and universities, they are also their "raw material," "suppliers," "co-processors," and "products." How can quality equal "student satisfaction" when its very process by design effects discomfort with conventional thinking, stretches the mind, and creates enough anxiety to force one to go beyond old performance levels? A Princeton theological professor is reported to have said to a ministerial student after hearing a graduating sermon, "You're too bright to be so certain."

If university faculty and staff think of student *needs* rather than just *satisfactions*, or *long-term* satisfactions rather than immediate ones, customer orientation takes on a different color. Furthermore, a customer orientation is powerfully effective in planning. Faculty and administrators should sincerely try to put the students' long-term needs ahead of their own interests, i.e., teaching one's dissertation or developing programs for ambition's sake.

Planning then becomes the most rational way to meet customer needs. Deming says a rational plan "requires prediction concerning conditions, behavior, comparison of performance of each of two procedures or materials." (1990, p. 9)

Constancy of Purpose

The first of Deming's fourteen points is **Create constancy of purpose toward improvement of product and service, with the aim to become competitive and to stay in business, and to provide jobs** (Deming, 1986, p. 23).

The question we must relentlessly ask is, "What does society need from higher education?" The aim is to make universities' systems and processes congruent with society's most fundamental need for universities (Batalden, July 6, 1990).

Quality improvement begins and ends with a continuing search for a profound understanding of customers' needs. This calls for intensive inquiry through scientific analysis and informed judgment of society's needs, short- and long-term.

Continuous Improvement

The effort to make "processes" congruent with "customer needs" is implemented through the famed P (plan) D (do) C (check) A (act on assessment or checking) cycle (see Figure 1). For example, a new course is planned to meet student needs. The course is taught (Do), and its results "checked" in terms of "student" needs. When the "checking" reveals that either identified "needs" were not met or had been misunderstood, appropriate "action" is taken to revise the course.

Ideally, this Shewhart-Deming improvement cycle rolls continuously in every "process" throughout the institution, reflecting "constancy of purpose" toward improvement of every service and product. "Constancy" not only means continuity over time but throughout the organization. So an institution is understood as a series of interlocking "processes." Each process has "suppliers" and "customers."

Imai in *Kaizen* points to this continuous, forever improvement of every process as the reason a visitor returning to a Japanese plant finds it completely different. In contrast, Japanese visitors to Western plants are amazed to find them essentially unchanged after a decade. Imai believes

American and European managers preoccupy themselves with dramatic innovations while neglecting continuous improvement in processes. By neglecting small incremental change, even the gains from the innovations erode (Imai, 1986, pp. 1-2).

PDCA and Course Improvement

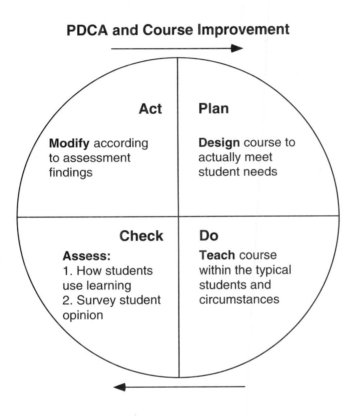

Figure 1 The Plan, Do, Check, Act (PDCA) Cycle

The task of institutional leadership and management is to orchestrate the processes toward commonly shared and understood goals. Deming (1990) describes cooperation among components of an organization as follows:

> The performance of any component is to be judged in terms of its contribution to the aim of the system, not for its individual production or profit, nor for any competitive measure. Some components may operate at a loss to themselves, for optimization of the whole system, including the components that take a loss (p. 5). Any system that results in a win, lose structure is suboptimized (p. 6).

The aim is to optimize the effectiveness of every process. But in an MBO system, one manager may meet his or her Objectives at the expense of other managers failing to meet theirs; "sub-optimization" results. For example, the Admissions Office may meet its quota-objective by admitting students unable to benefit from the instructional processes of a campus.

This focus on continuous improvement of every process to meeting internal as well as external customer needs requires us to change the way we think of organizational structure. The static, vertical command and authority structure gives way to a fluid one of continuously improving, interlocking processes.

Leadership

Why have managers? Deming says:

> For optimization, a system must be managed. Management's responsibility is to strive toward optimization of the system, and to keep it optimized over time. (1990, p. 4)

Deming also believes the leader's task is to remove barriers from the workplace that keep the worker from taking pride in his or her work. He assumes most people want to do the right thing and to take pride in their work.

If teachers and researchers are having about the same results across time, they are in a predictable system. Common causes rather than special causes account for their performance. Major changes in performance will come only through changing the system in which they work, not through exhortations to work harder or smarter or through individual rewards and punishments.

Management must be theory based according to Deming because:

> The theory of knowledge helps us to understand that management in any form is prediction. . . . Management acts on a causal system, and on changes in the causes. (1990, p. 2)

What should leaders do? Improve processes. This is not done by carrot and stick rewards and punishments of individuals. It begins by sorting out "common" and "special" causes of variation in a process (Nolan and Provost, 1990). The variation within control limits can only be reduced by changing the process because it results from common causes. Those variations not within the control limits result from special causes. No changes in the process will affect special causes, and dealing with special causes will not affect variation resulting from common causes.

Deming describes the two classical mistakes management makes in attempting to improve processes as follows:

Mistake 1. To treat as a special cause any outcome, fault, complaint, mistake, breakdown, accident, shortage, when actually it resulted from common causes. (Tampering)

Mistake 2. To attribute to common causes any outcome, any fault, complaint, mistake, breakdown, accident, shortage, when actually it came from a special cause (1990, p. 8).

Assume there are ten sections of basic mathematics and the students of nine instructors demonstrate similar achievements time after time. The tenth instructor's student achievements are consistently above or below the upper or lower limits of control of the other nine; the tenth instructor is not a part of the process of the other nine. Changes in the performance of the students of the nine professors will come as the common causes within their process are changed. The tenth instructor needs special attention.

The task of the department chair is to determine when instructional systems are in or out of control. For processes in control, the administrator aims to help instructors identify common, root causes of variation and to correct them. He or she serves the instructors by assisting them in understanding and changing the common causes of variation in their instructional processes. If the tenth instructor's students consistently test below the level of the others, the department chair works with him or her to identify the special causes of their different results. The same is true if the tenth instructor's students' performance consistently exceeds that of the other nine. What are the special causes of these consistently unusual results?

Hull, a theologian and Provost at Samford, sees "servant leadership" as the type of leadership required in quality improvement. He says Christ inverted the old view of top-down authority through the priest, father, and general. Christians are admonished by Paul: "Do nothing out of selfish ambition or vain conceit, but in humility consider others better than yourselves. Philippians. Each of you should look not to your own interests, but to the interests of others." Philippians 2:3-4 (NIV).

Christians are to follow Christ's example of emptying themselves (verse 7). Hull says the original meant "emptying himself of self" (Hull, 1990). The more leaders can put themselves out of the way to see the circumstances and needs of those with whom they work, the more they will be able to empower their colleagues to identify the barriers in their work environment that prevent them from taking pride in their work.

Statistical Thinking

Understanding variation is central to understanding quality improvement theory and techniques. Ishikawa (1985) summarizes the centrality of statistical variation as follows:

- In every work there is dispersion.
- Data without dispersion are false data.
- Without statistical analysis (quality and process analysis), there can be no effective control.
- QC begins with a control chart and ends with a control chart.
- Without stratification, there can be no analysis or control.
- Ninety-five percent of the problems in a company can be solved by the seven tools of QC.
- Statistical methods must become common sense or common knowledge to all engineers and technicians (p. 197).

Ishikawa defines the seven basic tools of quality improvement as follows:

1. Pareto Chart. The principal of the vital few and trivial many (or "many others").
2. Cause and Effect diagram. (This is not precisely a statistical technique.)
3. Stratification.
4. Check Sheet.
5. Histogram.
6. Scatter Diagram. (Analysis of correlation through the determination of median; in some instances, use of binomial probability paper.)
7. Graph and control chart (Shewhart control chart) (p. 198).

Distinguishing between common and special causes of variation is critical.

Variation in the performance of people is a result of common causes (in the system) and special causes attributable to the individual or the special causes outside of the individual's control. Obviously, it is important that the supervisor differentiate between the different types of causes. Without this perspective, it is easy to attribute all the cause of variation in people's performance to the individuals themselves and ignore the effects of the system. The forced ranking of people in an organization from highest to lowest based on some measure of performance is an example of the failure to consider the impact of common causes on individual performance (Nolan & Provost, 1990).

Deming's challenge to the performance reviewers and merit payers:

Solve: $P + S = M$ (With P as the only known)
P = performance of the individual
S = effects of the system
M= merit

Observations

It's not just a numbers game!

Deming observes that administrators often manage by numbers because they know how to count but do not know the work (Deming, 1986, p. 55). He also cites his colleague and friend Lloyd Nelson, who said the most important numbers about an organization are not only unknown but unknowable (Deming, 1986, p. 20). Deming is not Thorndike, believing, if it exists, it can be measured.

Funds for QIP in Higher Education.

Florida Power & Light has given the University of Miami significant funds to allow business and engineering faculty to learn about quality and to develop modules on quality to include in their courses. Banta, at the University of Tennessee-Knoxville, has a FIPSE grant to help us explore the application of quality improvement theory and techniques to higher education. But as far as I know, no institution has received major support from a foundation or government agency to pioneer an attempt to infuse continuous quality improvement into its academic and administrative processes.

No instant pudding.

Some say it takes ten years to make quality improvement normative in an organization's culture. Quality improvement consultants and training are in great demand in business and industry and the costs are high compared to what educational institutions are accustomed to paying. Furthermore, learning, adapting, and infusing quality improvement demand considerable energy and time added to that required for regular administrative chores.

Let's not slogan quality to death.

"Quality" will likely take the place of "excellence" in many slogans and on many signs. Some may opt for the words and not the pain. But I believe the long-term gains for those who learn and do it will more than compensate for the front-end costs of time, energy, and money.

QI and Japanese Higher Education.

Ellen Chaffee, Vice Chancellor for Academic Affairs of the North Dakota State Board of Higher Education, has taken a pioneering interest in applying quality improvement to higher education. She has developed a small but growing network of kindred spirits. In the most recent edition (July 3, 1990) of the network's newsletter, *Total Quality Management In Postsecondary Education*, she closed with the following summary of the use of TQM (total quality management) in Japanese universities:

> I had the privilege of spending two hours with Professor Masao Kogure in Tokyo a month ago at the Cambridge Corporation offices of Masaaki Imai. It was Kogure's 75th birthday. He won the Deming Prize for Individuals in 1951, is a Fellow of ASQC, and is internationally known for his work with service industries. My primary purpose was to learn about TQM in Japanese higher education.

> Kogure noted that every time TQM sought to enter a new industry, it encountered resistance we're not like the industry that is already using it. Moreover, once a company in a given industry has won the Deming Prize, other companies don't want to appear to be copying that company. So if they go into TQM, they call it something else.

> He said that, while professors love to teach and consult on TQM, no Japanese university is using it. Ishikawa was a university president for seven or eight years, and Kogure said, "I heard he tried it, but . . . he died." He cited professorial autonomy as a key stumbling block, and recommended using a different name for TQM, one that would be comfortable for professors. Drawing on his experiences with service industries, he recommends (a) start with the tools, then the managements side, (b) use quality circles, (c) expect tools to be more helpful for internal relations—those who deal directly with customers in service industries have so many unique encounters that tools have limited value for them, (d) use the "new 7 tools," with the relational diagram expected to be especially helpful, and (e) get all people in the university to focus on a single purpose, processes, and results.

Conclusion

If an educator is looking for a nifty new program to produce immediate, painless results to get quick attention, QI is not his or her ticket. On the other hand, for the educator interested in long-term improvement or even survival with integrity, QI is a powerful paradigm to focus and integrate strategic planning, assessment, faculty and instructional development, and administrative leadership. As for the Samford administrative team and myself, we believe QI's long-term benefits will greatly exceed its costs in time, energy, and money.

References

Batalden, Paul B. "Organizationwide Quality Improvement In Health Care." To be published in *Topics in Health Record Management.*

Chaffee, Ellen Earle. *Total Quality Management In Postsecondary Education.* North Dakota State Board of Higher Education, July 3, 1990.

Corts, Thomas E. "From One Customer To Another." Paper presented at the Samford University Quality Improvement Seminar, Birmingham, Alabama, February, 1990.

Deming, W. Edwards. "A System Of Profound Knowledge." May 11, 1990 (Unpublished).

Deming, W. Edwards. "Foundation for Management of Quality in the Western World." Given at a meeting of the Institute of Management Sciences in Osaka, Japan, July 24, 1989.

Deming, W. Edwards. *Out Of The Crisis.* Boston: Massachusetts Institute of Technology, 1986.

Hull, William E. "Leadership For Quality Improvement." Paper presented to participants at the Samford University Quality Improvement Seminar, February 16-17, 1990.

Imai, Masaaki. *Kaizen: The Key to Japan's Competitive Success.* New York: Random House Business Division, 1986.

Ishikawa, Kaoru. *What Is Total Quality Control? The Japanese Way.* Engelwood Cliffs, NJ: Prentice-Hall, Inc., 1985.

Juran, J.M. *Juran On Planning For Quality*. New York: The Free Press, 1988.

Nolan, Thomas W. and Lloyd P. Provost. "Understanding Variation." *Quality Progress*, May, 1990, pp. 70-78.

Seymour, Daniel. "Beyond Assessment: Managing Quality in Higher Education." Prepared for AERA, April 19, 1990. (HERI UCLA, 405 Hilgard Ave., Los Angeles, CA 90024-1521).

John Harris is Assistant to the Provost for Quality Improvement and Orlean Bullard Beeson Professor of Education at Samford University.

Chapter 3

How Quality Improvement Teams Work to Improve Processes in Departments and Administrative Units

Susan G. Hillenmeyer
Belmont University
Nashville, Tennessee

Quality teams are one element of a much larger strategic effort. The broader scope includes organization-wide knowledge, a quality management strategy, and systems-focused leadership. The application of a quality management strategy to institutions of higher learning is new; teams alone will not accomplish the transformation for quality, but without them, the action of transformation is impossible.

Quality in an organization may be born in the hearts and minds of senior leadership, but it *lives* in the work of teams. Quality teamwork is founded on committed leadership, education for all, carefully-planned strategy, and a culture for change. But without the efforts of people in all areas working together as teams, the quality transformation is not possible. Ishikawa (1985), famous for his work in quality in Japan as well as in this country, went so far as to say, "If there are no team activities, there is no quality control." Many think of quality teams as made up of the "workers" in an organization, those people who are "in the ranks." Quality teams work in *all* areas, and membership crosses traditional organizational chart lines.

A Caveat

It is important that readers understand the aim of this paper. References abound with advice to those who would begin QI (Quality Improvement) in higher education. In many cases, the advice comes from those who have not tried QI, or from those who suggest a manufacturing model will just transfer automatically to schools. This paper suggests that as with any change, struggle is a part of it; there is no "best" way. The basis for this work is a three-year strategic QI effort at Belmont University, almost two years of team operations, a few failures and several ongoing successes. Study of other institutions has been helpful, and we are grateful for their continued information sharing. There is a spirit of collegiality among those of us who study and learn together to find ways to make our institutions better through QI. This, then, is not *the* way, but *a* way, in hopes that others may benefit from what we learned.

Quality Teams Are Different

Setting up project teams or committees to solve problems is not new in higher education. What *is* new to colleges and universities is teams trained together in decision making based on collecting and understanding data. These teams differ from traditional college committees. Often, we in higher education administration have "filled the square" by allowing committees, task forces, and study groups only token input into decision making.

Quality teams are different because members have been empowered specifically to change processes in which they work. Senior leadership of the institution empowers teams, listens to them, makes organizational decisions on the basis of team data, and recognizes their efforts.

Committees usually have 10 to 15 members; teams usually have no more than seven. We in colleges often assume that if "the best and the brightest" are in a meeting together, they will come up with the best possible solutions. Quality teams, on the other hand, have a *method* by which they operate, collect data, and make changes.

Traditional college committees may bog down when they spend months studying and making recommendations only to be denied opportunity to make a change. The role of quality teams includes ongoing feedback loops with senior leadership; surprise recommendations are rare. Real value of any team comes when its contribution improves, or "optimizes," the institution through improved processes and customer service.

Two Types of Teams

There are two kinds of improvement teams, cross-functional and functional. This paper examines *only* the work of functional teams in departments and administrative units, but there is real need for both kinds of teams. One is not better or more sophisticated than the other; they serve different purposes. Functional, or within-work-area teams, focus on processes largely confined to individual areas. Of course, no department or administrative unit really operates in isolation. Processes "bump up" against other processes, providing input to, and receiving output from, those processes.

Most of the work done on any campus is cross-functional. Eventually, many quality teams will cross departmental or work-area boundaries. In the beginning, however, our teams are encouraged to select work processes over which they have control, or "own," within their work areas. Learning with members of one's own work group lets teams practice and effect changes together.

One particular advantage of department or office teams is that existing inter-departmental barriers do not hinder early team efforts. Team members know and already work with others on the team. They also know well the work they have in common and the inter-relatedness of what goes on in their area. An informal survey of other institutions having QI teams indicates work area teams may experience earlier positive results than do cross-functional teams.

Educating Teams

"Teamwork is not just telling people you want them to work together to solve problems," says Peter Reid in *Well Made in America* (1990, p. 169). Teamwork must be designed. The "best" quality education approach is centered around ways to improve work processes and the systems that contain them; it is *not* just an approach centered around learning quality theory and tools. Adults will learn things they believe will help them do their work, things that help them solve problems in daily work life. The training built around solving basic quality issues—the course that gives principles and practices for improving how people work—has much more impact than the dissemination of general theories for discussion.

We in colleges prepare people to absorb and integrate experience, but we do not always supply the experience. When members of a team *learn* together, each individual adds know-how, creativity, and specific skills to the team knowledge. What is known about adult learning suggests training intact work groups is most advantageous. People in a department or unit who trained together expected a team formed as the next step. Momentum and value seemed to be lost when new skills and abilities were not used soon after training was completed.

Teams need common knowledge and language about quality process improvement. Members are trained in analysis, synthesis, group participation, issue identification, problem solving, teamwork, statistical techniques, and other quality improvement tools. *How* team members should be trained can be debated. Method, in fact, may be idiosyncratic to each institution. Several organizations use cascading training; others rely on large-group instruction followed by team activity; others form teams and train members as they need a particular tool or skill while they work on a process.

At Belmont, we chose to work with smaller groups and complete the first level of training before forming functional teams. Our goal is common language, understanding, and "alignment of team members." In his masterful work, *The Fifth Discipline*, Peter Senge (1990) comments on team learning. He suggests *alignment* of a team is critical for "commonality of purpose, a shared vision, and understanding of how to complement one another's efforts" (p. 234). Part of the alignment can come from training in which the very act of learning together helps teams maximize their strengths.

The following are suggestions for department and work unit team training:

- Whenever possible, teach intact work groups
- Limit class size
- Involve senior leadership (Senior university leadership teaches Deming's 14 Points to all classes.)
- Have clear desired outcomes
- Create a climate for learning — no fear, trusting, collaborative
- Use knowledge of adult learning cycle — experiencing, processing, generalizing, applying
- Promote methods of quality — PDCA on learning processes, collect data, seek causes, communicate two-way
- Focus on long-term strategy: *coach* (not just deliver instruction); be process-centered; aim for win/win

Starting Right

Teams need "launching." Teamwork requires cultural change, particularly in academic environments where committee structure and "the way we've always done things" can hamper progress. Therefore, chartering teams is important because it provides a sense of accountability, mutual cooperation, and sense of purpose.

Teams, like institutions, live by their stories. Ceremonies to charter teams and celebrate their successes become part of QI. Celebration is not only good for team morale, it is good for QI in the entire institution. There is real power in team celebration; certainly the chartering by the president and steering committee can be a memorable event for teams.

Choosing the Issue or Project

In most cases, QI functional teams are problem-solving or issue-solving teams. Teams receive issues in two ways. Sometimes, an advisory group such as a steering committee *selects* a functional team to work on an issue they perceive as important to the institution. Most often, however, choice of an issue is collaborative. Steering committee, department or unit leadership, and members of the group come together to select an area for improvement. (Notice the word *issue* instead of *problem*. Although it probably does not make a difference in the results of teamwork, we prefer *issue* and *opportunity for improvement*.)

Forcing a topic on a team is counterproductive. It becomes another example of "do what I say" instead of collaborative effort. Joint selection and early guidance help avoid problems. The bent is to select much larger projects than teams can manage easily. Early on, the steering committee and facilitators can help teams narrow the focus and select improvement projects.

Our broad criteria at Belmont include being sure the process is important to the work of a given area and has a positive impact on the customers of the institution. Later in quality efforts, alignment of processes, identification of strategic processes, and *Hoshin* planning help determine team projects.

Several teams use the very helpful book by Peter Scholtes, *The Team Handbook* (1988). Scholtes gives readers common errors in selecting projects:

- Selecting a process no one is really interested in
- Selecting a desired solution instead of a process
- Selecting a process in transition
- Selecting a system to study, not a process (p. 3-2)

It is tempting to limit functional quality teams to administrative parts of the organization. Granted, working on processes in accounting, mail delivery, telephone handling, and housekeeping seems easier than studying how to use quality methodology to improve instruction in courses. If quality is to improve higher education, the quality improvement strategy is applicable to *all* our processes, including instruction.

Team Members

Putting people together and calling them a team will not work. People enter teams just as they enter organizations, asking themselves, "Where do I belong?" and "What difference do I make to the team?" Take care in selecting a team; avoid the pitfall of selecting only those who are not as busy as others. Volunteers, people who really want to serve, should be considered seriously. Also, choose people who *do* the work, not just those who supervise it. The most vocal complainants about a process are often good team members. They realize they *can* make a difference, and remember, they care enough to complain!

Clear definitions of roles help ensure early success. There are four major roles:

- Team Member — makes decisions, improvements; empowered to change processes
- Steering Committee — provides resources, empowers,

and supports the team effort; "clears a path in the organization"
- Quality Coach or Facilitator — keeps the team focused on the project, helps with group process, tools, and techniques
- Team Leader — runs the team, makes arrangements for meeting place, time, etc.

Waterman (1990) describes an informal test one of his clients applies to the choice of a team: "We asked ourselves, 'Will they be respected? How will they deal with others? Can we put the team's mission, the team leader, and the team members on the bulletin board? Will our people acknowledge that we picked the right team for that problem?'" (p. 20) Department and administrative teams need such credibility.

The role of the steering committee or advisory council is critical for encouraging team activity, providing resources to make team activity possible, and helping establish guidelines. This group recommends policy changes, suggests areas for attention, develops measures for determining team effectiveness, and keeps teams active after the "honeymoon" of early successes.

Team leaders have varied responsibilities. At Belmont, making sure administrators, department chairs, and deans pay attention to team progress is a task in itself. These leaders' main role is keeping teams studying and improving processes in their work areas. They negotiate throughout the organization on behalf of the team.

Early on, teams need much guidance from facilitators. The appropriate analogy here is one of making gravy. As anyone knows who has tried to make gravy for the first time from a recipe in a cookbook, it is well-near impossible. Quality teamwork, like making gravy, requires an experienced "cook" working alongside a novice. Our experience has proven that especially in teamwork, modeling is most important. Scholtes (1988) counsels that the role of the facilitator should decrease as teams move through time together. We at Belmont concur, with the exception of time when statistical process control elements are added. A quality-trained statistician is an important resource to the team and may work more time with the facilitator and team as they begin SPC.

Expectations

After the team is selected (or volunteers), answering another question is critical: "What do we expect the team to accomplish?" Although the steering committee may have an idea, team members who *do* the work will be able to give valuable input. Consider, "Is the expectation real in light of resources (time, personnel, money), and does the team believe, given those resources, the job of improvement is doable?"

The third important question to be answered is, "How is the work of this team important to the institution?" Senge (1990) and Paul Batalden (personal communication, July 1991) speak of alignment of teams and processes within the organization. The first time a new team meets at our institution, we ask, "How does this issue or process impact our primary customer?" Teams must take time *with* leadership to discuss, affirm, and investigate the issue of importance to the department, administrative area, institution, and its customers.

A caution: Remember the old saw, "Be careful what you wish for; it might come true." Teams can dramatically improve work processes, but momentum for the entire QI process can be lost if teams do not have the autonomy to function and act.

Consider a team studying the distribution of payroll checks. They found people stockpiling time and needed the authority and flexibility to change work schedules. Although there is no intention to advocate wholesale "team governance" of the campus, there must be a regular feedback loop between managers who are not part of the team and the functional team itself. There should be no surprises when teams report recommendations for improvement. Waterman (1990) concludes, "Nothing destroys morale faster than managers setting up teams and not giving them proper attention." (p. 19)

Studying and Improving Processes

Functional teams on Belmont's campus are made up of no more than seven people who meet to study and improve a work process all have in common. Most organizations working on QI have some sort of stepped process guide for improvement. These guides usually have five to nine steps and are designed to help teams know "when to do what" as they study and improve processes. At Belmont we use SOLVE-PDCA (see Table 1). This guide, modeled after one used at Hospital Corporation of America, became the map for viewing work as a process and studying it for ongoing improvement.

Table 1   SOLVE-PDCA: Five Steps to Improving a Process

SELECT A PROCESS TO IMPROVE
  1.1 The process
      1.1.1 is important to the work of your area.
      1.1.2 is a process over which you have control.
      1.1.3 has a clear owner.
      1.1.4 has identifiable boundaries within your area.
      1.1.5 has direct impact on external customers.
  1.2 Write a Process Improvement Statement.

ORGANIZE A TEAM TO WORK ON THE PROJECT
  2.1 The team has
      2.1.1 a leader. (In most cases this person is the owner of the
             process; if not, he/she understands the process thoroughly.)
      2.1.2 a recorder.
      2.1.3 a timekeeper.
      2.1.4 a board or flip chart recorder.
      2.1.5 no more than seven team members. (preferably 3-5)
  2.2 Team members are directly involved in the process.
  2.3 Team members view this project as priority and part of
      their real job. It is not considered an intrusion on their normal
      work.

LEARN THE CURRENT PROCESS
  3.1 Be sure the boundaries of the process are understood.
  3.2 Develop a FLOWCHART of the process.
  3.3 Eliminate waste and rework.
  3.4 Identify suppliers and customers. (TRIAD)
  3.5 Identify inputs and outputs. (TRIAD)
  3.6 Determine customer/supplier needs.

VERIFY CAUSES OF VARIATION
  4.1 Collect data on the process.
  4.2 Prepare a RUN CHART and identify any existing trends.
  4.3 Prepare a CONTROL CHART and identify all special causes.
  4.4 Eliminate special causes. (PDCA if necessary.)

ENTER IMPROVEMENT PROCESS
  5.1 BRAINSTORM about common cause variation.
  5.2 Use the FISHBONE diagram on possible causes.
  5.3 Gather data (CHECKSHEET) on causes.
  5.4 PARETO causes and select those to be improved.
  5.5 Begin PDCA for improvement of the process.

Table 1   SOLVE-PDCA: Shewhart or PDCA Cycle

PLAN THE IMPROVEMENT
1. Determine what improvements need to be made.
2. Specify what aspects of the project will have the greatest impact on customer needs. (KEY QUALITY CHARACTER-ISTICS)
3. Determine how, when, and where to begin.
4. Empower the people involved.
5. Decide how to begin implementation on a small/test scale.

DO THE IMPROVEMENT ON A LIMITED SCALE
1. Begin the pilot improvement.
2. Collect data for analysis.

CHECK THE RESULTS OF THE PILOT PROJECT
1. Analyze data for results.
2. If effective, move to ACT stage.
3   If ineffective, begin PDCA again.

ACT TO CONTINUE IMPROVING THE PROCESS
1. Standardize the improvement.
2. Consider the following questions:
    a. Do policies and/or procedures need to be changed?
    b. Is training necessary?
    c. Are all impacted people and departments aware of changes being made?
    d. Should the owner of the process be changed?
3. Begin PDCA for the next step in process improvement.

It is our observation that when new teams flounder, often they have not followed the process improvement guide. An administrative team was sure they knew what their customers wanted and spent time and considerable effort collecting data *unrelated* to what their customers perceived to be most important. The team *believed* customers needed and wanted rapid turn-around time of large data processing jobs.

When data was finally collected from those customers, most had planned well ahead for those large jobs and had several days of lag time built in their plan. Unknowingly, the team was tampering with the system by collecting data on turnaround time of large jobs and then forcing the system to turn those jobs around quickly at the expense of shorter computer runs.

That team, back on track after skipping the step about determining customer needs, was able to focus on where real improvement was possible and important to customers. The team improved turnaround time of short runs, added value in the form of different kinds of reports, formatting, and packaging of orders for pickup.

A stepped guide is not only helpful, it may prevent rework and lost momentum. Now, facilitators insist new teams follow the guidelines "to the letter." Later, with some experience and practice, they are better able to innovate.

Working Together

Quality teams are based on *new* kinds of relationships. Teams learn about group interaction, group process, consensus building, and meeting skills. They focus on improving work, and the leader-manager's role becomes one of helping people do the best possible job. Waterman (1990) cautions, "No matter how objective, honest, and focused teams try to be, they do not have management's perspective." (p. 19) Both perspectives — management's and the individual team member's — contribute to improving processes in departments and work areas.

Teamwork brings to mind championship athletic teams in which each member's performance contributes to the effort of the team as a whole. Because Belmont's forte is its music school, we use the analogy of a wonderful choral company. Among its members are gifted soloists, but for a successful group performance, each member contributes to the overall brilliance of the work. When this analogy was used in one team training session with faculty in our School of Music, a member commented, "In other words, you don't just want my participation to make *me* feel good, you want the benefit of my thinking." That feeling of responsibility is key. If a team member is not participating, the team is missing the benefit of what that "soloist" adds to the performance of the work.

Quality work area teams *change* departments and administrative units. Teamwork becomes "part of the job," contributes to joy of work, and encourages responsibility for improvement. Consider our team of instructors planning a new course in music theory. One, a music theorist and computer programmer, finds ways students can reinforce learning in the computer laboratory and then programs the computer to capture all responses for later analysis. Another member studies team learning and plans ways for collaboration among students. A third designs ongoing data collection methods for improvement of instruction. This music school team will continue study and improvement of the class on the basis of what the team discovers in the fall 1991 semester offering.

Critics have said that such methods are just good teaching and colleague collaboration, but they are not *just* those things. Data collection, striving for consensus, and decision making are different. Although teams, like individuals, experience ups and downs, a synergy emerges unlike traditional committee work or collaborative efforts usually seen on campuses. Dr. Deming (1986) teaches us that top management has the *ultimate* responsibility for quality through systems in place in the institution. The leader of the organization can give the "quality vision" and provide systems, policies, and an environment for change. But it is in *groups* collaborating with their knowledge, skills, and ideas that synergy accomplishes major improvements.

According to Robert Reich of Harvard, " . . . we must begin to celebrate collective entrepreneurship, endeavors in which the whole of the effort is greater than the sum of the individual contributions. We need to honor our teams more, our aggressive leaders and maverick geniuses less." (1987, p. 78.) A lapel button seen recently said, "None of us is as good as all of us." Perhaps that sums up the value of work area quality teams for colleges and universities.

Table 2 illustrates work area teams operating at Belmont University in the fall of 1991.

Barriers to Team Success

It has not been entirely smooth sailing for quality teams at Belmont University. In its simplest form, learning means changing. Change is serious business in higher education; tradition bound, we often resist it without even knowing why. People at Belmont waited for the latest program, "quality," to go away. After all, hadn't the leadership had short-term programs before?

When it became clear that QI was not going away and teams began to form, there were several difficulties. First, because of the internal system itself, people were not able to give teams the needed priority. Meetings were canceled when things were hectic, and team leaders heard mixed messages, "Quality is important and I want your team operating, but get this report finished by tomorrow morning." Second, there was a tendency to focus on relieving job frustrations through team activities. In other words, "What will make my job easier?" Early on, the *customer* was not first in team focus.

In one instance, a team formed according to the old organizational chart. It was too large and because of its makeup, it acted exactly like a confrontational committee. The joke was, "Well, it looks like the organizational chart showed up again." The group dynamics doomed the team before it could be effective.

Table 2 Departmental and Administrative Work Teams

Team Areas	Process Selected for Improvement	Expectations of Improvements
Admissions	Response to Applications	Quicker turnaround time to students, streamlined internal paper flow, less employee frustration
Admissions	Telephone Response	Fewer re-routed calls, more timely, accurate answering of incoming calls, better availability of answers
Campus Security	Availability of Parking	Increased availability of parking spaces, fewer violations, fewer community complaints, improved fac/staff/student relations
Career Services	Resumé Distribution	Improved efficiency in sending our resumés to employers, less re-work, more accurate gathering of information
Dean of Student's Office	Residence Hall Room Assignments	More timely notification of students, improved inter-office communication
Development	Alumni Computer Mail List	Less frustration, happier customers, less time and material lost, improved accuracy of posting
Development	Donor Receipts	Improved turnaround time from unknown to one day (standard), and improve accuracy
Event Scheduling	Campus Event Notification (CEN)	Improve scheduling system, fewer problems with events, more complete CEN, better prepared events
Financial Aid	Mail	Accuracy in mail dates, fewer lost materials, more satisfied staff, students, and parents
Financial Aid	Stafford Loan	Streamline Stafford Loan process, clarify staff responsibilities, more accurate processing
Food Services	Cafeteria Services	Improved service to students, less variation in quality of food, less waste, more satisfied customers
Plant Operations	Work Order/CEN	Improve control of work orders/CEN to assure a scheduled, timely response
Registrar's Office	Early Registration, Location and Phone Registration	Increase in percent of students registering early, smoother registration for students and faculty
Registrar's Office	Grade Posting	Checklists established, more timely posting, more accurate posting
Registrar's Office	Transcript Holds	Smoother, more accurate system of removing "holds" on transcripts and grade mailers

Table 2 Departmental and Administrative Work Teams (Cont.)

Team Area	Process Selected for Improvement	Expectations of Improvements
Student Services	Disciplinary Procedures in Residence Halls	Efficiency and consistency in handling cases, improved relationships with students
Treasurer's Office	Long Distance Telephone Service	Improved long distance service to Belmont customers, fewer lost calls
Treasurer's Office	Payroll Distribution	More timely delivery of checks, more accurate distribution, increased employee satisfaction
Treasurer's Office	Reconciliation of Bank Deposits and Cash Receipts	More accurate reconciliation, less time required for process, streamlined process
Tuition Benefit	Waiver System	Improved knowledge of ways resources used, recommendations for improvement of benefit system
University and Printing Services	Bulk Mail	Smoother flow of work, improved efficiency of handling mail, less waste
University and Printing Services	Typesetting through Printing	Smoother flow of work, less waste, less re-work, better communication among workers in process

Guard against superstructures; simple operational guidelines, reporting structures, and meeting formats ensure spending time on improving processes, not complicated politics and procedures. The final difficulty is one of breaking old habits; it is a challenge to stay focused on a given project for many months. Data collection and study of a process takes time. This change in "time mindset" is difficult for teams at first; they are used to quick fixes and acting on hunches. Quality teams are often long-term commitments.

Problems continue as we live through the awkward, "teenage" stage of implementing quality improvement. Quality must become the way we work, not just the work we do in team meetings. In the administrative work areas and departments where teams formed over a year ago, there is some change toward quality as a way of working. Dr. Deming reminds us this is a strategy for the long haul. In higher education, it may take even longer to see a change in the way we do business.

Making a Difference

Teams require genuine, not superficial, management involvement, and a commitment to change. We found, as did Edwin Choate (1990) of Oregon State University, implementing quality improvement in higher education is not as easy as we thought it would be. There are strong and complicated barriers to its success — tradition, language, funding of startup efforts, time constraints, and lack of system support.

Despite all the barriers, our teams have made positive differences. They reduced waste and rework in processes studied. Data indicate teams are improving processes affecting students. There is a very real appreciation for the opportunity to learn something new together. The training "alignment" seems to have been remarkably successful. In several cases, barriers between departments came down; the result was much improved service to students as quantified by customer surveys. Almost unanimously, those trained reported cooperation and teamwork increased as a result of the quality effort.

Sharing the Story

We are searching for new kinds of stories, those illustrating winning efforts by the team with the best blend of talent, not the one with the most talented individual. Management presentations and team celebrations make an impact. Dramatic department and work area improvements like a 300 percent improvement of processing time for applications and stream-lined payroll check distribution get people's attention. Employee contributions and ideas are being taken seriously. Our leadership recognizes it has an under-used resource—the knowledge and skills of work area teams. As these teams come to recognize their worth and "optimize" the systems they work in, we believe their work will be more challenging and interesting. In the long run, teams will be a catalyst for change, our vehicle for improvement.

References

Baker, Edward M. "The Chief Executive Officer's Role in Total Quality: Preparing the Enterprise for Leadership in the New Economic Age." Paper presented at the Conference on Quality, Madison, WI, April, 1989.

Choate, L. Edwin. "An Analysis of Oregon State University's Total Quality Management Pilot Program," Oregon State University, 1990.

Deming, W. Edwards. *Out of the Crisis*. Cambridge, MA: Massachusetts Institute of Technology, Center for Advanced Engineering Study, 1990.

Ishikawa, Kaoru. *What is Total Quality Control*. New York: Prentice-Hall, 1985.

Reich, Robert B. "Entrepreneurship Reconsidered: The Team as Hero," *Harvard Business Review*. May-June, 1987.

Reid, Peter C. *Well Made in America.* New York: McGraw-Hill, 1990.

Scholtes, Peter R. and other contributors. *The Team Handbook: How to Use Teams to Improve Quality.* Madison, WI: Joiner Associates, 1988.

Senge, Peter M. *The Fifth Discipline.* New York: Doubleday/Currency, 1990.

Stayer, Ralph. "How I Learned to Let My Workers Lead," *Harvard Business Review.* November-December, 1990.

Waterman, Robert H. *Adhocracy: The Power to Change.* Knoxville, TN: Whittle Direct Books, 1990.

Susan Hillenmeyer is Vice President for Quality and Professional Development at Belmont University. Dr. Hillenmeyer heads the Center for Quality and Professional Development, instructs teams in QI, and serves as a facilitator for those teams. Additionally, she directs the internal quality efforts at Belmont and serves on the Quality Steering Team.

Chapter 4

Longitudinal Student Databases:
A Critical Tool for
Managing Quality in Higher Education

Peter T. Ewell
National Center for Higher Education Management Systems
Boulder, Colorado

Information on basic processes is as much a fundamental requirement of Total Quality Management (TQM) in higher education as it is anywhere else. Despite the wealth of data about students contained in their computers, many colleges and universities currently know little about how their most basic process—undergraduate instruction—actually operates. Partly this is because of the way data are organized, itself a consequence of past management requirements. So long as students were seen primarily as accounting units whose individual status needed to be periodically checked, registrar's databases sufficed to support institutional operations. There was little need to examine overall patterns of instruction and student experience, and to therefore go beyond discrete student record files.

But as outcomes have become increasingly salient, students must be treated as "customers" and instruction as an integrated process. The national assessment movement that emerged in the mid-eighties was one response to this development (Ewell, 1984). Another was the growing prominence of enrollment management as a conscious attempt in uncertain times to shape the future (Hossler 1984). Both responses, however, have been limited in effect, the first primarily because it in practice has tended to emphasize end-point testing which adds little value to the educational experience, and the second because it tends to divorce the "processing" of students in such arenas as admissions and student support programs from the institution's main business of instruction.

In this context, TQM represents an important new metaphor for change, and longitudinal databases a critical tool for realizing its potential. The purpose of this chapter is to explore this potential by, (a) noting the particular conceptual benefits of applying TQM concepts to managing enrollments and the resulting need for new kinds of information, (b) specifying the requisites and structure of an appropriate institutional database, and (c) demonstrating some potential applications and benefits of this approach through example. Throughout (as is the case for any application of TQM principles), it is important to emphasize that there are no universally "right" answers; each institution will need independently to determine its own requirements, assess its own information environment, and proceed accordingly.

A. TQM as an Approach to Managing Enrollments

While there are many dangers in modeling undergraduate instruction as a "production line," some points of comparison are compelling. First, the process is linear and, at least in principle, proceeds according to a defined plan intended to enhance the abilities of incoming students in specific ways consistent with defined outcomes. Terms such as "enrollment pipeline" prominent in enrollment management research (for example, Rumpf, 1978; Hossler, 1984; 1986; Hossler, Bean and Associates, 1990), and "value-added" in student assessment (for example, Astin, 1978; 1985) strongly reflect this underlying structure. More importantly, the dynamics of enrollment have strong industrial parallels highlighted in the language of TQM. Student failure or voluntary dropout from this perspective can be easily seen as "scrap"; instructional costs are incurred but do not result in a finished product. Similarly, remedial instruction can be seen as "rework"; additional costs must be incurred later in the instructional process to accomplish objectives that should have been achieved by previous, already paid for, activities. Finally, the architecture of a curriculum or instructional design itself consists of a set of integrated, interrelated activities that build upon one another much like an industrial production line; where this fails in practice, research suggests, quality suffers. Despite an alien terminology, therefore, industrial concepts appear to fit.

But equally important are some caveats of the "production line" analogy that limit the applicability of TQM concepts to collegiate instruction. First, students are different from typical industrial "raw materials" in that they can talk to us about what is happening to them. Information collected directly from students about their experiences is thus of primary importance in both monitoring instruction and in improving its delivery. Its presence can give us a major advantage over the more passive production processes typical of manufacturing, and its inclusion in an enrollment management database is mandatory. More importantly, students are more than raw materials in the process of instruction itself. They also serve as "customers" who expect to receive particular services and benefits, and who will behave accordingly if they do not receive them. Information about their basic needs and about their satisfactions and dissatisfactions with particular provided experiences is thus particularly important in enrollment management. Students are also part of the "workforce." Though advised by college personnel, students themselves typically make most of their own curricular choices and are free to manage their time and effort in pursuit of instructional goals. Knowing something about both of these student "production management" activities is thus equally critical to meaningful improvement.

Within these caveats, TQM concepts remain broadly applicable in guiding comprehensive undergraduate improvement. In addition, as enrollment and student flow patterns have become increasingly complex in recent years, the need for better information about underlying processes has escalated. The dynamics of enrollment at most higher education institutions have moved far away from the traditional four-year attendance patterns and structured curricula typical of three or four decades ago. For most institutions, major changes in enrollment dynamics have taken place in at least four ways:

1. Students are increasingly attending part-time and will frequently interrupt their enrollment for one or more terms. Not only does this lengthen the overall time required for completion, but it renders completion points unpredictable; instead of arriving at the end of the instructional pipeline together, students who enter college simultaneously will complete at widely varying points in time.

2. Curricula and course-taking patterns are increasingly determined not by predetermined curricular plans, but by individual student choices; students frequently change programs, decide not to enroll in appropriate prerequisite courses, or engage in elective study, resulting in vastly different patterns of underlying experience. In fact, in typical undergraduate curricula, no two students will likely have taken an identical set of courses.

3. Students are increasingly engaging in activities outside the curriculum which, for better or worse, have an important bearing on their experiences and outcomes. Overall "time-on-task" has decreased due to the prominence of employment and family commitments. Similarly, job and extracurricular activities can either help or hinder educational progress, depending upon their particular linkages with instruction.

4. Students are entering postsecondary study with widely divergent backgrounds, abilities, and patterns of previous instruction. On the one hand, this means that the task of instruction becomes more difficult because it cannot be targeted at a known ability level; the result is often a decline in standards. On the other, it means that withdrawal and failure rates are high, with the consequent need for "rework."

Managing improvement under these four conditions requires quite different kinds of student information systems than have traditionally been available to college and university managers. At the same time, it may require major changes in the "information infrastructure" in terms of which existing data are collected and organized. A first problem is the basic term-oriented architecture of most current student records systems. Because the file structure of such systems consists of individual semesters or terms, establishing the kinds of linkages across files needed to meaningfully track students can be technically daunting. Also, because the function of such records systems is to process individual transactions for later retrieval, there is often little attention paid to making sure that data are coded in such a way that they can be meaningfully aggregated. Finally, such databases are increasingly "live," in that current records are being constantly updated with the latest information; while this practice is optimal to inform individual retrieval and intervention, it considerably complicates the task of consistently monitoring overall processes. All three of these conditions argue for creation of a free-standing longitudinal tracking system designed specifically to inform comprehensive quality improvement (Ewell, 1987).

At the same time, many of the kinds of data needed to understand student flow are not resident in student records databases. Important data on student entering conditions—for instance placement test scores or high school course taking patterns—are stored in different offices, and often not in machine-readable form. Survey data obtained from current or former students is generally archived in yet another location and format—if it is kept at all. Particularly important here from the standpoint of TQM are "customer" data on the level of satisfaction with services provided, and "market" data on the placement and performance of graduates. Finally, information on key student experiences occurring outside the regular curriculum—for example, library use, use of available tutorial services, or participation in campus activities—is usually maintained by the units responsible for operating these functions themselves. While only a few data elements from each of these sources may be appropriate for inclusion in a longitudinal database, those that are may be of particular importance in understanding what is happening; the difficulty is that they are scattered across the institution in unknown ways, with no means to link them together.

These two conditions—term-oriented record keeping and dispersed databases—underlie the growing interest in longitudinal student tracking systems. While the particular content of such systems may vary widely across institutions with different requirements, their basic structures are similar, and are outlined in the section that follows.

B. An Overview of Longitudinal Database Design

Few colleges and universities currently possess a formal tracking system although methodologies for best practice in longitudinal database design have been well established for some time (Wing, 1974; Endo and Bittner, 1985; Ewell, 1987; Terenzini, 1987; Ewell, Parker, and Jones, 1988). The intent of this section is therefore limited to providing a brief overview of the primary features of such systems, with particular reference to linkages with TQM.

The standard approach to generating statistics on persistence and degree completion—and the foundation for establishing a comprehensive student tracking system—is use of a cohort methodology. Rather than a particular term or academic year, the primary unit of analysis for this approach is an identified "cohort" of entering students—for example, all students beginning their studies at Institution X in the fall of 1991. Once identified, students remain a member of their assigned starting cohort regardless of their subsequent pattern of enrollment—including changes in load carried, degree objective, or interrupted attendance resulting in "stop-out" and re-admission. Statistics on student progress and experiences are generally calculated on the basis of the total number in the starting cohort—for example, the proportion of the cohort completing degree requirements within five years, the proportion completing general education distribution requirements by the end of their first two years, or the proportion initially assessed as deficient in writing who subsequently enrolled in and passed college-level writing courses. Because the longitudinal database also usually includes data about a wide range of student characteristics, moreover, performance statistics such as these are often broken down by numerous student subpopulations.

The structure of a cohort data file typically involves data of several different kinds. A first set of data elements, drawn largely from the student records database, is compiled once—at time of entry—and usually comprises the first portion of the longitudinal enrollment record for each student. Types of data generally included in this fixed portion of the record are data on student demographics, educational background, basic skills and need for remediation, and initial enrollment status (for example, initial program declaration, provisional admission, financial aid status, etc.). Additional data elements are added to the record at two points during every term that the student is subsequently enrolled. One set of elements is drawn from term enrollment files at the time of official census data, and reflects student behavior at that point; typical elements extracted at this point are total number of hours enrolled for, enrollment in particular designated courses of interest, and participation in identified experiences. Another set of data elements is added at the end of the term and reflects student performance. Types of data elements typically included are the number of hours successfully completed, numbers incomplete, grades earned (overall and in designated courses), and degree awards. Finally, a set of follow-up elements is often included that contains information on key post-enrollment activities, such as job placement and subsequent participation in postsecondary study; generally such elements are collected from students independently, through survey. Appendix A contains an abbreviated list of the types of data elements most commonly included.

Outputs of such a system are of several kinds. First, a set of standard reports is produced as each cohort reaches the end of a designated tracking period. Reports at the end of each year are most commonly used, with additional time periods determined by ongoing experience with the system. These reports are produced in a common format and contain basic information on cohort performance. If a statistical software package is used to create them, moreover, flexible reports can easily be run for any designated student population that can be described by the data elements in the system. This creates a powerful tool that enables local managers to investigate particular problems or to examine the progress of particular groups of students.

Technical requirements for establishing a tracking system can vary widely, depending on the system's size and complexity. Minimally, however, institutions must be able to:

- regularly extract relevant data elements from the existing student records system (and from any other data files that contain data elements of interest), and to "freeze" them at current values. Generally this is done using available data manipulation or report-writing software associated with the parent databases in which these elements normally reside.

- merge relevant data elements drawn from multiple terms and multiple data sources into a single file. Two operations are involved here: merging data across files at a single point in time, and regularly updating each cohort with new performance data each term; both require the use of a "key" element to match data across files (generally the student's Social Security number).

- quickly and flexibly calculate relevant performance statistics for designated student populations. Unlike cross-sectional student databases, most data elements in a longitudinal system do not mean much on their own; relevant reporting statistics instead must be derived from often complex combinations of base data elements. Because of the need for flexibility in such calculations, commercial databases or statistical software packages such as SPSS-X or SAS are often used.

Based on campus experience, four fundamental design issues frame the choices that must be made in designing a longitudinal database of this kind. The *completeness* issue concerns which types of students should be included in the system. Because many non-traditional students are single-term enrolled, some institutions elect only to track those students who are formally seeking degrees, or only those who express an intention to persist for more than one term. The *commonality* issue arises where a multi-institutional or multi-unit system is developed in common. The basic question here is the extent to which all participants will be operating a similar system with respect to data *coverage*, definitions of data elements, calculational procedures used, reports generated, and hardware/software configurations needed to manipulate records and produce reports. A similar issue arises when, as is increasingly the case, institutions elect to purchase or adapt a system already developed by another institution or vendor. The coverage issue concerns what data elements actually to include in the system, and which of these to actively track overtime. The major trade-off in this decision is the level of detail needed for specific management guidance in particular areas versus the overall size of the database; closer monitoring of processes may entail finer levels of detail, but may at the same time considerably slow down execution and produce major problems of data storage and manipulation. Finally, the coordination and control issue addresses the question of who will be responsible for the day-to-day operation and management of the system. Because the data elements needed to drive a meaningful tracking system are generally drawn from many places, a common solution is to make a single office responsible for coordination; often, in this respect, development of a tracking system constitutes an unintentional "audit" of an institution's data systems and may result in a major reorganization of the information function.

C. Some Applications of Longitudinal Data to Quality Improvement

Many linkages between longitudinal student tracking data and instructional improvement have been demonstrated in practice. While few of these have yet occurred under the formal heading of "Total Quality Management," all are consistent with a philosophy of continuous improvement through process monitoring and statistical control. Three particular applications are presented in this section.

Before describing them, however, it is important to stress that longitudinal databases will have little impact in the absence of an overall management strategy for improvement. Like other pieces of information technology, tracking systems are acquired for many reasons. Sometimes they are put in place because specific funding was available; sometimes as part of a system-wide initiative (Adelman, Ewell, and Grable, 1989). But those that have had a lasting impact have arisen in response to a particular, widely expressed operational problem—for example, effective placement, minority success, improvement of general education, or improvement of basic skills (Bers, 1989). In such situations, databases can be specifically configured to address particular problems and to meet the needs of specific institutional constituencies with sufficient motivation to follow through on the many commitments needed to make the system work.

It is also important to emphasize that when implemented, longitudinal data systems fulfill two distinct functions in guiding improvement. The first is an overall monitoring function, generally accomplished through periodic summary reports. Typically, these reports document the progress and performance of a particular cohort group in key areas such as persistence, grades earned, credits completed, proportion of requirements fulfilled, etc. Generally they are designed so that comparative indicators of performance for particular population groups can be easily scanned for aberrant values that might indicate a problem. To facilitate this process, summary reports are often produced in graphic form. Such reports, of course, do not contain sufficient detail to determine the reasons *why* an aberrant performance may be occurring nor, concomitantly, what ought to be done. Instead they signal the presence of a problem to managers and staff at many levels in much the same fashion as a TQM control chart. Like a Pareto chart, moreover, they also indicate where the problem is most often occurring.

Once a problem or anomaly is detected, a well-designed longitudinal database can then be used to investigate it more thoroughly. A major advantage of configuring such systems in a statistical software package is that detailed follow-on analyses can be quickly and flexibly executed that examine the behavior of a particular population, that define performance in different ways, or that include new variables in the analysis. Where, as is often the case, this analytical power is available to local unit managers through data downloaded to a microcomputer, benefits of the system for quality improvement can be particularly enhanced.

As institutional experience with longitudinal databases has grown, three particular applications have proven fruitful: supporting institutional retention programs, improving the effectiveness of initial placement and remediation, and improving curricular "connections" through such processes as placement and prerequisite course structures. As noted earlier, each of these areas evokes a production line parallel highlighted in TQM terminology—for instance, reducing "scrap" and "rework," or improving internal "customer-supplier" networks within the production process.

Each is briefly described and illustrated below.

Cohort methodologies have been applied to monitoring and improving student retention programs for some time. In the past, however, they required time-consuming methods and tended not to result in a widely accessible management-oriented database (for example, Endo and Bittner, 1985). More recently, the ready availability of easily-manipulable longitudinal databases has led to major improvements in institutional retention by allowing easy recognition of where and why particular problems are occurring (Bers, 1989). Most changes in retention and completion rates at a given institution, it turns out, are due to changes in the mix of student clientele served; they are not the result of changes in the ways particular types of students are behaving. Once specific types of students are identified and disaggregated for analysis, many institutions have found the behavior of these groups does not change significantly from cohort to cohort. One private liberal arts college that recently implemented a cohort tracking system, for example, discovered and documented five distinct student population groups that experienced stable but fundamentally different enrollment patterns over time (NCHEMS, 1991). Similar recent efforts at community colleges have led to the development of explicit student typologies for guiding intervention (Sheldon and Grafton, 1982; Aquino, 1989).

Factors that affect enrollment behavior within each student population, moreover, may be quite different from one another, and may consequently have quite different implications for policy or intervention. In the private college mentioned, for instance, substantial gender differences in performance were apparent within one population but not in others: the same programmatic approaches could not therefore be applied generically to all populations. As in TQM, a general lesson here is disaggregation and local application. It is critical for effectiveness to get both analysis and improvement efforts down to the level of specific units and student clientele groups if enrollment management efforts are to be successful.

Similarly, to be effective in improving retention, longitudinal systems ought to contain information on specific interventions and on initial student intentions, as well as summary data on academic performance. One community college, for example, now regularly includes in its tracking system term-by-term data on each student's interaction with the Learning Assistance Center—including the number of contacts, the nature of the contact, and any follow-up that may have occurred. This enables a more complete picture to be drawn of student experience and its effects. Several others include data on student intentions—both overall and intent to persist—collected on entry (Walleri and Japely, 1986). This enables managers to readily distinguish between intentional "non-persisters" and probable "dissatisfied customers".

Cohort methodologies have been more recently applied in the evaluation of instructional effectiveness—particularly in the areas of initial basic skills placement and remediation. Increasingly, because of changing demographics, institutions are finding that students arrive in college deficient in basic skills. Absent initial assessment and appropriate placement in remedial instruction, such students often fail freshman courses in large numbers. And if remedial instruction itself is ineffective, students may need to repeat such courses several times to acquire the skills needed to succeed. Primary applications of longitudinal databases in this context have been to monitor and evaluate current placement policies, and to assess and improve remedial instruction.

The first application generally involves periodically determining the overall predictive validity of the assessment instruments used in placement and examination of the cut scores to make particular decisions. Analytical procedures appropriate here are strongly reminiscent of those used by manufacturing enterprises to determine quality standards for supplied raw materials: the subsequent fates of "inputs" of varying qualities are monitored through the production process to determine how and at what levels differences in initial quality are causing quality problems later on in the process. One public university, for example, streamlined its cumbersome procedures for testing students' writing when it became clear the procedures did not better measure potential academic difficulty than a far simpler procedure. Not only were costs saved, but the exercise also helped faculty and staff focus more clearly upon the specific skills needed to succeed in college-level writing (Ewell, 1991).

A second application in this arena is to provide the data needed to support continuous instructional improvement. Several major multi-institutional student tracking systems, for instance, have been explicitly designed to provide comparative performance data in subsequent college-level work for students who, (1) were assessed as deficient in a particular basic skill area and who were later "fully remediated" as defined by the institution, (2) those assessed as deficient who were not fully remediated and, (3) those assessed as proficient on entry (Ewell, Parker, and Jones, 1988; Adelman, Ewell, and Grable, 1989). Comparing these statistics across the three populations—broken down by demographic or other subpopulation variables as appropriate—allows an initial determination to be made of how well remediation appears to be working for which types of students. Disaggregating further by section or type of instruction within those receiving remediation, moreover, allows further determinations to be made about which modes of delivery seem to be working best.

One curious result of such application is that institutions often discover they are not following their own policies. Many students thus appear to avoid "required" prerequisites and find themselves in difficulty as a result (NCHEMS, 1991). Longitudinal course-taking analyses at one public university just implementing a student tracking system, for instance, revealed surprising numbers of students who took basic composition courses as seniors. At several community colleges with explicit basic skills testing and directed placement policies in place, moreover, considerable numbers of students were found to have escaped their effects; often these students had withdrawn or were in sufficient academic difficulty that they required costly "rescue efforts" to give them a chance to succeed. Many sound policies affecting instructional workflow in higher education, it appears, like their counterparts in industry (Walton, 1989) are not "working" because they have never really been tried.

This observation leads to a final fruitful area of application also reminiscent of industrial practice: improving the coherence of the production process as a whole. As diversity has increased in higher education, so have student curricular choices—both with respect to major fields and with respect to individual sequences of courses. Simply keeping track of what is happening here can be a major challenge—but a needed one for systematic instructional improvement. One resulting application of longitudinal databases is to monitor behavioral sequences and patterns of course-taking, particularly in general education. One public comprehensive college now implementing a new core general education program thus incorporated into its student tracking system the capability to continuously provide information on the manner in which students fulfilled core requirements and the apparent impact of different course-taking patterns on subsequent performance. Another public university is using longitudinal data to assess the impact on student course-taking behavior of new foreign language requirements for the baccalaureate.

Not only do such data allow general evaluation of how well new policies are working but, once particular behavioral patterns or sequences are detected, they can also help support a process of course-to-course articulation to ensure better continuity. Consistent with TQM, this often works best at the local "work-unit" level of schools and departments. In one engineering school, for instance, longitudinal data first signalled a problem for minority students in a particular set of engineering principles courses (Ewell and Chaffee, 1984). Further analysis revealed that, pressured to complete programs in five years, such students were enrolling in these courses despite the fact that they lacked necessary prerequisite skills; though against official policy, advisors were allowing such placements on a case-by-case basis to "help" students succeed. Longitudinal performance information not only dramatically pointed out the detrimental impact of this behavior, but also enabled faculty and staff to think through a set of alternatives that included directed placement, additional tutoring and study sessions, and a new peer advisement program. Interestingly, in developing these alternatives, departmental work groups used a technique similar to the "fishbone diagram" commonly applied in TQM.

Examples such as these suggest the critical importance for academic improvement of consistent data on instructional processes and student behavior over time. Comprehensive longitudinal databases provide exactly this kind of information in a flexible, timely manner—tailored for use by faculty teams and unit managers. Used appropriately, such systems provide a fundamental foundation for effectively applying total quality management techniques to enrollment and instructional issues. In most cases, they require little new data and relatively modest up-front investments. To date, the colleges and universities that have made such investments with a commitment to continuous improvement have been well satisfied with the results.

References

Adelman, S. I.; Ewell, P. T.; and Grable, J. R. "LONESTAR: Texas's Voluntary Tracking and Developmental Evaluation System." In T. Bers (ed.), *Using Student Tracking Systems Effectively, New Directions for Community Colleges #66*. San Francisco: Jossey-Bass, 1989.

Aquino, F. J. "A Five-Year Longitudinal Study of Community College Student Behaviors: Toward a Definition of Student Success and Student Failure." Paper presented at the Association for Institutional Research, Baltimore, MD, April, 1989.

Astin, A. W. *Achieving Educational Excellence: A Critical Assessment of Priorities and Practices in Higher Education*. San Francisco: Jossey-Bass, 1985.

Astin, A. W. *Four Critical Years: Effects of College on Beliefs, Attitudes, and Knowledge*. San Francisco: Jossey-Bass, 1978.

Bers, T. (ed.) *Using Student Tracking Systems Effectively, New Directions for Community Colleges #66*. San Francisco: Jossey-Bass, 1989.

Endo, J. and Bittner, T. "Developing and Using a Longitudinal Student Outcomes Data File: The University of Colorado Experience." In P. T. Ewell (ed.), *Assessing Educational Outcomes; New Directions for Institutional Research #47*. San Francisco: Jossey-Bass, 1985.

Ewell, P. T. *An Evaluation of Minnesota's Postsecondary Quality Assessment Initiative, 1987-91*. Boulder, CO: National Center for Higher Education Management Systems, 1991.

Ewell, P. T. "Principles of Longitudinal Enrollment Analysis: Conducting Retention and Student Flow Studies." In J. A. Muffo and G. W. McLaughlin (eds.), *A Primer on Institutional Research*. Tallahassee, FL: Association for Institutional Research, 1987.

Ewell, P. T. *The Self-Regarding Institution: Information for Excellence*. Boulder, CO: National Center for Higher Education Management Systems, 1984.

Ewell, P. T.; Parker, R.; and Jones, D. P. *Establishing a Longitudinal Student Tracking System: An Implementation Handbook*. Boulder, CO: National Center for Higher Education Management Systems, 1988.

Ewell, P. T. and Chaffee, E. E. *Promoting the Effective Use of Information in Decisionmaking*. Boulder, CO: National Center for Higher Education Management Systems, 1984.

Hossler, D. *Creating Effective Enrollment Management Systems*. New York: College Entrance Examination Board, 1986.

Hossler, D. *Enrollment Management: An Integrated Approach*. New York: College Entrance Examination Board, 1984.

Hossler, D.; Bean, J. P.; and Associates *The Strategic Management of College Enrollments*. San Francisco: Jossey-Bass, 1990.

National Center for Higher Education Management Systems (NCHEMS) "Enrollment Analysis and Student Tracking: What Have We Been Learning?" *NCHEMS Newsletter*, Vol. 2, May, 1991.

Rumpf, D. *Undergraduate Retention: Description of Student Flow Including Applications*. Amherst, MA: Office of Budget and Institutional Studies, 1978.

Sheldon, S. M. and Grafton, C. L. "Raison d'Etre: Students." *Community and Junior College Journal* #52, November, 1982.

Terenzini, P. T. "Studying Student Attrition and Retention." In J. A. Muffo and G. W. McLaughlin (eds.), *A Primer on Institutional Research*. Tallahassee, FL: Association for Institutional Research, 1987.

Walleri, R. D. and Japely, S. M. "Student Intent, Persistence, and Outcomes." Paper presented at the Association for Institutional Research,
Orlando, FL, May, 1986.

Walton, M. *The Deming Management Method*. New York: Putnam, 1986.

Wing, P. *Higher Education Enrollment Forecasting: A Manual for State-Level
Agencies*. Boulder, CO: National Center for Higher Education Management Systems, 1974.

*Peter T. Ewell is a Senior Associate at the National Center for Higher Education
Management Systems in Boulder, Colorado.*

Appendix A

CATEGORIES OF DATA

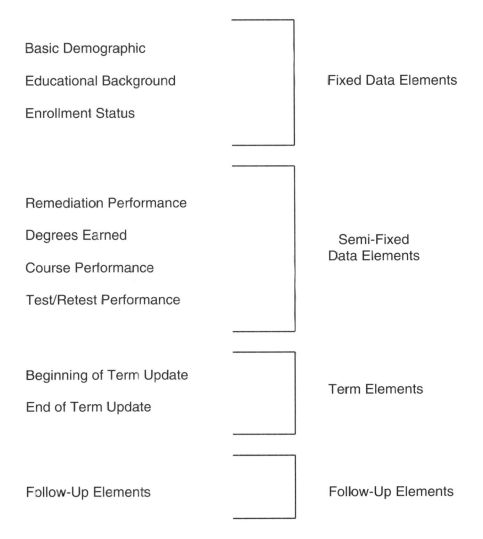

Basic Demographic

Educational Background

Enrollment Status

Fixed Data Elements

Remediation Performance

Degrees Earned

Course Performance

Test/Retest Performance

Semi-Fixed
Data Elements

Beginning of Term Update

End of Term Update

Term Elements

Follow-Up Elements

Follow-Up Elements

Chapter 5

QI Tools for Planning Instruction, Developing Courses, and Administrative Processes

Casey Collett
GOAL/QPC
Albany, Oregon

Erin Rogers teaches management courses in an urban community college. She wants to make this, her tenth year in teaching, her best ever.

Paul Gonzalez is the Dean of Sciences and Engineering at a small private college. He has high hopes for the curriculum design team he sponsors as they initiate their third project: the development of an interdisciplinary capstone course for seniors in engineering.

Lee Sung and Michael Stone supervise two sections of the Admissions Department in a large state university. Their units have embarked upon a long term quality improvement effort with a goal of substantially reducing response time to students applying for admission.

In each of these hypothetical situations, an individual or a team is creating a better way of doing something. These "better ways" could be called processes—specifically, processes for instructional planning, for course development, and for effective administration.

Erin, Paul, Lee and Michael could use a variety of approaches to improve their processes. They could use the "munitions method" in which people take their "best shot" at creating a better way, trying one idea at a time (the hip shoot) or many ideas together (the shot gun or buck shot approach). While the munitions method may be exhilarating, it can be a costly and less than predictable method of hitting the improvement target.

The Method

Another way to plan and create better processes involves the wise use of a Quality Improvement (QI) method and some tools. The seven-step method is:

1. What are the issues? Envisioning the perfect process.
2. Where do we currently stand?
3. Where do we concentrate our efforts?
4. What is our plan?
5. Who will be responsible?

6. What could go wrong? How can we prevent/fix it?
7. When and how will we review our plan?

Erin Rogers has a defined instructional planning process, which includes the following steps:

1. Course identified for instruction
2. Customers/stakeholders (e.g., student, colleague, administration) identified
3. Customer/stakeholder needs identified
4. Customer/stakeholder needs verified
5. Course vision developed
6. Resources (materials, current knowledge level) assessed
7. Action plan identified
8. Plan carried out
9. Plan reviewed, course finalized
10. Course conducted
11. Course outcomes assessed

Erin used **The Method** above to improve this existing process, but the same method can be used to develop or create brand new processes.

The Tools

Each step of the method is accompanied by a QI tool. These tools capture the thinking and discussion that occur during the QI process. They are discussion aids, not "coffee grinders" into which ideas are fed and answers emerge. They add objectivity to the QI discussion process, and they stand as a permanent record of how QI decisions were made.

The Affinity Diagram, Interrelationship Digraph, Tree Diagram, Matrix Diagram, and Process Decision Program Chart are five of the Seven Management and Planning Tools (Brassard, 1989). With their roots in operations research and total quality management in Japan, these tools are ideally suited for working with "idea data" generated in QI efforts. One additional tool, the Spider Diagram, is useful in the assessment of the current status of multiple factors.

Step 1. What are the Issues? Envisioning the Perfect Process.

Erin had no outstanding issues or problems with her current instructional planning process, so she began her QI efforts by creating a vision of the perfect process. She used a tool called the *Affinity Diagram* to brainstorm ideas for a better way and to group those ideas into meaningful categories. Erin began her visioning process by asking herself, "What are the elements of the ideal instructional planning process?" She used 3x5 cards to record her responses, one idea per card. Erin quickly generated 50 ideas, such as:

- Process is flexible enough to accommodate all courses I teach.

- It includes a way for me to get feedback about my teaching to aid continuous improvement of the process.

When she was sure she had recorded all of her ideas on the 3x5 cards, Erin displayed the cards on her desk and began moving similar ideas together. She continued this activity until she had six clusters of ideas, which she titled and summarized as follows:

Vision Elements for My Ideal Instructional Planning Process

Cluster Titles	Main Theme in the Cluster
Excellent Outcomes	effectiveness of instruction
Rich Set of Measures in Place	ways to measure the health of the planning process as well as its outcomes
Constantly Improving	evidence of QI mechanisms
Open System	periodic calibration with peers; evidence of new ideas
Easy to Operate	efficiency, repeatability of process
Partnership with Stakeholders	connection with students, fellow faculty members, and administration

Step 2. Where Do We Currently Stand?

Now Erin asked herself, "Where do I stand in relation to each of the six vision elements?" To answer the question, she used a *Spider Diagram* (see Figure 1).

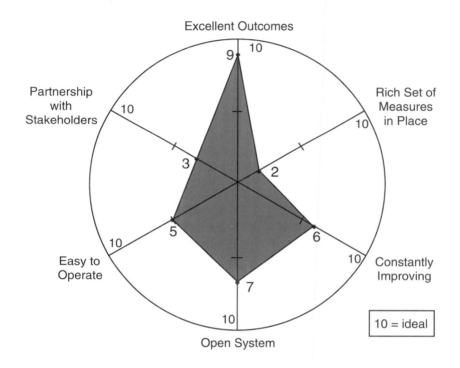

Figure 1 Erin's Spider Diagram: Current Status on Six Vision Elements

This tool displays a picture of the gap between the current situation and the ideal, using a 10-point rating scale (0 = low, 10 = perfection or achievement of vision). In rating each of the six vision elements, Erin used the following rationale:

Category	Rating	Rationale
Excellent Outcomes	9	Formal and informal assessments of my outcomes by students and administration have been quite favorable. I have received outstanding teaching awards three of the past 10 years, and students recommend my courses to peers.
Rich Set of Measures in Place	2	I have only outcome measures in place; no measures of the health of the planning process itself.
Constantly Improving	6	For the past 10 years, I have reviewed outcome data and made adjustments to my process each year. It appears to be working, but I need to be more systematic about QI.

Open System	7	I talk with peers and review literature to keep my instructional planning process current.
Easy to Operate	5	Could be better, but a fairly efficient process.
Partnership with Stakeholders	3	I need to make a more concerted effort to account for student, peer and administration needs in my planning process.

Step 3. Where Do We Concentrate Our Efforts?

Now having an idea of where she stood, Erin used another tool to help herself decide where to concentrate her efforts. This tool, the *Interrelationship Digraph*, illustrated causal relationships among the elements of Erin's vision. Each vision element is compared to all others with the question, "Does one of these elements cause or drive the other?" Causal relationships are shown with arrows leading from the cause to the effect (see Figure 2).

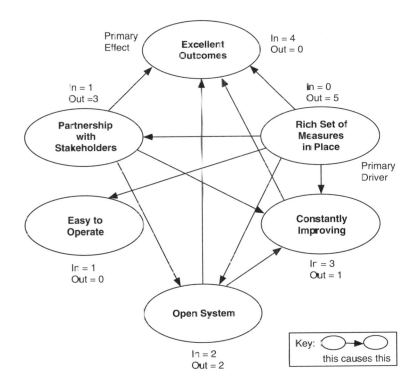

Figure 2 Erin's Interrelationship Digraph on Six Vision Elements

By counting the numbers of arrows going into and out of each vision element on the Interrelationship Digraph, Erin learned several things:

1. *Easy to Operate* is a fairly independent element, tied to the others by only one arrow.
2. Having good *Measures in Place* and maintaining *Partnership with Stakeholders*, with 5 and 3 causal arrows, respectively, are driving forces in achieving her vision.
3. *Excellent Outcomes* is a result (effect) of all the other vision elements.

Based on her analysis of the Spider Diagram and the Interrelationship Digraph, Erin chose to concentrate her QI efforts on getting a Rich Set of Measures in Place in her instructional planning process.

Step 4. What Is Our Plan?

Erin needed a tool to help her plan how to get a rich set of measures in place. The tool she used is the Tree Diagram, which breaks concepts into fundamental components and displays steps of a plan for achieving each component. Erin's tree looked like this:

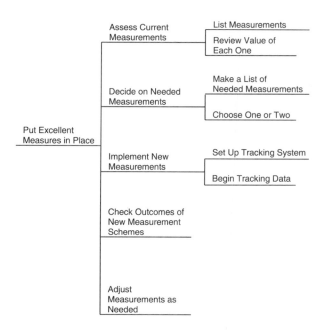

Figure 3 Erin's Tree Diagram

Step 5. Who Will Be Responsible?

This step was simplified because Erin was the only person carrying out the plan. In a situation of shared ownership, teams can use a Matrix Diagram to answer the questions of "Who is responsible?" and "To what extent?" Steps of the plan are displayed on the Y axis of the matrix and names of work units go across the X axis. Any symbol can be used in the nodes of the matrix to designate ownership (or joint ownership) of a step of the plan. Figure 4 shows the use of a double circle to designate significant responsibility, a single circle to show moderate responsibility, and a triangle to show a small amount of responsibility in carrying out a step of the plan.

Plan Step / Person Responsible	Sue	Joe	Martha	Kim
1	◎	◎	◎	◎
2		◎	◯	
3			◎	△
4	△		◎	
5		◯		◯

◎ = significant responsibility

◯ = moderate responsibility

△ = small amount of responsibility

Figure 4 Matrix Diagram Assigning Responsibility for Planning Steps

Step 6. What Could Go Wrong? How Can We Prevent/Fix It?

Before she implemented her plan, Erin asked "What could go wrong? What are the barriers at each step of the way?" She used a tool called a *Process Decision Program Chart (PDPC)* to "troubleshoot" her plan and to develop countermeasures, both contingency plans and preventive mechanisms, for the most probable and serious sources of failure.

Erin examined each branch of her Tree Diagram in sequence to identify potential barriers. For example, the PDPC for the second branch of her Tree looked like this:

Tree branch	What barriers might I face?	Countermeasures
Decide which measurements	Choose wrong measures	Pilot test my choices
I need	Too many measures	Start with only one

Erin decided to pilot test one additional measure during the first term that she implemented her new instructional planning process.

Step 7. When and How Will We Review Our Plan?

With her improvement plan complete, Erin was ready to begin implementing the changes to her instructional planning process. She committed herself to a formal quarterly review, in which she will take the time to consider her progress and to reflect on how she may improve her process in the future.

This example has illustrated how an individual might use a QI method and tools to improve an existing instructional planning process. The same QI approach is useful to teams as well. In the curriculum design example, Paul Gonzalez might find his team emphasizing the Affinity and Tree Diagrams for envisioning and planning a perfect capstone engineering course. The Matrix Diagram would be extremely useful in defining roles and responsibilities in the implementation process. The Admissions team could use an Interrelationship Digraph to zero in on the driving force for delays in the response process. Having used a Tree Diagram to map out a QI plan, the inter-unit team could use the Matrix to assign clear ownership for plan steps and the Process Decision Program Chart to anticipate pitfalls in the steps of the plan.

Quality Improvement in higher education calls for individuals, departments, and inter-departmental work units to view their work as processes — processes that can be defined, characterized, stabilized, and improved.

A reliable method and the sensible use of tools enhance the effectiveness of teams and individuals in obtaining and maintaining the QI results they seek.

References

Brassard, M. *The Memory Jogger Plus+™*. Methuen, MA.: GOAL/QPC, 1989.

After earning a doctorate in counseling (Purdue '79), Casey worked as an internal TQM consultant at Hewlett Packard for nine years. In 1989, she established her own consulting firm, emphasizing TQM application in higher education and government. As Western Regional Director of GOAL/QPC (a non-profit research firm in total quality methods), Casey has co-authored two texts on daily management and an application report on TQM in higher education.

Chapter 6

Quality Standards and Support Systems in Successful Publication of Scholarly Research: A Process Analysis

Robert G. Batson, Ph.D.
University of Alabama
Tuscaloosa, Alabama

I. Introduction

University faculty engage in many scholarly pursuits over the course of a career. Most institutions expect a certain level of scholarly activity, as evidenced by publication in scholarly journals in the faculty member's discipline. Administrators use this evidence to explain the value of the institution's research endeavors to various constituencies, and as one input to tenure, promotion, and merit raise evaluations. For the faculty member, no matter how much satisfaction is experienced conducting the research, the results are valued by peers and administrators only after it is published in an appropriate journal. More importantly, faculty scholarly research is the most significant form of sponsored faculty professional development. Lindquist cites "old reliables such as research grants, personnel policies favoring publications, sabbaticals, course load reductions, travel moneys for professional meetings, visiting scholar programs" as contributors to faculty scholarly development. These resource allocations and rewards occur in the context of an underlying process, and it is through process understanding that improvements, if possible, will become evident.

The process of conceiving, conducting, and ultimately publishing one's work, as depicted in Figure 1, is deceptively simple to those outside the system. However, a detailed analysis of the process—the purpose of this article—reveals many "customer-supplier" relationships upon which the scholar's research efficiency and effectiveness are dependent. The method we choose to illuminate the nature, timing, and criticality of each "customer-supplier" relationship is to take two research paradigms, literature search/synthesis and laboratory experimentation/deduction, and subject each to a process analysis.

To set the stage for the following sections, let us start by answering the question, "Who is the customer for a published academic paper?" No doubt, the *ultimate customer* is one or more of: (1) a colleague in the discipline of the author, located at another academic institution; (2) a government employee or agency; (3) a researcher in industry or consulting. However, these customers are represented by the journal editors and referees who screen submitted research results to determine those of sufficient value and quality to become part of the permanent record of the discipline. So, journal editors and referees are the *initial customer* for submitted articles, and in an unbiased arena each article is evaluated against these general criteria:

- Is the topic appropriate for the journal?
- What is the value of the research contributions?
- Did the author follow standards for the discipline and the journal itself?
- Will the topic, approach, results, and exposition delight the ultimate customer?

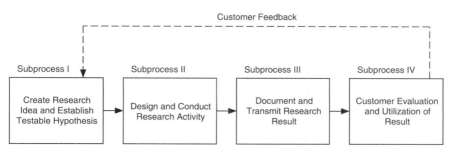

Figure 1 A Process Model of Scholarly Research

An academic purist might be concerned, or even alarmed by the discussion of the publication process and customer satisfaction described in the two paragraphs above. Some academics prefer the dated view of the *faculty member as craftsman, working alone* in "splendid isolation" to satisfy none but himself. The more pragmatic view put forth in this article, no doubt influenced by the author's research into the quality improvement philosophy of Dr. W. Edwards Deming, is one of the *faculty member as process manager*, striving for customer satisfaction while upholding internal ideals and standards. Rather than debasing the research endeavor, we believe the following analysis highlights the respective roles of faculty member, support staff, and administrators. Such user-server-funder triads are endemic to academic institutions (e.g., library services, health services, publication services, placement services). By uncovering the complex customer-supplier relationships that control the researcher's efficiency and effectiveness, we not only intend to converge on actions for process improvement, but also hope others will follow with similar process analysis for other institutional processes.

The remainder of this paper is organized around the research process model depicted in Figure 1. In Section II, we decompose each subprocess into functions the faculty member must perform. At this level, it is fairly straightforward to identify where standards are applied by the faculty member, and later by the editor and his or her referees. The source of each standard, how it is recorded (or at least learned from others), and the means whereby it is communicated and assured must be understood by the researcher. Success in scholarly publication depends both on the quality of the research, and on the quality of the process that brings it to the point of delivery to the customer.

The process analysis illuminates both faculty functions and standards. To meet standards, the faculty member is shown in Section III to be dependent on three critical support systems: (1) Internal Peer Review System; (2) Research Support System; and (3) Publication Support System. Each of these is discussed in enough depth to illuminate key *internal suppliers* to the faculty member. We conclude in Section IV with implications for faculty members and administrators who must cooperate to improve the scholarly output of the institution.

II. Subprocess Decomposition and Quality Standard Identification

Figure 1 depicted the process of scholarly research as four subprocesses, each generating information needed to engage in the following subprocess. Most researchers typically are at work on several projects—each potential publication could be in any one of the four stages. We intend to map out the progress of a single idea as it progresses through subprocesses I, II, III, and IV. In fact, some researchers like to see an idea through from start to publication submission, and will not start on a new idea until the current idea has either resulted in a publishable paper, or has been discarded. We do not intend to compare research strategies here. However, in the subprocess models presented below, we do accommodate two research paradigms:

Paradigm A: Literature review, critique, and synthesis.
Paradigm B: Laboratory experimentation, analysis, and deduction.

Paradigm A might be said to be more characteristic of the humanities, whereas paradigm B is more often found in the biological, physical, and social sciences. Needless to say, both paradigms are used extensively in academic research regardless of discipline. In fact, many papers begin with a comprehensive literature survey and then continue into either new theoretical or laboratory discoveries; therefore, both paradigms may well apply to one research effort.

We now decompose each subprocess into researcher functions. Where there is a difference in the paradigm A and B functional flows, parallel paths will be shown. Standards applied to a step will be discussed as they are encountered.

Subprocess I: Decomposition

As indicated in Figure 2, research ideas may originate in several ways, including customer feedback on previous publications or presentations, discussions with colleagues or students, or simply through the mysterious instant of personal creativity. Campbell has suggested that the subconscious mind works upon various information one has stored, surfacing solutions to persistent problems, or presenting novel ideas that the conscious mind may choose to note or ignore. Connolly states that "creativity seems to require two things: (1) A prior immersion in the problem in all its aspects in order to generate many relevant ideas, and (2) an evaluation or verification phase to decide which, if any, of the ideas generated are any good."

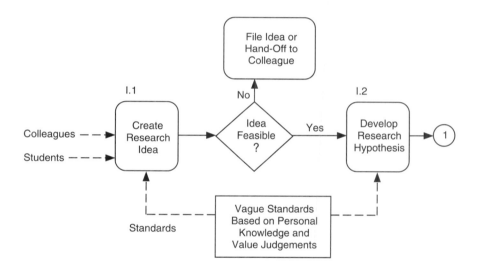

Figure 2 Subprocess I Model

As indicated in Figure 2, this evaluation of ideas by the faculty member narrows the pool of potential research topics he/she might investigate. The standards applied are based on the researcher's knowledge of the discipline and the customers, and may vary occasionally to admit a whim, or an intuitive "hunch." The novelty of an idea and its potential appeal or value to the ultimate customer no doubt are accounted for in the evaluation of ideas, but terms such as "novelty, appeal, and value" are inherently subjective. Hence, their effective application depends on the degree to which the researcher knows:

1. The current status of research in the discipline, and
2. Both the initial and ultimate customer.

Losing touch with the current research in one's discipline can therefore lead to poor selection of research ideas. It can be said that only by interacting with colleagues who are "on the cutting edge" and through a serious investment in research reading can one retain currency. The role of the "trusted peer" (see Section III) can be critical in screening ideas before any commitment to pursue them. Pursuit of ideas with low appeal to customers and/or low probability of publication can thereby be avoided.

Given a research idea that looks promising, the researcher must then decide whether pursuit of the idea is feasible at the present time. Feasibility here means:

1. The degree of difficulty is appropriate.
2. The research idea is of higher priority than others on file.
3. The research resources to carry out the research are available.
4. The time is available to pursue the idea.

Note that the researcher again must make an evaluation. Criteria 1 and 2 are personal—the researcher must know his or her ability and limitations, and his or her other ideas. Criteria 3 and 4 are related to teaching and service loads, and to the research support system at the institution (or institutions the researcher can access). These, or course, are controlled by administrators, but for the faculty member involved in the decision the byword is "know your time constraints, and know your research support system." Some ideas must at this point be filed away or transmitted to colleagues or students for their idea files. The reasons might include:

- research resources inadequate to pursue idea
- outcome of research too risky for this point in my career
- idea judged to be of minor interest—perhaps suitable for master's thesis at later date.

In posing a research hypothesis, the researcher in a sense commits to pursue the idea into at least Subprocess II. The standards applied are still subjective, but because the researcher foresees the need to design and conduct a research activity, the hypothesis will be posed in such a way that the state of the discipline, the ability of the researcher, and the availability of time and resources predicted will give some probability of success in proving or disproving the hypothesis. The level of success probability some researchers require is 0.8 or 0.9; others are satisfied with 0.5 or even less. Once again, personal and somewhat vague standards apply. However, there are standards of proof that are currently accepted in each academic discipline. The researcher must be completely cognizant of these standards, for they form not only the basis for his research hypothesis, but the quality criteria for Subprocess II—Design and Conduct the Research Activity— which we discuss next.

Subprocess II: Decomposition

As illustrated in Figure 3, both literature-based research and laboratory-based research may be viewed as three-step processes. Each discipline establishes "generally accepted research practices" which scholars in the discipline must follow if they expect to publish. These standards slowly change as a discipline matures. For example, in its early stages (1920-1950) industrial engineering principles were almost all empirically-derived from either observing or experimenting with work methods. After 1950, the advent of operations research provided a basis in the mathematical sciences for development of the more sophisticated research methods of computer simulation, resource allocation models, network flow models, and others. The required strength of evidence in both literature survey and experimental work has changed dramatically in the second 40 years of this discipline's evolution.

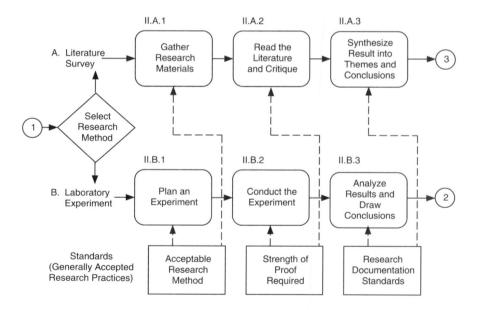

Figure 3 Subprocess II Model

Scholars learn how to plan, organize, conduct, and document their research from the graduate student experience. Experiences in the first few years of employment may enhance their understanding and sharpen their instincts. It is particularly important to developing scholars that they have both an outlet for and critical review of their research results. University departments or divisions often provide a "working paper" series for just this purpose. Progress reports to sponsors or to research symposia, memoranda to colleagues, and publication of short non-refereed articles are well-known forms of documenting preliminary research results. The faculty member typically uses one or more of these semi-finished products as the basis for preparing an article for submission to a refereed journal.

Subprocess III: Decomposition

Once the decision to write an article is made, the scholar must decide upon a target journal (Figure 4). This decision is typically made just prior to or during the writing of the article. Essentially, the scholar must select a target journal that best fits the kind of research result that has been achieved. Although editorial statements tell part of the story, to feel confident about the goodness-of-fit of the article with a journal, the scholar should be familiar with:

- The contents of recent issues of the journal
- The types of articles accepted, and any evidence of preference for one type of article (e.g., theory vs. application, survey vs. experiment) over another
- Particular lines of research the journal editor likes to feature.

For example, the journal *Management Science* has a long history of publishing articles related to decision theory and utilization of subjective probability estimates in decision making. To submit such an article to other journals of management science/operations research, one would be losing the benefit of this historical editorial bias, which boosts the probability of acceptance of such articles. Furthermore, potential consumers for the research result might look only in *Management Science*, thereby costing the scholar in utility and citation of his work.

Once the journal is selected, the author must abide by two other strictly enforced standards:

- Format and style requirements
- Procedural requirements.

Of the format and style requirements, perhaps the most important are writing style and manuscript length. For example, the research publication of the Institute of Industrial Engineers, *IIE Transactions*, instructs authors to:

"Keep all contributions as brief as possible consistent with clear, concise writing. Summarize or cite, do not repeat, arguments already available elsewhere, and make references to related previous work. The Editor will give priority to shorter papers; authors submitting more than 20 typewritten pages can anticipate delays in publications, extensive revision and deletion, or rejection."

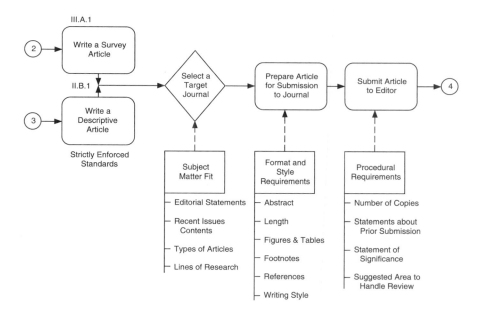

Figure 4 Subprocess III Model

Ignoring such editorial pronouncements would doom a paper, except those few brilliant or exceptional papers that define a new field or prove/disprove a long-standing hypothesis. Most journals also ask for a brief "statement of significance" to help the editors judge whether to even enter the paper into the refereeing process. *IIE Transactions* editorial policy states that the authors statement "is intended to help expedite the review process and succinctly communicate the essence of the paper directly to the Referees." An author who cannot put his paper in context in a convincing manner runs the risk of "striking out before he gets to bat." In some sense, the value judgment about the importance of the research that was made Phase I must now be explained to highly knowledgeable judges in order to pass from Subprocess III to Subprocess IV.

Subprocess IV: Decomposition

Editors handle submitted papers through an organization of associate (or area) editors, who, in turn, coordinate the review and decision on editorial action through a network of referees. As shown in Figure 5, papers are either accepted "as is," sent back to the author for revision (with instructions), or rejected. Although rejection of work that took perhaps several years to complete is a depressing experience, the reasons for rejection are directly traceable back to the standards the author should have applied from Subprocess I through Subprocess III. No one succeeds with every publication; most experienced faculty can attest to having papers rejected for one of the following reasons:

- Little novelty or creativity
- Little value to advancement of the discipline
- Research method(s) questionable or invalid
- Inadequate knowledge of other work in the field
- Subject matter doesn't fit journal
- Failure to follow format and style instructions
- Failure to follow procedural instructions.

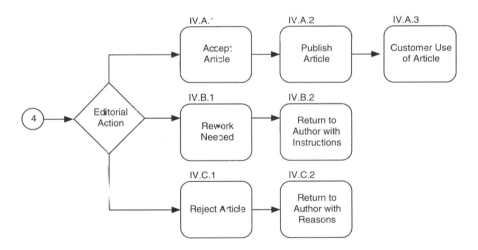

Figure 5 Subprocess IV Model

Better understanding of the research-publication process, as modeled here, can help the faculty member improve the probability of acceptance of a submitted journal. In the next section, we discuss certain key support systems that supply the author with services in the research-publication endeavor. These, too, are critical to the quality of the work and, hence its chances for publication.

III. Critical Support Systems and Suppliers

As mentioned in the introduction, university administrators provide funding for a number of support services on campus. Three of these systems, if properly constituted by the administration and utilized by the faculty member, can increase the probability of acceptance of an article to be submitted for editorial review. These three systems will be called:

- Internal Peer Review System
- Research Support System
- Publication Support System.

Internal Peer Review System

A system of internal peer review can intervene in Subprocesses I and II by providing a type of process quality assurance that can prevent faculty from misjudging the value of a research result, and from drawing unjustified conclusions *prior to* presentation of results to the initial customer. Peers become, in effect, surrogate customers who provide early feedback to the scholar on the quality of hypotheses and procedures.

Faculty often turn to a "trusted peer," either at his home institution, his Ph.D.-granting institution, or someone he has met in the profession, for judgment of whether a creative idea (Stage I) is too hard or too easy, whether it duplicates or contradicts existing knowledge, and most critically—what value will the research result provide if the research hypothesis is proven. In Stage II, some institutions provide a panel of peers that review proposed research for safety, use of human subjects, and sometimes the validity of the research method. Important conclusions, such as a major discovery in medicine or physics, may be reviewed for both faculty and administration information prior to preparation of a formal paper for release to an appropriate journal. The supplier in the peer review system is clearly the person(s) performing the review; in a larger sense, the supplier is the institution that encourages such reviews and promotes their effectiveness by paying the peer, assuring standardized reviews and reports, avoiding any appearance of "policing" the author, and so on.

Research Support System

This system is the most important of the support systems, and also the most expensive to maintain. It is important in two critical ways:

1. It often delineates what kind of research a faculty member may attempt, in that it weighs heavily upon the judgment about what research topic is feasible;

2. It provides the means whereby the faculty member accomplishes
    the research.

An interesting asymmetry appears when we consider that the scholar
engaged in a literature review (flow path A in Figure 3) uses research
resources in step II.A.1, whereas the scholar conducting laboratory experimentation uses research resources primarily in step II.B.2 of Figure 3.
Furthermore, comprehensive articles typical to the sciences and engineering require both research resources. In other words, a good library with no
laboratory is limiting to a scientist, just as is no library but good laboratory
resources. Fishbone diagrams suggesting key suppliers in the research
support system are shown in Figures 6 and 7. Note that the suppliers for
literature survey research are informational in nature (Figure 6), whereas
for laboratory research (Figure 7) they are primarily physical (materials,
machines, methods, manpower) in nature.

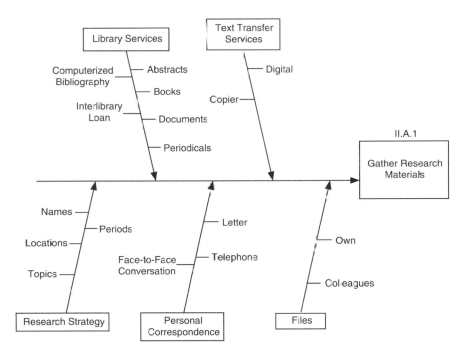

Figure 6 Literary Survey Research Support System

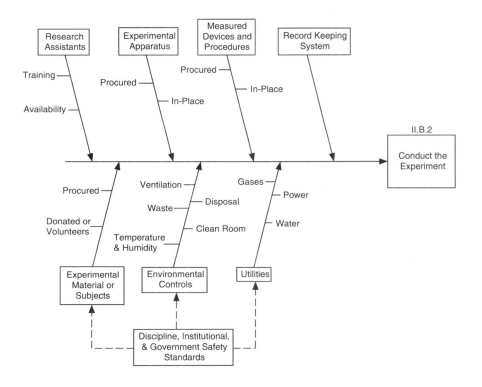

Figure 7 Laboratory Research Support System

Publication Support System

Recall the strict standards concerning style and format that journals impose on prospective authors (Figure 4). The scholar must interpret these requirements not only for his own use as writer, but also must translate and convey selected portions of the journal's requirements to a variety of suppliers who are helping him prepare the article for submission. This translation and apportioning out of requirements requires extensive people skills, and in this role the scholar becomes a process engineer—conveying process specifications and assuring they are met in the final product. Listed below are the key publication support suppliers and the corresponding pitfalls which await the inexperienced author in the absence of high quality publication support.

Publication Support Suppliers	Result of Poor Quality Suppliers
Graphic Arts	Unacceptable art work
Proofreading Services	Misspelled, Misused Words
Editorial Services	Poorly Worded Sentences, Paragraphs, and Sections
Typing Services	Typographical Errors, Poorly Presented Text
Reproduction Services	Poorly Copied Articles for Submission

IV. Implications for Researchers and Administrators

There can be no scholarly endeavor without the research-active faculty member. Creative ideas, a commitment to the discipline, and a deep sense of purpose keep researchers active in their fields. The act of submitting one's work for publication has been shown to be the end result of a series of subprocesses, each with some form of standard which the faculty member must discern and apply. Thus, the researcher is at once a process planner, process engineer, processor, and process quality inspector.

Although certain support services were shown in Section III to be critical for the success of the research activity, and its subsequent submission for publication, *it is clearly the funder of such services (the university administration) that through its actions largely determines the success or failure of its research-active faculty.* We conclude this paper with lists of actions for improvement for each major player in the scholarly endeavor.

Researcher Actions to Improve the Process

- Know your subject area, even articles not yet in print.

- Know your customer (initial and ultimate).

- Evaluate the potential value of a successful research activity prior to starting.

- Use acceptable research practices, and document everything.

- Know your target journals.

- Write many drafts and follow the editorial "instructions to authors" religiously.

- Find "trusted peers" who will review your preliminary research ideas before you commit to them—reciprocate.

- Use internal peer review, outlets such as "Working Paper Series," and professional meeting presentations to:

    - get your research results organized
    - get feedback from your colleagues.

- Find out exactly what research support systems and publication support systems exist at your institution (perhaps prior to even accepting the position).

- Properly manage whatever research and publication support systems you have. Inform administrators of your unmet needs.

- While using the services available, evaluate supplier effectiveness.

- Work with the so-called "funder" (your administrators) to improve the effectiveness of these suppliers—which may require that you start and lead a supplier quality improvement team.

Administration Actions to Improve the Process

- Understand the *customer-funder-server triad* that applies to most every organizational relationship found in universities.

- Study the process and accept responsibility to help your faculty succeed.

- Don't sit back and wait for tenure and promotion processes to "winnow out the unworthy."

- Improve the process to improve the results. Continued improvement of the support systems in Section III is an obligation of administration.

- Set up peer review systems to help the faculty member, not to provide information to rank or categorize the faculty member's research potential. The same may be said for peer review of teaching effectiveness.

- Assure all suppliers provide consistent quality that meets or exceeds faculty expectations, and the expectations of the next process (the editorial review).

- Train supplier personnel in the extended process.

- Avoid hiring faculty into programs for which you are unwilling to provide the support services to help that person succeed.

References

Campbell, D. T. "Blind Variation and Selective Retention in Creative Thought as in Other Knowledge Processes," *Psychological Review*, Vol. 67, 1960, pp. 380-400.

Connolly, Terry. *Scientists, Engineers, and Organizations*, Brooks/Cole, Monterey, California, 1983.

Deming, W. Edwards. *Out of the Crisis*, MIT and Cambridge University Press, Cambridge, Massachusetts, 1985.

Ishikawa, Kaoru. *Guide to Quality Control*, Asian Productivity Organization, UNIBUB, New York, 1982.

Kume, Hitoshi. *Statistical Methods for Quality Improvement*, AOTS, New York, 1987.

Lindquist, Jack. "Professional Development," Chapter 41 in *The Modern American College*, Arthur W. Chickering and Associates, Editor, Jossey-Bass Series in Higher Education, San Francisco, 1981.

Robert G. Batson is a Professor of Industrial Engineering at The University of Alabama, where he teaches and performs research in statistical quality control and operations research. Dr. Batson has been a proponent of increased education in statistical methods for undergraduate engineers, and has developed a curriculum of quality-related courses within the M.S.I.E. program at Alabama. He consulted from 1986-89 with the President's Office on enrollment prediction and management, using both statistical and optimization methods.

Chapter 7

A Total Quality Management (TQM) Organizational Behavior Course

Jose Eulogio Romero-Simpson
University of Miami
Miami, Florida

This chapter was made possible thanks to the University of Miami Institute for the study of quality improvement in manufacturing and service, and Florida Power and Light.

I.   Introduction

"Total Quality Management" (TQM) has generally been described as a "new way of perceiving and doing business." It is a philosophy which views human, technical and engineering subsystems as intertwined through a closely-knit value structure clearly geared to satisfying the customer. TQM stresses the need for the constant improvement of products and/or services through the involvement of the entire work force. TQM's thrust is process improvement rather than quantity of goods produced. A major school of thought of quality improvement is that of William Edwards Deming, an American statistician to whom the "Japanese miracle" is greatly attributed. According to reputed authors, TQM holds great potential for improving the economic situation of the United States and other countries of the world. Due to this situation, the teaching of TQM in Business schools seems imperative.

II.   The Inclusion of TQM in Organizational Behavior (OB) Courses

Christopher Hart, a Harvard Business School Professor, states the following: "For quality . . . there is as yet no predetermined body of knowledge to be taught and there is a crying need for organized course material." (Hart, Testimony)

The field of organizational behavior is in as primitive a situation with respect to quality as other fields contained in standard MBA curricula, with the exception of operations management. According to Hart, Cornell is the only university with an organizational behavior course touching upon quality.

III.   Including TQM in Organizational Behavior Courses

In order to test Hart's assertion, the author examined twelve representative Organizational Behavior textbooks (Arnold & Feldman, 1986; Baron & Greenberg, 1990; Cohen et al., 1988; Hellriegel et al., 1986; Johns, 1988; Kolb, Rubin & McIntyre, 1984; Kreitner & Kinicki, 1989; Lau, 1989; McAfee & Champagne, 1987; Moorehead & Griffin, 1989; Randolph & Blackburn, 1989; Szilagyi & Wallace, 1990 and Vecchio, 1990). None of these textbooks covered its topics from a TQM perspective. The references to quality were fragmented and consistently related to "quality circles" and "quality of work life." The emphasis on the external or the internal customer, which is characteristic of the TQM philosophy, was clearly missing. The enhancement of productivity through performance is seen as an end, rather than quality improvement for ensuring customer satisfaction.

IV.   Purpose of the Paper

The main purpose of this paper is to describe the development, implementation, and evaluation of a course called "Advanced Organizational Behavior" (AOB). This course was offered under a TQM perspective, with a strong emphasis on the Deming philosophy . This paper will also address the reader's attention to some warning signals when implementing TQM. It will conclude with some specific recommendations for those instructors who may be interested in offering an organizational behavior course under this perspective.

V.   Procedures

These were the procedures followed:

1. A review of the TQM literature to seek the most substantive assumptions and principles consistently shared by known authors in the field;
2. The development of instructional guidelines stemming from basic assumptions and principles;
3. The selection of pertinent instructional materials;
4. The implementation of the course; and
5. Course and course components evaluation by its users.

VI.   TQM Guidelines Applicable to Instruction

A critical assessment of the TQM review yielded the following instructional guidelines:

1. An orientation to the customer (student);
2. Commitment of management (instructor) to quality and willingness to accept the responsibility for the system's "well-being" and improvement;
3. The crucial role of education and self-improvement for accomplishing any type of change;
4. The spirit of "KAIZEN," or constant improvement through efforts of the entire work force (students and instructor);
5. A process orientation, as opposed to product orientation;
6. The importance of a stimulating environment, free of fear;
7. A teamwork approach;
8. The use of communication rather than inspection to overcome obstacles, improve the system and achieve quality;
9. The relevant role of statistical thinking and the use of traditional/ad hoc tools to measure/reduce variation; and
10. A personal commitment of each author to the diffusion of TQM rooted on a conviction of its value.

VII. Brief Description of the Course

The AOB course was offered to management majors who had already taken a basic organizational behavior course and thus were familiar with its different topics.

The course, the attending members, the instructor, the classroom and the available resources are viewed comprehensively as a "learning organization" comprised of several interconnected teams modelling a TQM organization. Topics considered particularly critical for management majors were covered by student teams via exercises and simulations.

Mission of the Course

The basic mission of the course was twofold:

1. To help each student improve his/her ability to learn and help his/her fellow team and class members along the way; and
2. To improve the quality of the course as a learning system by offering suggestions and recommendations pertaining to its content, modules and procedures, among others; this effort was geared to making sure that the new "generation" of students (external customers) be exposed to an improved learning system.

Worker-Organization Bonding: an Ideal Module to Teach QI

The course covered its different units from a TQM perspective. Most emphasis, however, was given to the worker-organization bonding (organizational socialization). As an introductory unit, it offers the instructor a unique opportunity to acquaint the students with a different philosophy from the beginning. TQM calls for a different set of values and norms such as cooperativeness, as opposed to competitiveness, and team effort, as opposed to individual effort only. It also calls for different roles from the instructor and the students. The instructor's role is that of a "learning enhancer." Students are expected to gradually assume responsibility over their learning and that of their fellow team members and classmates, and, in general, over the improvement of the overall learning system.

VIII. Course Implementation

Students of "Advanced Organizational Behavior" were exposed to TQM concepts quite early, during the "Worker-Organization Bonding" unit. They practiced such concepts throughout the entire course. Different media were used for this purpose such as readings, films, and tapes. Also, "Personal Application Assignments" (PAAs) were used as learning tools. Finally, students were exposed to pertinent role models—as close to their age as possible—from which they could infer some basic TQM values. These models were either live or "conveniently packaged" in a video cassette.

A standard *learning routine* was applied throughout the course period. These were the steps that each student had to follow:

1. Study the specific topic and exercise to be covered in class;
2. Join a multiple-style team; the instructor "assembled" the team to maximize problem-solving skills;
3. Participate in an experience related to the topic: either a case study or a simulation;
4. Actively participate in a team discussion and in the formulation of the conclusions;
5. Elect or become a team representative to share the team's conclusions in public;
6. Participate in a discussion involving all members of the class leading to specific conclusions pertaining to the subject matter; and
7. Write a Personal Application Assignment (PAA) containing the above points to be presented at least two days after the learning experience.

IX. Course Evaluation

The course was evaluated by multiple-style teams to get more balanced reactions. A questionnaire containing eight crucial items, relating to Deming's 14 points and applicable to a learning setting, was developed. Both items and outcomes will be presented and discussed later. A complementary evaluation, more subjective in nature, was done through the final PAA, where students offered suggestions and recommendations leading to an improved version of the course. Oral spontaneous remarks from the students were also taken into consideration.

X. Results of the Evaluation

Table 1 Team's Evaluation of Eight Crucial Items Related to the Course

ITEM	TEAM NUMBER					
	1	2	3	4	5	$\overline{X}$
1. Absence of Fear	5	4	5	5	5	4.8
2. Learning Useful Things	5	5	4	5	4.6	4.7
3. Responsibility for Own Learning	3	4	4	4	2.5	3.5*
4. Improving Problem-Solving Skills	5	4.8	4	5	4	4.6
5. Quizzes	5	5	1	4.6	3	3.7*
6. Working in Teams	5	4	5	5	5	4.8
7. Leadership Exercise	5	5	5	3	3	4.2
8. Films	4	5	5	4.5	2	4.1

$$\overline{X} = 4.3$$

* Under 4.0

As can be observed both in Table 1 and Figure 1, six of the eight items related to the course received an evaluation higher than 4 (over 5) by the participants. Two items were evaluated low. These items were Number 3 ("responsibility for own learning") and Number 5 ("quizzes"). At this stage of course development, the scarcity of data did not allow the analysis of the variables for determining whether the system (AOB) was in statistical control and/or whether these two items accounted for special or for common causes of variation.[1] The outcomes do show, however, that the learners were least satisfied with the issue of quizzes and assumption of own responsibility for learning, expected from a TQM perspective. This fact was further clarified by the subjective information furnished by the students in their final PAAs. The analysis of this information was facilitated by the use of three analytical tools: (1) an **affinity diagram,** (2) an **interrelation-ship diagraph,** and (3) a **cause-effect diagram,** also known as Ishikawa's "Fishbone Diagram."

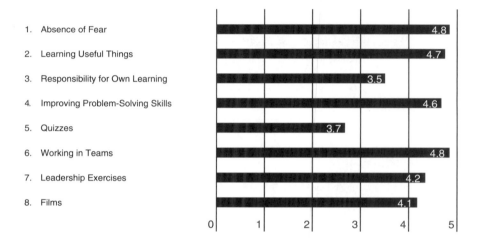

1.	Absence of Fear	4.8
2.	Learning Useful Things	4.7
3.	Responsibility for Own Learning	3.5
4.	Improving Problem-Solving Skills	4.6
5.	Quizzes	3.7
6.	Working in Teams	4.8
7.	Leadership Exercises	4.2
8.	Films	4.1

Figure 1 Team's Averages on Eight Crucial Items Related to the Course

The use of tools (1) and (2) greatly clarified the students' poor attitude toward quizzes and their reluctance to assume responsibility for their own learning. Tool (3) concentrated on the issue of quizzes and assumption of own responsibility. Outcomes of the evaluation appear in Figure 2.

XI.   Discussion

According to individual evaluations and the team evaluations by students, the course successfully enhanced the learning and application of OB concepts through a TQM approach since its early stages. Some key factors for this seem to have been: (a) the philosophy behind the course, (b) the instructor's commit-ment to it, (c) the emphasis on process orientation ("learning how to learn") and (d) the high receptiveness of and involvement by students.

Course Components Contributing to Course Effectiveness

The non-threatening atmosphere, or "free-to-learn climate" as described by a student, allowed students to voice their concerns, doubts and frustrations regarding the readings, exercises and other factors. Such "pinches" were handled immediately, in an orderly way, both by the instructor and by fellow students. The availability of an "escape valve" may partially explain the lack of serious discipline problems in the classroom. (Two students occasionally exhibited dysfunctional behavior; this, however, did not affect their fellow classmates' performance nor the class climate; the instructor dealt with each student after class on a one-to-one basis).

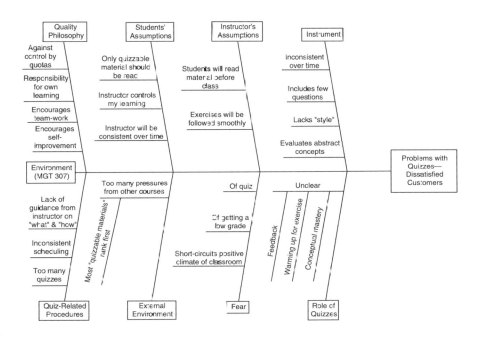

Figure 2 Cause and Effect Diagram for Quizzes

Teams proved to be useful "ice-breakers" and feedback enhancers among participants. The balance of learning styles of team members significantly enhanced effective problem solving.

The PAA proved to be a highly useful tool and compatible with the quality improvement philosophy due to its process and problem-solving orientation.

Individual Differences

Quality authors recognize the importance of "individual differences" when referring to working skills. The concept of "problem-solving style" fits nicely within the TQM philosophy and seems to be instrumental for efficient organizational behavior. Its main strength is that it recognizes differences among human learners in the way they perceive their environment and act upon it. This concept is particularly useful when applied to a "multiple-style, problem-solving team." Each student's style was determined through the application of the "Learning Style Inventory" (Kolb, 1976): the four styles are "accommodator," "diverger," "converger," and "assimilator." The instructor labelled each style as "bee," "dolphin," "beaver" and "owl," respectively (see Figure 3). This was done for didactic purposes.

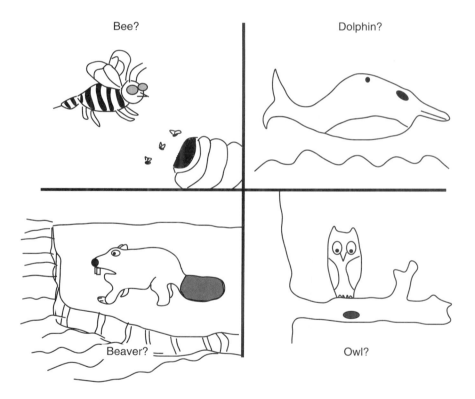

Figure 3 What is Your Adaptive Mode?

Students found the "animal typology" easy to remember and a useful tool for maximizing team effectiveness.

"RED FLAGS" FOR FUTURE APPLICATIONS OF A TQM/OB COURSE

Quizzes and the Assumption of Responsibility for Own Learning

Students felt uncomfortable with quizzes. They perceived quizzes as a "threat" to both their course grade and their final grade. However, they also perceived them as "a necessary evil." Every single student of the course—except one—considered that quizzes should be kept, but "handled with care," in future AOB courses.

Two revealing statements regarding the role of quizzes were: "Students of a specific course may be the victims of the tyranny of the urgent from other courses," and "Readings for AOB got knocked off the list for the new pressing item from another course (unless the readings for AOB were contingent to a quiz)." In other words, reading another course's materials became a priority if students were to be tested on them. This put AOB in a disadvantaged position respecting other courses.

The above situation illustrates a system where the grade has become more important than learning itself. Thus, students concentrate on those assignments which will eventually yield a higher grade upon an external criterion: that of the instructor. While doing this, students are leaving other materials behind which could interest them and help them become more effective learners. A great deal of energy is spent by students analyzing the consequences of being unprepared for the different courses they are taking to minimize their failures instead of gearing their energy to learning useful things. This is unfortunate.

Students, according to the above, would be operating under McGregor's Theory X assumptions (as opposed to Theory Y). Three students' quotes support this assumption.

"Students, given a chance, will try to get out of doing as much as possible."

"All people need external pressure to do something and quizzes are the external pressure that makes a student study."

"Quizzes force students to study."

Another student explicitly mentioned Theory X, refuting it:

> "The assumption that students don't learn unless they're forced to
> (Theory X) is an unfair one. Some will learn because they are
> interested and motivated and others will not learn."

However, only few "Theory Y" type statements like the above were found,
i.e., "Quizzes are distractors of real learning," and "Quizzes ruin the true
spirit of the class." Unfortunately the above comments did not include
recommendations. One student admitted that:

> "There was a shift from grades as an end per se to grades as
> indicators of real progress in class."

The same student, however added the following statement:

> "Due to the structure of the present educational system, the posi-
> tive outcomes of the shift may not be that appealing. After all,
> grades are everything, for they are the gateway to future prosper-
> ity. Thus, your effort in eliminating quotas might be in vain."

It is pathetic that grades, presumably indicators of learning, are pursued
as an end per se. It is also unfortunate that fear of failure and external control
take over motivation for improvement and internal control which are
crucial elements for real learning to occur.

Presence and Management of Fear

According to Deming (1988), fear should be driven out from a company
for everyone to work effectively. The AOB course as a "learning" organization is no exception to this plea. The subject of fear was originally handled
during the "Worker-Organization Bonding" module. The instructor and
the students used Sherwood and Glidewell's model of "psychological
contract" which appears in the initial chapter of Kolb et al.'s textbook (1984)
through which content and procedural specifications were outlined quite
early in the course (first three sessions). The contract specified content and
procedural issues (a clearly process-oriented instructional strategy).

Unfortunately fear was not totally driven out as desired.

Quizzes: An Ideal Way of "Building Up Fear"

Fear was hardly noticed beyond the initial sessions, but it recurred as soon
as the first quiz was announced. According to Gitlow & Gitlow (1987), two
of the three pitfalls to "Driving Out Fear" are: (1) Believing you have

eliminated fear when it still exists, and (2) Not planning for new fears that the philosophy will create. This is exactly what happened. Students had already been acquainted with and had started to experience a philosophy which preaches the avoidance of "inspection" to achieve quality. In spite of this, they were faced with "instructional inspections" as one student pointed out. The assignment of grades also reflected post-facto control procedures.

Under ideal circumstances a "pure" TQM-oriented course should not demand quizzes since they resemble external inspections. Quality, rather, should be built into the system. Each member of the system should feel pride in "workmanship." The inner satisfaction for his/her accomplishments should be reward enough. Each student should feel proud of gradually becoming a better learner.

Given that quizzes and grades do not fit in a TQM-oriented course, how does the instructor make sure that students study the assigned materials? Is there an available alternative?

As mentioned before, a significant number of students will only study the assigned materials if they are quizzed later on. This generalized practice leads the author to assume that the educational system may have conditioned this behavior.

How does a TQM course survive in a non-TQM system?

The AOB course with its specific rules may be perceived as a subsystem within a broader system which follows a different set of rules which at certain points conflict with the former.

As we have seen before, the main concerns or "disruptions" during the implementation of AOB were related to the issue of quizzes and students' assumption of responsibility for their own learning. These two closely related concerns, if handled inadequately, could become special causes of system variation.

What can be done to overcome these potential "short-circuits"?

An ideal strategy for avoiding conflict is to change the entire system, from a curricular structure to a TQM approach. This task, if not impossible, is demanding, time-consuming, and complex. A more sensible strategy would be accepting AOB within its systemic constraints and maximizing its effectiveness with some adjustments. This would prevent "short-circuits," rather than correcting them after the fact.

What specific adjustments can be done to the course to overcome the difficulties of quizzes and external control and yet keep its TQM orientation? At this point, the opinion of the instructor and of every student (except one) is that quizzes should be kept. The real issue is to determine the conditions under which quizzes should be given.

The following suggestion from an AOB student, pertaining to an ideal quizzing procedure, encompasses most of the learners' suggestions:

> "The wrong way is to tell a student to study a large amount of abstract material and test him/her on it in a few days without first having given him/her directions in what to stress or how to best approach the material. The right way is to give the material one week before the quiz, ask for input on questions, discuss the best approach to take in learning the information and wish the student good luck."

XII.   Basic Recommendations

Close attention should be given to the issue of "quizzes" and "external control." These issues should be brought up at a very early stage of the course, while establishing the psychological contract between the instructor and the students. It is important to develop a quizzing style which should also be communicated to the students at a very early stage of the course. Before a quiz takes place, the instructor should briefly offer an advanced organizer of the subject in question to the students and provide guidance with respect to those points considered focal. This becomes particularly critical when the readings have a high level of abstraction (which is not that uncommon). Ideally, the instructor should make a special effort in selecting the instructional materials which can be easily understood by the students.

Rules of Thumb for Maximizing Success of TQM-Oriented OB Courses

1.   The course should be as relevant and appealing as possible to the students in light of the set of objectives mutually agreed upon between students and instructor;
2.   The students should thoroughly enjoy the process of learning and actively participate in it;
3.   The terminology should be geared to the semantic and experiential level of the learners;
4.   The concepts should be explored within situations which are familiar to the learners;
5.   The learners should take active responsibility in their own learning; and
6.   The classroom should become a stimulating environment where transactions among students and between students and the instructor are the rule, not the exception.

XIII.   Final Comments

The teaching of "Advanced Organizational Behavior" under a TQM perspective proved to be both a challenging and a gratifying experience for both junior and senior learners (students and instructor, respectively). Its implementation was greatly enhanced by the instructional materials, most of them stemming from David Kolb's experiential learning theory. This theory, although not directly related to TQM, is compatible with its assumptions and values. PAAs (Personal Application Assignments), which were initially taken with suspicion by the students, became a great asset to the course. Other course components, both tangible and intangible, which were useful were: the use of multiple-style teams, the use of the "psychological contract" for handling "pinches" (*"warusa kagen"* in Japanese) and the "free to learn climate" established in the class, among others.

It seems important to point out that the feedback given by the AOB students is the result of an unprecedented effort on their part to evaluate the course both from an individual perspective and from a team perspective.

Throughout approximately 20 years as an instructor, the author has never witnessed such zeal and dedication of students to improve their particular learning system. This seems greatly due to the spirit of "kaizen" (constant improvement of the entire work force) which the students assumed early in the course. They learned to work within a team perspective, while experiencing the thrill of going "beyond themselves" for a worthy cause: the betterment of their course for the sake of future generations of students. Although—or perhaps precisely because—this was particularly done for the benefit of future students (prospective customers), their own learning was reinforced.

The nature of the course, which is process-oriented ("learning how to learn") and the instructor's specific instructional philosophy, seemed to have significantly eased the inclusion of TQM concepts.

Epilogue

The author, in his role as instructor, has acquainted his students with an alternative way of learning which is also unfamiliar to them. The question remains as to whether this approach will actually help the learners in future courses or experiences. The author is concerned that students might have developed a set of expectations which will not be fulfilled in future courses. The students will certainly compare and contrast this experience to that of other courses.

The usefulness of the course within a broader perspective is an issue which cannot be neglected when considering the implementation of future TQM-oriented courses. The development of a TQM global business curriculum bearing its most important assumptions should be seriously considered. Representative organizations of the business world such as IBM, Motorola, Ford, Florida Power Light and even branches of the Federal Government have shifted to a TQM-oriented approach. Business schools cannot get behind. They should take active steps for satisfying the present needs of the business community through an innovative TQM curriculum. This is a challenge yet to be met.

References

Arnold, Hugh J. & Feldman, Daniel C. *Organizational Behavior*, McGraw-Hill Book Company, New York, 1986.

Baron, Robert A. & Greenberg, Jerald. *Behavior in Organizations*, Allyn & Bacon, Boston, 1990.

Cohen et al. *Effective Behavior in Organizations*, Richard D. Irwin, Inc., Homewood, IL, 1988.

Gitlow, Howard S. and Gitlow, Shelly J. *The Deming Guide to Quality and the Competitive Position*, Prentice-Hall, NJ, 1987.

Hart, Christopher. Testimony Before the Congressional Committee on Science, Space and Technology, April 20, 1989.

Hellriegel, Don, Slocum, John W. & Woodman, Richard W. *Organizational Behavior*, West Publishing Company, St. Paul, 1986.

Johns, Gary. *Organizational Behavior: Understanding Life at Work*, Scott, Foresman and Company, Boston, 1988.

Juran, J.M. *Managerial Breakthrough: A New Concept of the Manager's Job*, McGraw-Hill Book Company, New York, 1964.

Kolb, David, Rubin, Irwin M. & McIntyre, James M. *Organizational Psychology*, Prentice-Hall, Inc., Englewood Cliffs, NJ, 1984.

Kreitner, Robert & Kinicki, Angelo. *Organizational Behavior*, Richard D. Irwin, Inc., Boston, 1989.

Lau, James B. & Shani, A.B. *Behavior in Organizations: An Experiential Approach*, Richard D. Irwin, Inc., Homewood, IL, 1988.

McAfee, R. Bruce & Champagne, Paul J. *Organizational Behavior: A Manager's View*, West Publishing Company, St. Paul, 1987.

Moorhead, Gregory & Griffin, Ricky W. *Organizational Behavior*, Houghton Mifflin Company, Boston, 1989.

Randolph, W. Alan & Blackburn, Richard. *Managing Organizational Behavior*, Richard D. Irwin, Homewood, IL, 1989.

Scholtes, Peter R. et al. *The Team Handbook: How to Use Teams to Improve Quality*, Joiner Associates, Madison, 1988.

Szilagyi, Andrew D. Jr. & Wallace, Marc J. Jr. *Organizational Behavior and Performance*, Scott, Foresman, Glenview, IL, 1990.

Vecchio, Robert P. *Organizational Behavior*, The Dryden Press, Chicago, 1988.

The content of this paper is based on a presentation delivered at the 1990 OBTC Meeting, University of Richmond, Virginia, June 13, 1990.

Endnote

1 Common Causes of variation are random or due to chance; thus, at this point, it was decided to leave them the way they were. Intervention at this point could have increased variation, thus tampering a system which appears to be in statistical control. Special causes of variation need to be traced back to the process in order to establish corrective measures.

Jose Eulogio Romero-Simpson is Associate Professor of the Department of Management, School of Business Administration, University of Miami.

Chapter 8

Demythologizing Quality Improvement for Faculty

Mark Baggett
Samford University
Birmingham, Alabama

Why would faculty members, bred in the rarefied atmosphere of some noble academic discipline, embrace the principles of Quality Improvement, which often seem couched in the language of crass commercialism? Despite the impressive inroads of QI into the academy, the question still needs an answer. A reluctance, if not refusal, persists by faculty members to invest professionally in Quality Improvement.

However, the inescapable fact about Quality Improvement applied to higher education is that there already exists a strong tradition of QI, a tradition that faculty members participate in and live by. It involves accreditation standards that require faculty members to assess student performance, library holdings, and criteria for student admissions. These accepted practices of higher education are nothing more than ingrained attempts to insert quality into the processes by which the university functions. What remains is for faculty to acknowledge that tradition of quality, and then to identify and, yes, invest, in a more formal articulation of those principles. Before acceptance, then, must come a recognition of the alliances between QI and the academic process.

First, faculty members must confront the myths about Quality Improvement and its progenitor, W. Edwards Deming. The principal apprehension is that the application of QI strategies means importing structures from "foreign" soil, namely the business world. The assumption is that a heavy-handed, indiscriminate importation of these techniques is merely another way of distracting faculty from their real responsibilities of teaching and research. At best, these techniques are thought to be time-consuming, inconvenient, and irrelevant. At worst, they are thought to reinterpret and to taint the purer mission of the academy.

At Samford, a Southern Baptist-affiliated university of 4,200 students with professional schools in law and pharmacy, faculty members have had an ample opportunity to critique QI ever since John Harris arrived on campus in 1989. Harris has conducted seminars and workshops on Total Quality Management (TQM), including a fairly intensive course entitled "Student First Quality Quest" for most faculty members, administrators, and staff personnel, who participate over the course of a semester. Harris's efforts have received an enthusiastic endorsement from President Thomas Corts and Provost William Hull, as well as from spearpoint faculty members in various disciplines who have in turn helped conduct the workshops. The quality quest has, it is true, been met by apathy and even antipathy in some quarters, but the large percentage of Samford faculty have kept an open mind and waited to judge the fruits of the efforts. It has helped that this discourse has become a part of a larger conversation within Samford and among its constituent groups, all of whom are concerned with clarifying the mission of the University as it celebrates its Sesquicentennial.

Still, Samford faculty members are like those at other schools: burdened by our teaching responsibilities, which seem to give ever-fewer opportunities for scholarly research, and distracted by a growing number of administrative duties. The atmosphere is one of suspicion of "paper shuffling," "make-work projects"—the general charges of peripheral tasks interfering with real work. For Quality Improvement to survive and prevail at Samford, its advocates must satisfy a range of impressions and misinformation.

Myth #1. *That Quality Improvement is content-poor, that it is an empty box decorated by bells and whistles, and signifying nothing.*

The impression by humanities faculty in particular is that Quality Improvement smacks, at best, of business methodology clumsily imported to academia, or, at worst, of slick marketeering that plays for a popular, transitory audience. Why, we sometimes ask, is there always such a trade imbalance in our fields, and we are inevitably importing from business and education, in particular? Why can't the guiding philosophy partake of humanities studies and instruction?

One answer is that administrations traditionally have reflected a humanities bias, and that administrators (such as those at Samford) come from humanities backgrounds to a significant degree. Only recently has a secular management philosophy made strides in higher education.

Faculty participants in the seminars and workshops soon realize that QI comes with as little suprastructure and jargon as any program, even those in their own disciplines. Yes, there are Deming's 14 Points, and yes, there are a handful of utilities to become familiar with (fishbone diagrams, for instance). But for the most part, QI allows the participant to discover his or her own structure and processes, in order to understand the bases on which present decisions are made. In fact, there is little "importing" at all, aside from the quality paradigm (another word that soon loses its intimidation factor), and there is much less jargon than in the first few pages of the average textbook.

Myth #2.   That QI is not about quality at all, but uses this mask to conceal a simplistic, unsophisticated, and ultimately quantitative approach.

As an English professor, I tended to equate QI with those computer programs that purport to "assess" one's writing effectiveness. The notion of "quantifying" critical judgments left me frustrated. After all the spellchecks, percentages of passive verbs, average sentence lengths, and number of dependent clauses, the fact is that no machine can measure the *quality* of a sentence. Is the same true for the processes of higher education? Perhaps. But surely some aspects of higher education can be isolated and measured reliably: the number of graduates finding jobs, going to graduate schools, the number and amount of gifts; the number of active alumni. And if the assessment data is not wielded as a sword, departments and faculty members can learn significant things about the way they teach.

Our English Department has just begun to add a data-component to our decision making. We are studying the effectiveness of preliminary courses on student performance in upper-level courses; we are studying the effects of placement on student progress; we are studying the comprehensiveness of our curriculum, as it can be measured on graduate school aptitude tests; we are studying the optimum use of our physical space and of class size; we are studying the demands on our clerical staff. In all these things, we are uncovering the underlying structure—a data structure—of our department and realizing that the structure can be manipulated, and furthermore, that *we* can manipulate it for better results. We are finding that quantifications, which are just one part of Quality Improvement, can be useful, and that they need not threaten our basic enterprise.

Myth #3.   That decision makers are not interested in assessment data, but are merely looking for some "performance" criteria, however crude, to justify hiring and firing decisions.

The buzzwords that disturb faculty most profoundly are "results" or "effectiveness" or "performance." In the typical humanities professor's mind, these words signal a material litmus test against which the professor is judged. The notion of strict performance standards in a medium which is essentially abstract and intangible is frightening because it raises the threat of losing jobs, losing departments even, when academic units don't "measure up" to a standard they don't understand and can't control. Furthermore, we want to believe every department's distinctive contribution should be measured in the context of the university's mission. This English Department, for instance, graduates student teachers; this one prepares its students for graduate school; this one serves an adult learning community. How can performance criteria measure each consistently?

The answer, again, is that Quality Improvement focuses on process improvement. In many ways, departments define their own performance criteria and measure themselves according to their own rules. The implications of the results are not directed toward personnel, but toward processes, and process improvement is a goal on which every faculty member should insist.

Samford has addressed this issue in a recent attempt to link assessment results with budgetary planning. The ambitious proposal creates a faculty-staff panel for monitoring the process of budgetary planning and seeks to drive budgetary planning from faculty perspectives upward. Such a proposal, as you can expect, puts Quality Improvement on the spot. Will already-shorthanded departments be penalized for falling short on their assessments? Will some "marginal" academic units be phased out?

The answer is no. We hope to formalize a holistic budgetary process that will stimulate constant improvement without a corresponding fear of punishment. Indeed, the departments with the most pressing needs may justify the largest increases in funding. At the same time, there will be a corresponding award for "breakthroughs." No one is saying, nor should they say, that all programs will survive perpetually, or that programs will not be redirected. Academic units live under those realities now. The point is that by adding budget and planning criteria, departments are forced to examine their processes and to seek improvement. One of the benefits of the proposal is that "breakthroughs" and improvements may not be budget-related at all; that is to say, departments may find ways to improve their programs without spending money.

Myth #4.   That Quality Improvement is just an excuse to add another administrative layer to a bloated bureaucracy, at the expense of teaching faculty.

Answering this myth depends on the intentions and integrity of university leadership, and on the academic credibility of the QI person or persons. Ostensibly, QI could be carried out on a university campus among teaching faculty and staff, although few faculty would welcome the administrative burden. At Samford, we have one person and one administrative assistant who fill this role, but they fill other roles as well. In every respect, John Harris has served as a facilitator; the projects on which he works—such as Senior Seminars and national Peer Reviews—are projects that the departments have accepted themselves, and on which Harris's office provides guidance, coherence, and clerical support. Like any good assessment officer, his ideal situation would be to eliminate the need for its office. Faculty members trained in QI are helping him discover that goal by leading workshops themselves, by helping to disseminate Samford's findings, by participating in grant proposals and in administering grant funds. When one considers the administrative strata for admissions, student affairs, university relations, and business affairs, the Quality Improvement office seems streamlined in proportion.

Myth #5. *That Quality Improvement detracts from the ultimate goal of teaching and learning by preserving the institution rather than serving its customers, or students.*

The issue is really quite complex. Ford Motor Company exists to serve its stockholders. True, the company serves its stockholders best when it serves its customers best. And customers will ultimately define and determine what is "best," no matter what Ford stockholders or executives want to tell them. Still, in a real sense, the customers are used, and manipulated, to serve stockholders and to preserve the corporate structure.

The purpose of a college or university, we argue, is more transparent. Its customers (a word whose connotation as "students" is still a long way from being universally accepted) are not "used"; they are intrinsically a part of the institutional structure. They are customers, stockholders, and products all at once. It is true that an institution of higher learning may survive, even seem to thrive, when its students are not served efficiently or when they are not successful. The charge against well-endowed research institutions whose faculty work on publications while graduate students teach undergraduates is such an example. But ultimately, the institution's success depends on the success of its graduates.

Educators, especially teaching faculty, express a consistent dislike for equating students with "customers." This dislike is rooted in many of the honorable concepts by which faculty think of themselves and their work. But part of the dislike can be traced to the disturbing notion that faculty members are responsible for their students, even beyond college. The truth is that faculty do not universally accept, or want to accept, that idea. Yet it should not be threatening to us. Our professional goals should extend beyond the classroom, beyond our own professional advancement even, and should include a professional responsibility for students. No one is saying we should rise or fall according to their career success. But faculty members can be persuaded to see themselves as components in a larger process whose success is judged according to many components. For their part, QI advocates should be persuaded not to insist on QI methodology and terminology in every instance, especially when they meet with resistance. Surely, these are secondary matters that shouldn't jeopardize the entire process.

Ultimately, we need visionary administrators who approach faculty honestly with the demands of running a university in the 20th and 21st centuries. Faculty investment is the crucial issue, and it will not come through passive acceptance. Speaking as a faculty member, I believe the administration, through its decision making, must first demonstrate its own commitment to quality improvement. Faculty must perceive that commitment in the administration's treatment of faculty, and in the response to issues of faculty-importance: teaching load, tenure and promotion, and academic support. Although faculty members in their disciplines may work on the cutting edge, they are traditionalists by and large when it comes to justifying the university as an institution. They are less avant-garde and more old guard of academic traditions. The more administrators can understand what faculty do and how they think, the quicker those administrators can slay the dragon of misperception and debunk the myths of quality improvement.

Mark Baggett is Associate Professor of English and Law at Samford University.

Chapter 9

Total Quality Improvement in the Basic Sciences: A Retrospective Case Study

Ronald N. Hunsinger
Samford University
Birmingham, Alabama

Introduction

Quality control has long been part of standard operating procedure in many clinical—and analytical—chemistry laboratories. The reason for these repetitive measurements of known standards is simple. They tell the technicians that their procedures, reagents, and instrumentation are all trustworthy, and therefore that their results are credible. Likewise, quality control measures have for years found applications in industrial processes. After all, a small dysfunction or two along the assembly line can result in an accumulation of defective products at the end of the line. This results in increased production cost, decreased profits and dissatisfaction among customers.

While quality control is still needed in many disciplines, Deming, Ishikawa, Scherkenbach, and others have broadened the whole quality concept so as not only to assure the processor that the results are acceptable, but also to allow for continual improvement in quality. This revolution, sometimes referred to as TQI (Total Quality Improvement), has encompassed not only the industrial production lines, but also the whole corporate process. As Daniel Seymour (1991) notes, "Quality has evolved from a narrow technical discipline, focused on the detection of manufacturing flaws, to a broader field that encompasses all stages, from design to production to market." Basically, the system involves a number of sequential problem-solving steps in a closed feedback loop which are designed to continually improve processes:

1. Select a critical process
2. Survey customer(s)
3. Select an issue
4. Diagram the process
5. Establish process performance measures
6. Diagram causes and effects
7. Collect data on causes
8. Analyze data
9. Develop solutions (PDCA)
10. Standardize improvements

In a seemingly unrelated development, higher education has entered an era of assessment. Accreditation is no longer based on counts of books in the library or the number of earned doctorates on the faculty. Instead, accountability of the educational processes designed to produce the "educated person" is becoming more and more the focus. This means that no longer can professors indulge in complete academic freedom, as it relates to content and pedagogy. They will assume more direct responsibility for the competency of their product.

In light of these pending paradigm shifts in higher education, what is to be the reaction of the faculty? The purpose of this chapter will be to show how corporate-style quality improvement (QI) techniques can be applied directly to improving teaching effectiveness in higher education.

What is Teaching Effectiveness?

Historically, educational theorists have sought to answer this question by examining three basic aspects of the learning process: cognition (higher thinking skills), emotion (feeling), and response (behavior). In recent times, the pendulum has swung from the operational analysis sparked by the work of Thorndike and Skinner to an intense interest in cognition and hierarchies of higher order thinking skills. The evidence of this transformational process within the field of psychology, as it applies to learning, can be seen in the repletion of the current literature with articles on the teaching of critical thinking skills. What has endured from the earlier Skinnerian era, which still provides a base for teaching and learning, can be summarized by what Miller and Dollard (1950) describe as the three psychological components of the teaching/learning paradigm — cues, engagement, and reinforcements. Walberg's analogy (1990) of these three components with the physiological processes of input, integration, and output suggests that they are closely linked with the very biological basis of learning.

Indeed, there are data (Walberg, 1990) which show that cues, engagement, reinforcement, and corrective feedback have highly significant effects on learning by students. Let us elaborate briefly on the importance of each:

Cues

- clearly show what is to be learned and may need to include strategies which can be used to learn the material (unfortunately, the latter is often lacking in college classroom settings). Syllabi, lectures, directions, handouts, textbooks, brief overviews of larger blocks of material given at the beginning of a unit, course objectives and goals, pre-tests, etc., are all examples of cues. Ideally, as the learner advances, fewer cues should be needed.

Engagement

- is the actual process of learning the material. It is the progressive process of synthesis, analysis, and evaluation by the learner; the point at which one internalizes the material presented. From a teaching standpoint, it is the point at which professors move from a typical lecture format to methods which prompt thinking on the student's part, i.e., the asking of thought provoking questions, which require deeper thinking about the material, the "who, what, when, where, why, how" questions, problem solving, or the introduction of case studies.

Feedback and Reinforcement

- are the corrective processes which remedy incorrect or inadequate responses. When given in an appropriate, clear, and immediate manner, feedback and reinforcement can effectively signal students as to what to do next. They are markers of the progress being made by the student.

A more pragmatic view is that it is a very difficult task to define precisely what constitutes good teaching. Some may even assess that good teachers are "born" and not "created" by some training process. Others view teaching skills as simply "icing on the cake," with the "cake" being the subject matter expertise brought to the classroom by a professor. In this view, content is all-important. Essentially, the total burden of the learning process is shifted to the students. They must attend the lectures, take the notes, read the text, motivate themselves, judge what is important, learn it, store it, retrieve it at the appropriate time, and finally integrate it into the whole of their educational experience. The professor is simply the expert who "hands down" the knowledge. If learning does not take place, then it must surely be the students' fault. They should work harder!

At the opposite end of the spectrum is what has been called the "technocratization" of higher education (Goodlad, 1990). In this model, the professor is not necessarily a real expert in the subject. Instead, he or she has an array of skills (informal or formal) in pedagogy, but only a limited or general knowledge of the subject matter. This approach is not always undesirable, depending upon the nature and goals of the institution in which a professor is employed and the needs profile of its constituency.

To aid us in our discussion of effective instruction, let us pragmatically view the ideal teaching paradigm in terms of three elements (seen in Figure 1).

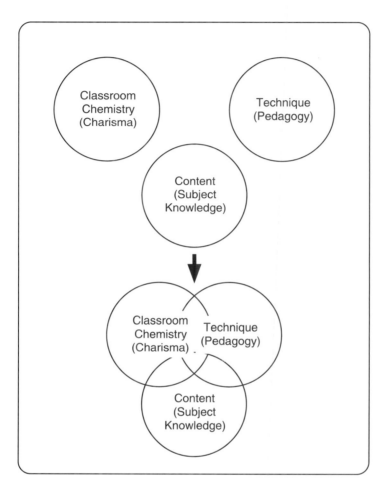

Figure 1 Elements of Good Teaching

We will now examine more specifically how quality improvement can be applied to effective instruction. To do so, we will describe the basic philosophy of our QI program in the Department of Biological Sciences and look at one particular teaching unit as a retrospective case study.

The QI Paradigm

Our QI paradigm in the Department of Biological Sciences at Samford

University stems from three emphases: customer, process, and statistical analysis. Modeled similarly to our effective teaching elements (*vide supra*), we believe that optimal effectiveness for an academic unit occurs when all three emphases become operational (shown in Figure 2):

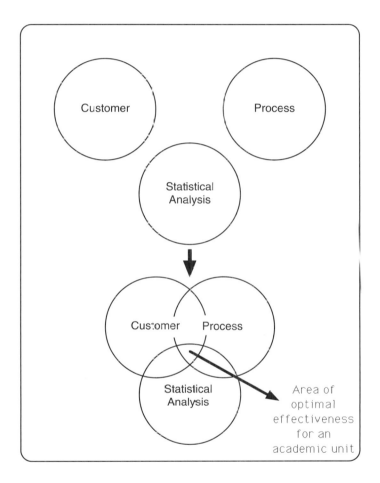

Figure 2 Area of Optimal Effectiveness for an Academic Unit

Our academic applications of QI arose from interactions with J. Edward McEachern, M.D. Dr. McEachern heads Clinical Quality Improvement at West Pace Ferry Hospital in Atlanta, GA, and is a member of the Hospital Corporation of America's Quality Resource Group. In a nutshell, our basic operating philosophy is echoed in that of the West Pace Ferry Hospital, "... create [an] environment for continuous improvement and then enable all employees (faculty) to improve their individual and group processes by giving them the tools they need."

A Retrospective Case Study

As a case study, let us consider a course taught in the Department of Biological Sciences at Samford University. Long before quality improvement policies and theories were introduced at Samford, this class was one of several "service courses" offered by our department. This means that it was not a part of the curriculum for biology majors, but was offered by the department, as a service, to non-biology majors, e.g., nursing students.

There is nothing particularly unique about such a service course arrangement. Indeed, many nursing schools associated with smaller colleges and universities have such agreements with the science departments. Beyond a matter of professional courtesy, the rationale for offering such courses is that it eliminates duplicity within the system while at the same time, allows for a greater concentration of budgetary efforts within the anatomy and physiology division of the department.

Historically at our institution, even though this course was offered as a service, there had been very little interaction between the Biology Department and the School of Nursing. Only limited communication had occurred between the two entities of this case study, usually occurring during some crisis (e.g., someone complaining after not doing well in the course). Upon receiving in-service QIP training from the Samford University Quality Improvement Office, various external customers—medical and other off-campus graduate and/or professional schools, various cooperative laboratories, and governmental agencies—and internal customers—Samford's School of Nursing, School of Pharmacy, Department of Psychology, and Sports Medicine Program—were identified by our department.

After consulting with Dr. Catherine Collett of Collett Associates, we decided to survey one of our internal customers, the Ida V. Moffett School of Nursing. This choice was based upon growing perceptions of problems with our service course for the Nursing School. Our customer indicated the following product and service needs:

BIOL 106 (Nursing Anatomy and Physiology) should give Associate Degree nursing students the basic knowledge of the anatomical and physiological sciences to successfully complete clinical courses and to pass board exams.

The following measurements and expectations were indicated:

1. Reduce the number of failures (i.e., those who make below a grade of "C")

2. Strengthen the mastery base of the "C" students

3. Increase performance on the National League of Nurses (NLN) board exam for Anatomy and Physiology.

An issue statement was then formulated:

"Increase the mastery level of students as indicated by NLN Anatomy and Physiology Exam performance."

All three measurements and expectations were deemed urgent. Immediately, new information was gained through this first step in the QI methodology, e.g., previously, we had not been aware that the Nursing School had been monitoring our course through the NLN exam. We had not been apprised in the past of the performance ratings of the nursing students. Thus, vital feedback about the quality of our course had been missing.

After the customer survey, we felt that the situation provided an excellent opportunity for applying the process improvement techniques learned in a recent training session conducted by Collett and Associates. An issue statement was then selected. In order to implement the process improvement technique, an academic QI team was formed involving the professor who taught the course, the Department Chair of Biological Sciences, the Dean of the School of Nursing, and the Chairs of the Nursing School's Curriculum Committee and Admissions Committee. Thus, ownership of the actual course, the suppliers of the raw material for the process, and the customer for the finished product were all represented. The next step was to gain some idea of what our current academic process looked like in a flowchart (Figure 3).

Subsequently, our academic QI team engaged in an organized brainstorming process to devise a "fishbone" cause and effect analysis. The specific effect reflected our original issue statement and was succinctly expressed as low NLN performance. In essence, all team members felt that if these scores could be improved, then this would be a broad indicator that student mastery of the material in the course was also improved and chances were better that performance in subsequent courses in the nursing curriculum would be improved (Figure 4).

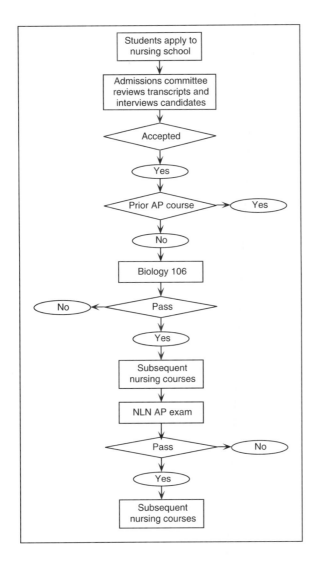

Figure 3 Flowchart of Current Academic Process

A Pareto analysis of data collected on our students showed that the variable which contributed (or at least correlated) the most with poor NLN scoring was the long time period which elapsed between the completion of

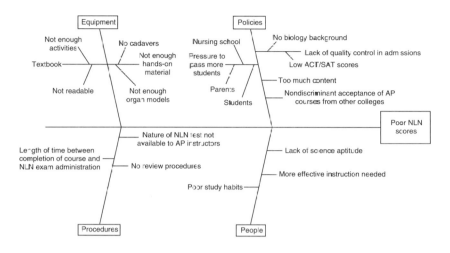

Figure 4 Cause and Effect Graph for Low Anatomy
and Physiology NLN Scores

the Anatomy and Physiology course and the actual administration of the
NLN exam in Anatomy and Physiology. Beyond this, other factors were
also identified (Figure 5).

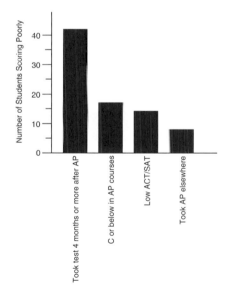

Figure 5 Pareto Chart of Students Scoring Poorly

After careful analysis of the current process, a PDCA cycle (Figure 6) was designed and agreed upon by the entire QI team:

1. Give NLN at the end of the course
2. Give some incentive to study for the NLN exam
3. Use mastery system in the course
4. Increase admissions standards
5. Establish prerequisities for the AP course

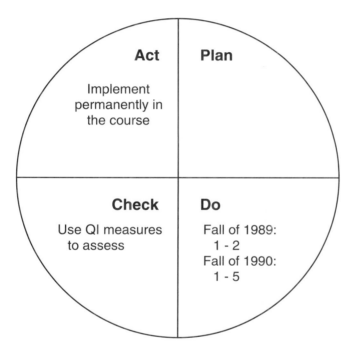

Figure 6 PDCA Cycle for the NLN Exam

A redesign of our process reflected improvement over the previous process flowchart (Figure 7).

Figure 8 shows scatter plots of the scores from year to year following our implementation of the PDCA. As one can see, consistent progress has been made in the general scoring pattern of the students as we have gradually implemented change. Notice, in particular, increases in the number

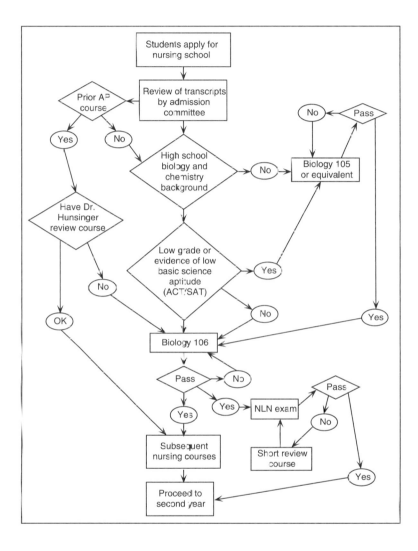

Figure 7 Flowchart of Redesigned Process

of students scoring above the national average. Lower scores (i.e., those falling below the LCL) represent special causes, not common causes, to the system's variation. These are borderline students, with respect to Nursing School Admission Standards, who have been allowed into the Anatomy and Physiology class on a probationary status. In addition to the measured progress in our system, there is a feeling of cooperation, team-work, and pride in our QI group. The fear and fault-finding mentality is no longer in existence. No doubt a spin-off from our efforts to improve quality in our basic science offerings, it should be noted that the Ida V. Moffett School of Nursing students ranked first in the nation among 877 nursing programs because of its 100 percent passage rate on the National Council Licensure Examination for Registered Nurses. QIP in academia works!

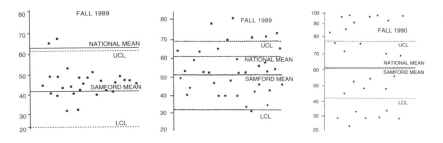

Figure 8 Scatter Plots of NLN Scores from 1988-1990

References

Goodlad, J.I. "Studying the Education of Educators: From conception to findings." *Phi Delta Kappan, 71,* 1990, pp. 698-709.

Miller, N. and Dollard J. *Personality and Psychotherapy.* New York: McGraw-Hill, 1950.

Seymour, D. "Beyond Assessment: Managing Quality in Higher Educa-tion." *Assessment Update,* 3 (1), January-February, 1991, pp. 1-2.

Walburg, H. J. "Productive Teaching and Instruction: Assessing the Knowl-edge Base." *Phi Delta Kappan, 71,* 1990, pp. 470-478.

Ronald N. Hunsinger is a professor of Biological Sciences at Samford University. He holds a Ph.D. in Toxicology from the University of Mississippi. Dr. Hunsinger teaches in the areas of neurobiology, anatomy, and physiology, and conducts research in the areas of reproductive and developmental toxicology.

Chapter 10

Statistical Thinking and Techniques: A General Education Requirement

Mary H. Hudson
Samford University
Birmingham, Alabama

Abstract

Learning and applying the statistical thinking theories and techniques of the Deming management philosophy of Quality Improvement in introductory statistics courses can produce quality general education graduates for the 21st century. Advantages for the graduate who experiences a statistics course with emphasis using the Statistical Process Control (SPC) methodology include: (a) replacing fear of mathematics with statistical critical thinking, team problem solving, and writing and communication skills that enable learning for a life time, (b) statistical interpretations and analysis of data using reasoning skills that are imperative survival skills necessary for the competitive job market, (c) statistical foundations with the Quality Improvement (QI) philosophy which can contribute to improving disciplines and attitudes. The implementation of this new paradigm for statistics courses will require new attitudes for both students and teachers, new methodology of management and teaching, and new context for the course.

Introduction

Due to the intense world competition in the job market, and the demands made by industry and service jobs, the college graduate who understands and can solve problems using the Deming Quality Improvement (QI) philosophy may gain the upper edge for success in the 21st century. In other words, a general education graduate who becomes skilled in the use of Statistical Process Control (SPC) tools and techniques will have several advantages over the graduate who takes only a maximum of two traditional mathematics courses, neither of which is statistics.

There are many reasons for this conclusion, some of which have been offered by students doing projects in a statistics course this past spring. Comments from students in statistics classes representing arts, social sciences, education, business, physical sciences, and paralegal, whose requirements include two mathematics courses, one of which is statistics, emphasized the importance of "doing." One student's project involved a survey on exercise where she is employed. She wrote, "I learned that much statistical work went into the gathering of information. . . . I learned how to sample randomly and representatively. I decided against the interview survey since it would be time consuming and attitudinal in content. I placed my survey forms in the break room. I had hoped for thirty responses from the one hundred people in our office. I obtained only fifteen responses which could be used. I obtained seventeen responses, two of which were not true responses. The people in my office enjoy playing jokes and thus two responses resulted which could not be used in the project as I had suspected from the beginning." (E. W. Hudson, Statistics Project, May 14, 1991) Another comment from a student's project on safety and security for a college campus wrote, "This statistics project was definitely a learning experience. It proved to me that statistics is part of the real world, and even everyday things. I found out the answers to some questions I was interested in, too. Even though I discovered that I could not be a statistician, overall, it was a positive experience."(J. A. Fleming, Statistics Project, May 7, 1991) A third student who surveyed four different grocery stores made the comment, "I feel like I have learned a lot about statistics in the process of compiling this project. Many aspects of the course have become clear to me when I was able to use them in something outside the book. This project enabled me to `tie up the loose ends' in this class."(L. A. Homesley, Statistics Project, May 7, 1991)

One advantage of a statistics course with SPC emphasis is process learning, which contributes to methods of analyzing and interpreting data and graphs using both inductive and deductive reasoning, critical thinking, and problem-solving team interaction skills that provide foundations for learning for a lifetime. However, the student's learning of these skills may be hindered by fear of the course. In fact, it may be the most feared of all mathematics courses required in higher education today. Therefore, if students achieve the first advantage, fear of the course must be removed by management.

1. Learning for Life by Removing Fear of Statistics

Employing the Deming philosophy of statistical thinking may not only remove the student's fear of the course, but also produce quality learning. The intrinsic value of statistics in daily applications is worth the effort. Moreover, applying the Deming style of quality to statistics courses can result in better productivity with high quality and lower costs.

The QI philosophy emphasizes management, which, in this case, revolves around the teacher's responsibility. Suppose the management of a statistics course includes one of Deming's 14 Points, "Drive out fear, so that everyone may work effectively. " (Deming, 1986, p. 23) This is not an easy task. A positive approach is to build a student's confidence, while driving out fear. Achievement of this task begins with daily personal encouragement and nurturing as a mentor, placing more emphasis on student input in team learning, having less emphasis on multiple choice tests with right or wrong answers, and implementing more interaction and communication by emphasizing problem solving case studies and projects.

Blum (1991) agreed with the report of the National Research Council which stated casual teaching, curricula context, and invisible instructors are some of the problems facing mathematics education today. In her words:

> The report concludes that teaching methods represent a major problem in mathematics education. Mathematics is often taught without context, so students see it as unrelated to other subjects or problems in the 'real world.' It is also frequently taught along a flawed model of teaching—blackboard lectures, template exercises, and isolated study—instead of through such methods as problem solving. (p. A16)

Primarily, the improvement of undergraduate statistics courses is dependent on continuous faculty training and learning of new ideas and innovations in statistics. On the other hand, superior knowledge based on the performance of the teacher does not necessarily produce learning on behalf of the student. Teachers must realize how students learn, and create an appetite and excitement for learning, especially statistics! Improvement in these courses is necessary to produce both satisfied students and employers.

DePalma quoted Voytuk, project director for the National Research Council's study on the mathematical sciences in the year 2000, "It is now possible to take the drudgery out of mathematics and get to more meaningful modern ideas." (p. B6) Also, DePalma stated:

> The new mathematics education tries instead to pump more students into the mathematics pipeline, not necessarily to create professional mathematicians but to help all students learn basic functions like reading graphs, understanding statistics, figuring probability and thinking in logical ways. (DePalma, 1991, p. B6)

For a student, removing fear may mean removing the fear of failure, fear of humiliation, or fear of a substantial waste of time and economic resources. A reinforcement of this idea came this past spring semester from a fearful graduating senior in a statistics course. She stated, "Thank you for helping me overcome my *fear* of math. I am eternally grateful to you." (E. W. Hudson, personal communication, July 4, 1991) Removing such fear might be like the feeling that a rookie has when hitting a home run instead of making a strikeout in a professional league baseball game. Removal of fear is efficacious!

In many elementary statistics courses, non-scientific majors are intimidated and overwhelmed with concepts and formulas that are irrelevant to their mode of thinking. Even mathematics and physical science majors cannot always relate classroom learning to practical solving of problems. Anxiety and frustration prevent understanding, and meaningless memorization results in low scores on competency examinations. Moreover, when a student completes the course, the lack of interconnectedness between statistical concepts in the classroom and real life situations lowers performance and confidence levels.

Realizing the significance of employing Deming's philosophy in education, some educators, Harris, Hillenmeyer, and Foran, (1989) applied Deming's 14 Points in a fundamental new way of thinking and acting with quality assurance for private career schools. They stated:

> To bring about significant improvement in a school's or college's educational quality, three major changes will have to occur at the same time: the adoption of outcomes assessment, systematic instructional design, and quality assurance. None of these is easy or inexpensive. The path of least resistance for the short run is to make no changes at all. Or an institution may try to implement one change at a time, which is usually easier than making several changes at once. But in this case, each of the changes is interdependent on the other two, so one is not likely to be sustained without the others, necessitating making three large changes at once.

However, these three changes may not be as monumental as they first appear if quality management becomes the controlling principle. (Harris et al. 1989, p. 3)

2. Training for the 21st Century

Another advantage of an SPC course is the practical and necessary training one receives for the job market. In the 21st century, college graduates will need the knowledge of statistical concepts with a focus on the interpretation of data by specifically using the ideas of SPC. Employers are demanding that college graduates become trained wholesome workers with SPC knowledge to solve real-life problems. Wilcox quoted Butler, owner of the South Carolina-based Quality Control Services Company:

> In Japan, . . . production workers, before they even see the shop
> floor, get three months of statistical training. That's our competi-
> tion. In this country, . . . there are about 500,000 manufacturing
> companies. Just think of all the people who need to have some
> training in SPC. We haven't even scratched the surface. (Wilcox,
> 1987, p. 43)

To prepare college students for this statistical training, mathematics must
be improved at all levels in the United States. Steen's report of a 1990 Joint
Task Force of the Mathematical Association of America and the Association
of American Colleges emphasizes this fact:

> One principal goal of the undergraduate mathematical experience
> is to prepare students for lifelong learning in a sequence of jobs that
> will require new mathematical skills. Departments of mathematics
> often interpret that goal as calling for breadth of study. But another
> interpretation is just as important: because mathematics changes so
> rapidly, undergraduates must become independent learners of
> mathematics, able to continue their own mathematical education
> once they graduate.

Most college students don't know how to learn mathematics, and most
college faculty don't know how students do learn mathematics. It is a tribute
to the efforts of individual students and teachers that any learning takes
place at all. Effective programs pay as much attention to learning as they do
to teaching. (Steen, 1990, p. 8)

So, it is obvious that a transformation needs to occur in the management
of teaching mathematics, particularly statistics, to produce an atmosphere
conducive for effective learning of important survival skills needed for the
job market. Deming (1989) suggests that transformation is required for
survival and can only be accomplished by management seeking long-term
commitment to new learning and new philosophy. In our highly techno-
logical and competitive world, one cannot resist change and expect to
survive, whether psychologically, emotionally, spiritually, intellectually,
or economically.

Survival is an instinct that has existed since the beginning of creation. It
became a daily priority to all persons of Desert Storm in the Persian Gulf.
Learning to use gas masks in preparation against missile attacks proved to
be a necessary methodology. Courage was demonstrated by the many
pilots who flew dangerous missions in the face of death. However, years of

planning, preparation, and training contributed to the low casualty rate of the troops in Desert Storm.

John Akers, chairman of IBM Corporation, and the Business Roundtable Education Task Force, stated in a most recent issue of *The Wall Street Journal*:

> The allied victory in the Persian Gulf was a stunning triumph of American technology, and of young Americans whose personal commitment, courage, discipline and technical skills had been vastly underrated. As our focus shifts back to the home front, now is the time for an equal commitment to rescue our educational system. America needs to follow Operation Desert Storm with Operation Brainstorm. . . . If American education is to produce more people who can compete in the marketplace, our schools should respect competition in the educational marketplace. (Akers, 1991, p. A22)

The new "Brainstorm" in the statistical field is the Deming style of quality improvement using the statistical process control ideas and tools.

3. Improving Disciplines and Attitudes

The third advantage that a QI course gives is a strong foundation for the continuing development of a student's disciplines and attitudes. Often, a student's inability to learn is blamed on persons or past experiences with mathematics. However, the problem may be a lack of personal discipline.

According to Senge (1990), learning disabilities can be overcome in learning organizations. His idea focuses on the building of learning organizations so that one will give up the illusion that the world is made of separate and unrelated forces. From these organizations, he believes people can develop capacities which help them learn together.

Senge also refers to new innovations in human behavior as components called disciplines. In his words, "a discipline is a developmental path for acquiring certain skills or competencies" (Senge, 1990, p. 10), and he suggests that anyone can develop proficiency through practice. However, he says, "To practice a discipline is to be a lifelong learner. You `never arrive'; you spend your life mastering disciplines. . . . The more you learn, the more acutely aware you become of your ignorance." (p. 11) Furthermore, he suggests the idea of systems thinking, which includes the disciplines of building shared vision, mental models, team learning, and personal mastery to realize its potential. As has already been emphasized, mathematics education in the United States is struggling for survival.

Would not systems thinking as the conceptual cornerstone of all learning create a new shift of mind for learning mathematics?

Creating a desire for learning mathematics and employing the Deming style quality statistics cannot happen overnight. It is a non-ending process of change; change in attitude for both the student and the teacher, methods of teaching, and content of the course. First, consider attitude change for both the student and the teacher.

Change In Attitude

Attitude is like taking a long trip through Europe on a train, and discovering the view is foggy due to weather conditions. Not seeing the scenery may cause one to feel sad, depressed, lonely, angry, dissatisfied, or discontent. However, on a clear day, the same scenery is viewed in a different manner. The clear picture stimulates and soothes one's feeling with a sense of pride and appreciation. What a difference a view makes! It produces a positive attitude!

Often, attitudes of students are developed from teachers, as children's attitudes may be reflected from their parents. A positive attitude of mutual respect between student and teacher is like a clear view. It produces an atmosphere for learning. However, if an attitude is negative, learning may be fatal. Therefore, attitude (the state of the mind) is of primary importance for quality learning.

Change In Statistics

In the specific area of statistics, the new paradigm is to study statistics using the Deming philosophy. SPC involves more than just control charts and graphs. It is a process of thinking to achieve quality and productivity.

In July 1990, at the University of Tennessee in Knoxville, 50 college professors across the U. S. attended a National Science Foundation Workshop on Integrating Quality and Productivity Concepts in Statistics Courses, a first for college educators, to learn about this new way of thinking.

One year later, changes are occurring on some college campuses using this new approach. In particular, at Samford University, a new pilot core curriculum including this new paradigm in statistics was implemented in the spring of 1992. Hopefully, this course will be a requirement for every general education graduate by 1995. The new methodology includes the seven basic tools of statistical process control along with team learning while emphasizing speaking, writing, critical thinking, and problem-solving skills as opposed to the memorizing of formulas and just number crunching without useful interpretations of the data.

Other educators are recognizing the importance for teaching SPC in statistics courses. At a recent meeting of the National Council Teachers of Mathematics in New Orleans, general interest sessions emphasized the importance and need for SPC in education. One topic, "Statistics, Industry's Key to the Twenty-first Century," provided teachers with first-hand knowledge and applications using SPC. Employers representing Mayo Clinic, Eli Lilly and Company, 3M Company, Alcoa-Fujikura, and St. Cloud University challenged over 200 high school and college teachers to implement statistical process control ideas in high school and college classrooms. It was emphasized that a large percentage of time and money is spent on in-house training of workers because of the lack of training prior to employment.

Change in the Methodology of Teaching Statistics

Next, changing the methodology for teaching statistics is laborious for a teacher who has used the traditional lecture method for many years. Teaching can be like stagnant water, not moving in any direction, and depleted of resources. So it is possible that the implementation of this new methodology could result in a "Failure Storm," if training, planning, and measuring are ignored.

Higgins and Messer's (1990) research found that SPC was best used in the improvement of instruction by solving problems as they occur, not when the course is over. They believe the goal is to reduce the need of final inspection, as in industry, by identifying problem areas and making corrections within the process. By looking at course evaluation questionnaires from previous years they were able to develop biweekly feedback forms to gain valuable input from their students in statistics courses and were able to make improvements before the end of the course.

The idea for continuous improvement is called KAIZEN by the Japanese and is the key to Japan's competitive success. Imai said:

> The essence of KAIZEN is simple and straightforward: KAIZEN means improvement. Moreover, KAIZEN means ongoing improvement involving everyone, including both managers and workers. The KAIZEN philosophy assumes that our way of life—be it our working life, our social life, or our home life—deserves to be constantly improved. (Imai, 1986, p. 3)

Quality learning demands ongoing improvement. Knowledge of assurance of quality teaching and learning is primary before a contract (registration and tuition) develops between a student and a college. The famous Japanese engineer, educator, and writer of many Quality Control books, Ishikawa (1985), suggests that when using quality control in management, a purchaser should consider several conditions before selecting its supplier. A classroom consists of the student as both a purchaser (before graduation) and a product (after graduation), and the teacher as the supplier. Consider applying similar conditions for a teacher/student relationship to those of Ishikawa (Ishikawa and Lu, 1985, p. 162):

1. The teacher knows the management philosophy of the student (who is required to take the course), and continuously gives eye contact and personal help to the student. They learn to cooperate.

2. The teacher has a stable management system that is well respected by others. The support from management (the Chair of the department, the Dean, and the Administration) allows freedom for the development and support of new techniques for teaching the course.

3. The teacher maintains high technical standards (for assessment) and has contact with employers to prepare students in the manner they demand.

4. The teacher can supply the raw materials. The teacher also possesses the statistical process control tools which enhance such process capabilities.

5. The teacher controls the amount of lecturing to deliver new ideas, and invests in other ways such as team learning and brainstorming to ensure the course produces practical statistical learning.

6. The teacher delivers with sincerity to implement the contract provisions (the standards and goals).

7. The teacher measures the raw materials often to check for defects to produce a quality product (the student) for the employer.

8. The teacher measures the performance of the product by measuring the employer's satisfaction of the product (the student). The employer will not be satisfied if the product is substandard or defective.

Change in Content

Last, but not least, a significant amount of change in the context is necessary if the new philosophy can be implemented to produce quality learning of statistics that is fit for use.

According to Juran and Gryna (1980), "An essential requirement of these products is that they meet the needs of those members of society who will actually use them." (p. 1) Also, they implied that the wide variety of uses means that products must possess multiple elements of fitness for use and referred to them as the quality characteristics: "Structural, Sensory, Time-oriented, Commercial, and Ethical." (Juran and Gryna, 1980, p. 2)

Applying Juran and Gryna's characteristics to a statistics course demands fitness for use in any profession. Thus, the designing and structuring requires recognizing the importance of useful trends and new ideas, including new tools for critical thinking, as well as the displaying and analyzing of data in charts and graphs.

Imai lists the seven basic tools for analytic problem solving as "Pareto diagrams, Cause-and-effect diagrams, Histograms, Control charts, Scatter diagrams, Graphs, and Checksheets" (Imai, 1986, p. 239-242). These important and useful tools are referred to as the Ishikawa tools. Written by Dr. Kaoru Ishikawa to introduce quality control practices in Japan, they contributed tremendously to Japan's successful economic development (Ishikawa, 1968).

Blumberg (1989) discusses the use of SPC control charts in educational settings and suggests that researchers who are not mathematically oriented can understand these techniques as opposed to other procedures often recommended in statistical research that are not easily understood.

The second characteristic, sensory, provides the element that stimulates and motivates the student (the product). If wetting the appetite for great ideas and books is created, then the beauty of learning may overflow like that of a melting ice cream cone.

The time-oriented characteristic of the course may be two-fold. The first may be yearly assessment from students, peers, and employers of graduates. It may be useful for the next year, but does not produce instant improvement. Besides, in industry, if a final product does not meet the specifications, it is returned to scrap, and enters the process again. Quality Improvement demands measurement before the end of the line to reduce costs while producing quality. When students do not meet the specifications (fail the course), are they considered scrap? Rerouting failures increases costs while lowering moral.

Friedman's research (1987) found that repeat examinations in introductory statistics courses improved students' grades, helped weaker students keep up with the course, and encouraged the learning of the course material. Positive feedback during the process was well-received by the students.

The second time-oriented characteristic involves the amount of time spent on descriptive statistics. Weaver's research (1989) gave an approach to introductory statistics that focuses more on descriptive statistics to encourage habits of systematic and critical quantitative thinking. For instance, in the social sciences, he said:

> When more time is spent on descriptive statistics, important skills are imparted and the whole enterprise can be defined and implemented around a set of substantive questions capable of drawing students into the study: An introductory statistics course can be a content course, in which important dimensions of social life are studied through quantitative methods. On that method side, the course is where students confront the realization that quantitative data most certainly do not speak for themselves, and that the same body of data can be (and often is) used to support divergent conclusions that are meaningful for social inquiry. (Weaver, 1989, p. 80)

The commercial characteristic, or warranty for higher education, is to output quality graduates at lower costs.

The last characteristic involves the ethical view. Producing a quality course is not only ethical, but demands the highest service possible for a teacher while developing a sense of pride. Shook's version (1988) of Honda's success emphasized service when he quoted Buck Rodgers:

> It's a shame, but in almost any field, when you get good service, it's an exception, and you're excited about it," says IBM's Buck Rodgers. ... "Every business is a service business, and it's the companies that think *service, service, service* that are most likely to succeed. (Shook, 1988, p. 83)

Colleges and universities exist to serve students. Humanism of personal concern, courtesy, honesty, and respect exhibited by a professor can create a state of euphoria that increases like an exponential function. Students are human beings, who not only expect service, but deserve service.

Shook also quoted Rich Port, a past president of the National Association of Realtors, who recognized service when he said, "A successful real estate salesperson will provide so much service that the customer will be ashamed to do business with anyone else." (Shook, 1988, p. 83) Furthermore, Shook stated:

> A definite correlation exists between the quality of a company's products and the pride of a company's employees. In short, people feel good about themselves when they know their product represents a good value to the customer. Similarly, people have low self-esteem when they work for a company known for inferior merchandise. The degree of pride people take in their work is directly affected by how they are perceived, or think they are perceived, by the community. (Shook, 1988, pp. 112-113)

Obviously, when one exhibits pride in teaching, feelings of accomplishment, happiness, excitement, and service follow and promote growth and inspiration in both the teacher and the student. However, a poor quality statistics course may result in a job loss or lack of tenure for the teacher.

Summary

1. Every general education college graduate in the United States needs an introductory statistics course with training in the new Deming-style philosophy of continuous QI with an emphasis on SPC tools and techniques for the job market.

2. Higher education personnel, faculty, and administrators not only need to learn the concepts of QI and SPC, but need to be *willing* to accept any change necessary for the implementation of this new paradigm in all educational services and academia.

3. The demand by employers is for colleges to produce trained, wholesome workers with useful statistical knowledge, who have also learned survival strategies including critical thinking, team problem solving, and writing and communication skills.

4. Continuous improvement in the methodology of teaching and the content of introductory statistics can generate quality graduates with foundations for learning for life. Applying the Deming philosophy over a period of time will result in quality output while increasing productivity and lowering costs for higher education.

References

Akers, John F. "Let's Get to Work on Education." *The Wall Street Journal.* March 20, 1991, p. A22.

Blum, Debra E. "Colleges Urged to Make Radical Changes to Deal with National Crisis in Mathematics Education." *The Chronicle of Higher Education.* April 17, 1991, p. A16.

Blumberg, Carol Joyce. "Applying Statistical Process Quality Control Methodology to Educational Settings." (ERIC Document Reproduction Service No. ED 306 285, TM 013 145) March, 1989.

Deming, W. Edwards. *Out of the Crisis.* Massachusetts: Massachusetts Institute of Technology. Center for Advanced Engineering Study, 1986, pp. 18-96.

DePalma, Anthony. "What? Math Without the Drudgery?" *The New York Times Education.* February 13, 1991, p. B6.

Friedman, Herbert. "Repeat Examinations in Introductory Statistics Courses." *Teaching of Psychology,* 14 (1), February, 1987, pp. 20-23.

Harris, J., Hillenmeyer, S., & Foran, J. V. *Quality Assurance for Private Career Schools.* Association of Independent Colleges and Schools, 1989, p. 3.

Higgins, R. C., & Messer, G. H. "Improving Instruction Using Statistical Process Control." *Engineering Education.* May/June, 1990, pp. 466-469.

Imai, Masaaki. *Kaizen, the Key to Japan's Competitive Success.* McGraw-Hill, 1986, pp. 3, 239-242.

Ishikawa, Kaoru. *Guide to Quality Control.* Quality Resources, 1968.

Ishikawa, K. & Lu, D. *What is Total Quality Control? The Japanese Way.* Prentice-Hall, 1985, p. 162.

Juran, J. M. & Gryna, F. M. *Quality Planning and Analysis.* (2nd ed.) McGraw-Hill, 1980, pp. 1-2.

Senge, Peter M. *The Fifth Discipline.* New York: Doubleday Currency, 1990, pp. 3-13.

Shook, Robert L. *Honda, An American Success Story.* Prentice-Hall, 1988, pp. 83-113.

Steen, Lynn Arthur "Challenges for College Mathematics, An Agenda for the Next Decade." *Focus, the Newsletter of the Mathematical Association of America, 10* (6), November/December, 1990, p. 8.

Weaver, Frederick S. "Introductory Statistics: Questions, Content, and Approach. Promoting Inquiry in Undergraduate Learning." *New Directions for Teaching and Learning, 38,* San Francisco: Jossey-Bass, Summer, 1989, pp. 79-85.

Wilcox, John. "Making it Right the First Time." *Training and Development Journal, 41*(10), October, 1987, pp. 39-43.

Mary H. Hudson has taught undergraduate mathematics at Samford University for 25 years. She is a member of the American Society for Quality Control and attended the National Science Foundation Workshop on Integrating Quality and Productivity Concepts in Statistics Courses at the University of Tennessee at Knoxville in July, 1990. She received training in the Samford-Student First Quality Quest Seminar in the fall of 1990 and was a member of the Samford University Cross-Functional Energy Conservation Team, participating in a presentation by this team to the Deming Style Quality Improvement Conference on Quality Improvement in Higher Education at Samford University in April, 1991. Also, she is presently a member of a core curriculum committee and is developing a pilot SPC statistics course and text for 75 freshmen to be implemented in the spring of 1992.

Chapter 11

Reducing the Hassle for Faculty Through QI

Billy J. Strickland
Samford University
Birmingham, Alabama

> Quality is never an accident; it is always the result of high intention, sincere effort, intelligent direction and skillful execution; it represents the wise choice of many alternatives.   Will A. Foster (McAlindon, 1989, p. 5)

Introduction

The primary goal of this article is to document certain hassles found in the Samford University School of Music and to present a case study of the treatment of one such hassle through quality improvement (QI). By examining the influence of hassles on faculty and improving the processes that are structural and behavioral, the university should be able to enhance quality in teaching and learning through QI.

> The long-term effects on improving teaching/learning will never be fully realized. However, certain facets will materialize. Presidents, administrators, and academic deans react to accurate data. If the information reinforces the views of these decision makers, the probability of change is meaningfully increased. (Strickland, 1991, p. 18)

Success of the Organization/System

What is the potential of the organization/system? When the head-of-the-class is viewed as "excellent," the system often perceives the same performer as "mediocre." There is still much to be accomplished, knowledge to be gained, and wisdom to be achieved. By developing and evaluating performance within the system, "institutions can effect positive change even if nothing else is done." (Seldin, 1988, p. 9)

What is the purpose of the organization? The higher education system must enable the faculty to teach, research, and serve customers, the end results being positive reactions and commitments from the customers and the marketplace. Our position should not limit the system, nor should the system limit our responsibility to learn and teach. The administration, faculty, and students must share responsibility for performance outcomes by continual assessment and improvement of performance standards. The purpose is to provide a "value-based, vision-driven environment" (Senge, 1990, p. 347) that promotes learning.

According to Deming, learning should be the focus of an optimal, continuous process by faculty, students, and administrators. Learning is the core of the organization anchored with critical performance standards. Yes, the organization must be about learning to ensure success (see Figure 1). Luther states,

> Natural talent, intelligence, a wonderful education—none of these guarantees success. Something else is needed: the sensitivity to understand what other people want and the willingness to give it to them. Worldly success depends on pleasing others. No one is going to win fame, recognition, or advancement just because he or she thinks it's deserved. Someone else has to think so too. (Luther, 1982, p. 7)

Deming? William Edwards Deming is the 91-year-old world-class quality management consultant "whose work led Japanese industry into new principles of management and revolutionized their quality and productivity" (Deming, 1986, p. vii). His 14 Points for management has transformed many companies from "crisis" to "quality." While the concepts have been widely used by business, industry, and various health enterprises, Samford University is leading a paradigm shift in higher education to focus on customer service. The Deming plan promotes optimal quality improvement of processes and procedures that range from the apex of administration to zeal in teaching/ performance.

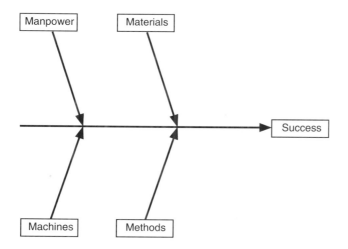

Figure 1 A Fishbone Chart Features the Goal and Components in a Cause/Effect Relationship

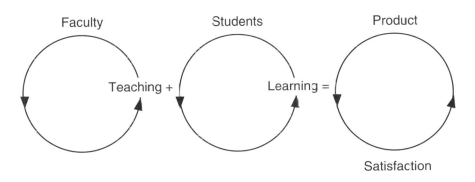

*Figure 2 The System of Higher Education as Shown
by Deming Quality Circles*

Success of the system results from an investment and commitment to meet and serve customer needs. We must identify those things that matter to our customers: quality programs, quality faculty, quality products, and quality performers (see Figure 2). We must "build the composite of people, skills, and organizational infrastructure that [is] needed to serve customers demand at high levels of quality." (Senge, 1990, p. 133) Sam L. Moore cites that "quality products and services evolve from quality work environments." (McAlindon, 1989, p. 71) "When you are making a success of something, it's not work. It's a way of life. You enjoy yourself because you are making your contribution to the world." (Granatelli, 1982, p. 23) "In short, a campus has many individuals who harbor casual opinions of the quality of work of others and share those opinions with friends or colleagues." (Seldin, 1988, p. 22)

Personal Mastery (Students/Faculty/Administration)

Orison Swett Marden writes "It is just the little difference between the good and the best that makes the difference between the artist and the artisan. It is just the little touches after the average man would quit that make the master's fame." (McAlindon, 1989, p. 49)

Deming says that the product should be designed by the producer. We should provide a definition of the "product" and empower them (products) with an appreciation for the teaching/learning system, provide optimal learning for them, and have a working knowledge of variation and psychology. The literature presents this caveat: "People learn what they need to learn, not what someone else thinks they need to learn." (Senge, 1990, p. 345)

To activate such a system, personal mastery should be achieved (See Figure 3). It is only obtained through experience, knowledge, and mentoring. Master teachers provide these. Why should students study with MASTER teachers? Master teachers have "profound knowledge." They will level with you. They are performers, make fewer mistakes (smaller variability), and are willing to risk producing quality performers.

What are the characteristics of an effective music teacher? The teacher:

- is trained in theory and performance practices
- effectively solves performance-based problems
- has good communication skills appropriate to his/her field (a conductor's skills differ from those of a composer)
- works within the parameters of the system
- understands the literature of music
- interprets performance practices
- works with various publics
- gets highly involved in the solution of departmental problems
- extends and develops performance methodology
- adapts quickly and effectively to new problems and challenges
- produces high-quality performers within the system
- cares about the finished product (the performer and the performance)
- fosters continuing improvement, seeks not to stifle it
- inspires student creativity and behavior
- creates a collaborative learning environment
- nourishes a love of and instills respect for world-class practitioners of the arts
- respects and affirms the strengths of his/her colleagues
- removes barriers that prohibit teaching/learning

Deming states in a recent *Wall Street Journal* article that:

> You learn only with theory. There's no experience without theory, nothing to record. So how could management improve? I know what management will have to do if it plans to survive. An example of a system well managed is an orchestra. The various players are not there as prima donnas—to play loud and attract the attention of the listener. They're there to support each other. In fact, sometimes you see a whole section doing nothing but counting and watching. Just sitting there doing nothing. They're there to support each other. That's how business should be. (The *Wall Street Journal*, 1990, p. R39)

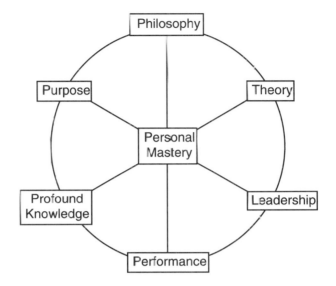

Figure 3 Components Leading to Personal Mastery

That's how higher education should be. The literature states that:

> Leadership strategy is simple: be a model. Commit yourself to your own personal mastery. Talking about personal mastery may open people's minds somewhat, but actions speak louder than words. There's nothing more powerful you can do to encourage others in their quest for personal mastery than to be serious in your own quest. (Senge, 1990, p. 173)

May points out that "in creating a climate that is conducive to teamwork, the administration should give its employees guidance in the fundamentals of teamwork, while still facilitating an individual sense of mastery." (May, 1991, p. 86)

Shared Vision for Learning/Performance

The Samford University School of Music defines quality of performance through a series of accountability factors. These factors are articulated by the faculty/administration through clear and concise expectations to students, faculty, and staff. The expectations must be met by professional and knowledge-based performances. We should remember that "quality products and quality service begin with quality thinking." (McAlindon, 1989, p. 52)

Performance standards should be based on "profound knowledge." How? Timely, quality performances are based on the expectations of the system. Through in-depth testing, the system will have data to establish continual improvement of the teaching/learning, or the data will indicate a paradigm shift where improvements can be implemented into the system.

The purpose of the School of Music is to focus and refocus on visions of teaching/learning for faculty and students. The focus should include visions of future trends in customers, program changes, and changes in the marketplace. For example, since the market projects fewer students graduating from high school during the next four years relative to the last twenty years and fewer students entering fine arts curricula, then the curricula should be supportive of the type of student available for the college experience in fine arts.

The purpose of the faculty is to learn, perform, teach, and serve. The purpose of the student is to learn, perform, and serve. To achieve student and faculty satisfaction, the quality of their performance must be the number one priority. Learning has to be the focus of the music component. The students must prepare themselves for any actions they even suspect they might face. The teaching/learning environment must provide students and faculty with optimum methods and materials, producing better performers and performances (see Figure 4). The literature reports that teachers "must serve as coaches and mentors, not necessarily problem solvers, helping students develop their own personal skills." (Senge, 1990, p. 111) "Research indicates that well-managed feedback may improve performance from 10 to 30 percent." (Seldin, 1988, p. 81)

When the system is equally fair to all, learning is expected of ALL students and faculty, integrity of performance is enhanced, and hassles are reduced to ensure quality within the educational process. We should provide quantifiable data of processes within our systems to aid in reducing hassle. The data should include:

- Number of complete and incomplete student and faculty files with lack list.
- Number of recitals/concerts performed.
- Number of calendar complications (changes, conflicts).
- Complaints from students and faculty/staff.
- Average length of employment for faculty and persistence for students.
- Number of students in music classes (major and non-major categories).
- Number of tests conducted by specific faculty.
- Number of tests by subject (theory, history, etc.).
- Number of students and faculty out sick or otherwise absent.

- Music library and recital hall usage.
- Frequency of over-booking recital hall.
- Piano maintenance chart.
- Turnover of faculty/staff/adjunct faculty.
- Number of applicants versus the number who matriculate.
- Number of majors on music scholarships with average $ amount.
- Number of students who receive no financial aid but persist to graduation and number of students who receive maximum financial aid and persist to graduation.
- Correlation of ACT scores and persistence to graduation.
- Comparison of ACT scores by majors, i.e., music education, church music, theory/composition, performance, bachelor of arts, and master of music.
- Number of freshmen and transfers who persist to graduation.
- Reduction of delay in awarding scholarships.
- Comparison of audition date and date of scholarship award.

"It's not what the vision is, it's what the vision does." (Senge, 1990, p. 154) We must say "farewell" to outmoded educational systems, and "welcome" systems that nourish, teach, and challenge forever. We must reduce the hassle for faculty to teach, research, and serve through quality improvement by bringing under control the higher education system.

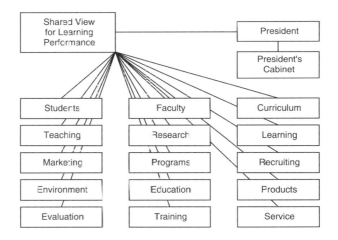

Figure 4 Quality Improvement Process Permeates the System

Reflections of the Faculty

In a recent brainstorming session, the Samford University School of Music faculty were asked, "What would free you to do better your job of teaching, research, and service?" The following items were submitted. A survey form was drafted and a sample of the faculty ranked the items. The rankings are as follows:

Table 1 A Listing of Responses from Faculty Survey Relative to Rank Order of Importance Regarding a Hassle-Free Environment

Rank	Variable
1	Security
1	Video/audio recording of recitals, etc.
2	Expertise and knowledge
3	Standardization & eventual reduction of faculty loads
4	Pride of workmanship
5	Performance environment
6	Leadership
7	Freedom of expression
8	Improved salary package
8	Teaching materials
8	Trained colleagues
9	Benefits
9	Support system (Library, periodicals, etc.)
10	Job expectations and evaluation
11	Openness to creativity
12	Support staff
13	Professional approach/concerns
14	Improved facilities
15	Improved studio and practice pianos
16	Better implementation of policies
17	Improved calendar process
18	Access to recording & music computer equipment
18	Sound proofing
19	Parking for faculty
19	System of painting rooms/studios
20	Reduce paperwork
21	Lobby/waiting room for visitors/parents/etc.
22	Elevator
23	Piano Laboratory
24	Improved restrooms

Ranking of variables from most important to least

What would happen if the above items of interest and conflict were met with concern, diligence, and steadfastness? Would morale be raised? Would faculty and students perform at a higher level of proficiency?

Case Study - SFQQ
(School of Music Student First Quality Quest Process QI team)

Faculty, students, and the university administration should be partners in the experience of teaching/learning. At the heart of a hassle-free system is a feedback process from faculty, students, and the administration. This process should serve as a method to view the hassle, plot the cause and effect, and implement the remedy.

The Samford University School of Music SFQQ Team (The Printer's Devils) embarked recently on the process improvement of duplicating. The following are the procedures used in the study.

Problem:

Faculty Purview: Present policy of 3 hours per day availability of copier is not enough time.

Staff Purview: Present policy presents major conflicts due to faculty and administrative demands for duplicating services.

Student Purview: Presently no access to duplicating machine in Buchanan Hall.

THE PROCESS: Total Quality Control of the Duplicating Process

A. Critical Process selected: Duplicating

B. Survey Customers:
    1. Faculty
    2. Staff
    3. Preparatory Department
    4. Chancellor's Office
    5. Students

C. Select the Issue:
    Access to the duplicating process

D. Diagram the present process:
    Flowchart (see Appendix)

E. Establish Process Performance Measures
    Present Copier statistics:
    Sharp SF-8100 purchased June 1988
    Copying ratio: ....20 copies per minute
    In use (Feb. 1991): ....33 months
    Total copies since purchase: 506,749
    Copies per month (506,749/33): 15,356
    Copies per workday (15,356/21): 731
    Copies per hour (731/8): 91

F. Diagram Causes and Effects:
    1. Machines
        a. Limited to one
        b. Demand by too many publics
        c. Breakdowns (always when I need it)
    2. Manpower
        a. Time (inadequate time for faculty)
        b. Too much lead time required for staff to do the job (up to 24 hours)
    3. Materials
        a. Quality—automatic feed often skews the paper until the copy is lost
        b. Colored paper desired (editorial comment: only white is recyclable)
    4. Methods
        a. Time—let the faculty copy any time machine is available
        b. Time—allot certain times for administration or "bump" faculty

G. Collect data on causes:
    1. Data on number of copies
        a. 91 copies per hour during 8 hour day
        b. Copier Usage
            Administrative...232,633
            Academic...237,782
            Chancellor's Office 5,930
            Preparatory Department 30,404
            TOTAL 506,749
    2. Amount of additional dollars funded through Samford University printing office.
        a. 1990-91 = $10,143.13
            1989-90 = $ 8,935.22
    3. Number of copies printed by current machine = 506,749
    4. Number of recitals/concerts over past two years = 88
    5. Number of ensembles = 14

6. Customers served by the printing process:
   a. Alabama Music Teachers Association
   b. Bands
   c. Chancellor's Office
   d. Community Choir
   e. Music
      1. Music Education
      2. Church Music
      3. Performance
      4. Theory/Composition
   f. Music Library
   g. Sacred Harp
   h. Workshops
   i. Preparatory Department
   j. Students
   k. Emergency use by Art and Speech/Drama Departments

H. Analysis of Data:

The School of Music ranked well in service but low in availability and convenience. Statistics show that faculty and administrative usage is just about equal.

Charts:
1. Fishbone: One suggestion was that faculty have access to copy machine at all times and the staff would have special times worked out for their needs. It remains clear that our basic problem is the availability of the copy machine to the faculty and staff which numbers forty or more people. This team feels that a second machine is really necessary. It remains to be seen if we could obtain one that would primarily pay for itself (a pay-by-copy machine).
2. Survey results (see Tables 2 and 3):

Table 2 A Ranking of Variables Relative to a Hassle-Free Environment Within the Duplicating Process

Ranked by Importance to Customer

1.	Ability to solve duplicating problems promptly	98
1.	Convenience of self-service hours	98
2.	Ease of duplicating	97

Table 2 A Ranking of Variables Relative to a Hassle-Free Environment Within the Duplicating Process (Cont.)

3.	Ability to fit duplicating service to meet your needs	95
4.	Ability to provide high-quality duplicating	94
5.	Convenience of duplicator location	92
6.	First-come, first-serve service	85
6.	Preference of self-service options	85
7.	Speed of the duplicator	83
8.	Availability to ALL customers	82
8.	Number of duplicators	82
9.	A wide range of related duplicating services (collation, staples, etc.)	75
10.	A good process	71
11.	Instituting competitive service charges for non-SUSM duplication	62
12.	The attractiveness of the location	59
12.	Preference for staff assistance in duplication process	59

Table 3 A Ranking of Variables Relative to the Present Duplicating Process Environment

Current Rankings for Rating SUSM

1.	The duplicator location is convenient	73
2.	The attractiveness of the location	71
3.	First-come, first serve service	66
4.	Ability to provide high-quality duplicating	63
5.	Ability to solve your duplicating problems promptly	61
5.	A wide range of related duplicating services (collation, staples, etc.)	61
6.	Preference for staff assistance in duplication process	60
7.	Speed of the duplicator	55
8.	Ability to fit duplicating service to meet your needs	52
9.	A good process for people like you	49
10.	Making it easy to do your duplicating	48
11.	Number of duplicators	44
12.	Availability to ALL customers	42
13.	Convenience of self-service hours	40
14.	Instituting competitive service charges for non-SUSM duplication	32

I. Develop Solution:
    1. Plan: New hours and new machine.
    2. Do: Institute plan. Use best options.
    3. Check (study): Use 1991-92 as test for comparison study of copying/printing.
    4. Act: Determine next action.

J. The Solution:
    1. Furnish one additional pay copier for staff, students, and faculty usage. The copier should be located in the most convenient site, i.e., music library or music office.
    2. Provide access to copier for faculty, staff, and students during normal office hours.
    3. Provide printer education for students, faculty, and staff by ABM consultant to maximize machine performance.

K. The Future:
    By implementing the solutions (J), the University would provide:
    1. Greater efficiency in printing.
    2. Higher quality and improved services (less hassle).
    3. Greater ability to serve all publics.
    4. From point five of the Deming system: To provide quality "improve the system of production and service."

The educational process should provide students, as much as possible, with rewarding and problem-free opportunities. Learning is the core of the postsecondary educational experience. By making changes in authoritarian or unresponsive management styles to styles that are based on trust, respect, constancy of purpose, and effective communication, quality teaching and enhanced productivity are more likely to be realized. (Smith, 1991, p. 81)

Questions for Future Research

Many questions remain. However, higher education must continue to question for optimal improvement and success of the system(see Figure 6). Answers need to be provided for the following:

Identify the administration's commitment to a quality hassle-free environment.

- What hassles would cause the organization to fail?
- What procedures would aid success?
- What are the hassles of the system as seen by our customers?
  By the faculty?
  By the administration?
- What are the strengths of the system?
- Are the goals of the student in line with the goals of the faculty?
  Faculty with administration?
  Programs with university?
- What programs show under-investment?
  Over-investment?
- What essential issues cross functional lines?
- How much of a risk should we implement?
- Is higher education a "hassle" institution or a "service" institution?
- If we know procedures that will produce significant improve-ments, how do we get the "leverage" to implement them?
- Are ample responsibility and opportunity given to the faculty?
- Should we develop teaching/learning of musical concepts by the case study method?
- Would simulation improve music management?
  How?
- Why use high-cost equipment when better equipment is available at a lower price?

The vitality of thought is in adventure. Ideas won't keep. Some-thing must be done about them." Alfred North Whitehead, 1861-1947. (Ashen, 1977, p. 18)

Questions from the literature include: "Are performance rewards—salary increase, promotion—based on meaningful criteria, standards, and evidence? (Seldin, 1988, p. 16) "What specific areas need improvement?" (Seldin, p. 20)

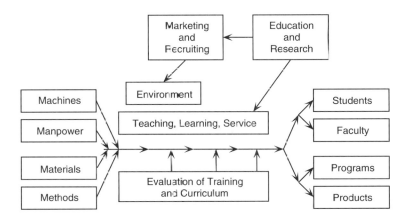

Figure 6 Use of the Deming Flow Diagram for Higher Education

Summary

The result of a hassle-free environment for teaching/learning is a spring-board to an academic culture with rigorous standards of "profound knowl-edge," equity, and ethics. So be it.

References

Ashen, M. "The Management of Ideas." *In Harvard Business Review: Manag-ing Creativity*. Boston: Harvard University Press, 1977.

Deming, W. E. *Out of the Crisis*. Cambridge: Massachusetts Institute of Technology Center for Advanced Engineering Study, 1986.

"Deming's Demons." *The Wall Street Journal*. June 4, 1990, p. R 39.

Granatelli, A. *Bits & Pieces*. Vol. I, no. 7, Fairfield, NJ:The Economics Press, 1982.

Luther, J. *Bits & Pieces*. Vol. M, no. 1, Fairfield, NJ:The Economics Press, 1982.

May, D. K. "Point Nnine: Break Down Barriers Between Departments." In R. I. Miller (Ed.), *Applying the Deming Method to Higher Education*. Wash-ington, DC: College and University Personnel Association, 1991.

McAlindon, H. R. *Commitment to Quality*. Lombard, IL: Great Quotations, 1989.

Seldin, P. *Evaluating and Developing Administrative Performance*. San Francisco: Jossey-Bass, 1988.

Senge, P. M. *The Fifth Discipline*. New York: Doubleday Currency, 1990.

Smith, L. G. "Drive Out Fear." In R. I. Miller (Ed.), *Applying the Deming Method to Higher Education*. Washington, DC: College and University Personnel Association, 1991.

Strickland, B. J. "An Assessment of the Attitudes of Samford University School of Music Graduates from 1979-1988 Concerning the Quality of Their Music Education." Unpublished doctoral dissertation, University of Alabama, Tuscaloosa, AL, 1991.

Billy J. Strickland is Assistant to the Dean of Samford University School of Music. He recently graduated (August, 1990) from the University of Alabama with a Ph.D. in higher education administration.

Appendix

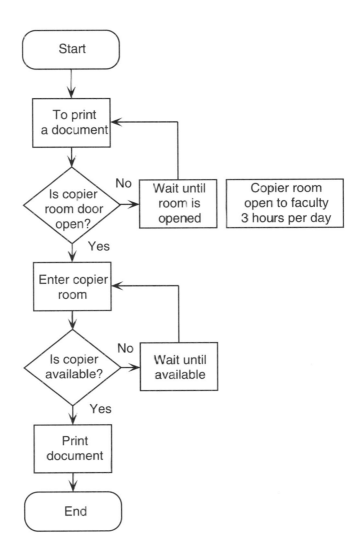

Flowchart of the Process of Duplicating

Chapter 12

Fear in the Classroom: Implications for QI

Janice R. Teal
Samford University
Birmingham, Alabama

The purpose of this report is multi-fold: to encourage colleagues to consider that there may be a better way of teaching; to explore the possibility that the processes of quality improvement may help find this better way; to investigate the role played by emotions (especially fear) in the classroom; to relate data obtained from an attempt to apply quality improvement tools in the classroom setting; and to lay the basis for a series of articles dealing with the subject of fear.

Listen to the conversations among professors at Samford University! Today, more than ever, terms such as "quality control," "quality planning," "quality principles," and "quality improvement" pervade the vocabulary. Statements such as " Do it right the first time" and "The customer is always right," along with the question, "Who controls the process?", have taken on new and more profound meanings. Names such as Juran, Deming, and Ishikawa, once known only to business majors, are now being used in such diverse disciplines as psychology, biology, art, and music.

Several years ago, Deming outlined the now famous 14 Points of quality improvement which are stated below:

1. Create a constancy of purpose for improvement of products and services.
2. Adopt the new philosophy.
3. Cease dependence on mass inspection.
4. End the practice of awarding business on price tag alone.
5. Improve constantly and forever the system of production and service.
6. Institute training.
7. Institute leadership.
8. Drive out fear.
9. Break down barriers between staff areas.
10. Eliminate slogans, exhortations, and targets for the workplace.
11. Eliminate numerical quotas.
12. Remove barriers to pride of workmanship.
13. Institute a vigorous program of education and retraining.
14. Take action to accomplish the transformation.

Coinciding with Deming's 14 Points, Peters and Waterman (1982) identified the following seven attitudes characteristic of excellent companies.

1. They have a bias for action: do it; fix it; and try it.
2. They stay close to the customer: learn from the people they serve.
3. They let imagination fly: allow creativity and practice risk-taking.
4. They recognize that productivity comes through people: respect the individual.
5. They stick close to the knitting: do what they know best.
6. They utilize simple forms and lean staffs: some billion dollar industries are run by staffs of less than 100.
7. They exercise loose-tight properties: bring autonomy down to the ground level while getting fanatic about the values they hold dear.

Throughout both of these philosophies, emphasis is placed on *customer*, *process*, and *quality*. The Quality Steering Team of AT&T, a long-time leader in industrial quality control, defines these terms in the following way:

1. CUSTOMER: the recipient or beneficiary of the outputs of work efforts.
2. PROCESS: a set of interrelated work activities characterized by a set of specific inputs produce a set of specific outputs.
3. QUALITY: consistently meeting the customers expectations.

Originating in industry, Quality Improvement (QI) has become an interesting concept that can be applied to settings outside the confines of industry. This report is concerned with the possibility of utilizing these same techniques in the field of higher education. Although reported attempts at applying QI to teaching are few, the practice of comparing education to industry is not altogether new. Juran and Gryna (1980, p. 10) made an interesting analogy between school and industry:

> Our schools are an industry supplying a service (education). Schools start with raw materials (students), apply a process (teaching), and turn out a finished product (graduates), although there may be some rejects. There are raw material specifications (minimum entrance requirements) and incoming inspections (entrance exams). There is a process specification (curriculum course outline); process facilities (faculty, laboratories, textbooks), process controls (reports, recitations, quizzes), and final product testing (exam inations).

Lindren (1969, p.133) compared the student to an employee and the college to a corporation. To the student he writes:

The student's role in college is not unlike that of an employee. You are given certain tasks to perform and are paid in terms of credit units completed and grades earned. . . . You are . . . expected to maintain certain minimum standards or quality in production and are given extra rewards for exceeding these minimums.

Even before QI had gained popularity in industry, Skinner was urging teachers to look at the method used in the classroom, noting that almost no effort is directed toward improving teaching, as such. According to Skinner (1968, p. 93):

Aid to education usually means more money and the proposals for spending it follow a few familiar lines. We should build more and better schools. We should recruit more and better students and hire more and better teachers. We should design new curricula. All this can be done without looking at teaching itself. We need not ask how these better teachers are to teach these better students in those better schools . . . or how curricula are to be made more effective.

Skinner contrasts contemporary educators with such names as Comenius, Rousseau, and Dewey in stating:

When teachers today complain, it is as consumers of education at lower levels. . . . Graduate school authorities want better college teaching and college teachers want to improve high school curricula." It is perhaps natural that consumers should turn to the shortcomings of plant, personnel, and equipment rather than to method.

The views of Skinner would not appear to be in disagreement with the findings of Quality Improvement since it is commonly reported that approximately 85% of all problems rest in the process, not in the people performing the task.

Skinner believed contemporary psychologists have spent too much time measuring the results of teaching while neglecting the study of teaching itself. He states:

What has been taught as pedagogy has not been a true technology of teaching. College teaching, indeed, has not been taught at all. . . . The beginning teacher receives no professional preparation. . . . No enterprise can improve self without understanding the processes of learning and teaching. (Skinner, 1968, p. 94)

Urging reforms in educational practices, Akers (1991) writes: "One point on which we all agree money alone is not the answer to better education."

Agreeing with Skinner, teachers need help! Perhaps it is time for education to turn to industry for this help—help found in the principles of Quality Improvement.

Exactly how can QI be applied to the classroom? Quite possibly each of Deming's 14 Points has direct implications. However, for the purposes of this paper, only point eight, dealing with the element of fear, will be addressed.

A strong case can be made for selecting fear for further study. Scherkenbach (1990, p. 75) writes that fear is the antithesis of the Deming philosophy. He notes, "Dr. Deming has found removal of fear should be the first of his fourteen obligations which top management starts to implement because it affects nine of his other points." Lindgren (1969) identifies the two major causes of failure in the classroom as attitudes (emotions) and deficiency in one or more skills. He believes that attitudes take precedence over aptitudes in determining whether learning will occur. According to Carr (1991), 90% of high school dropouts result from feelings, not intellectual difficulties; in the workplace, 70% are fired from the job due to personality conflicts, not incompetence. Marks (1967) found that entering students who fear failure are three times more likely to drop out of school than those who don't report such fear. Students consistently identify fear as one of the major obstacles to learning and performance.

To understand fear, we need to understand emotion. Traditionally, psychologists have divided the psyche into three component parts: cognitive (thinking), response (behavior), and affect (feelings). Some contemporary psychologists describe human behavior as all we think, feel and do. Preferring to study the more intellectual processes (thinking) and observable processes (doing), most psychologists have attempted to hide emotions rather than study them. Goode (1991) reports that "fear, joy, anger have been seen as peripheral and of interest mostly when they interfered with thought or become deviant or extreme. . . . Today, in disciplines ranging from psychology to neuroscience, the study of emotions has moved center stage." We are now beginning to understand that how people perform in school or any other place depends not only on how capable they are, but how capable they feel they are.

The study of emotions has followed several themes. Consistent with QI principles of today and beginning with James over a hundred years ago, psychologists have sought an operational definition of emotions. It is common to define emotion as a response to stimuli that involves physiological arousal, subjective feelings, cognitive interpretations and overt behavior. Considering the complexity of the concept, it is not astonishing that there is no single operational definition of emotion. (Pettijohn, 1989)

Apart from attempts to define the term, others have tried to classify emotions. Among these have been McDougall (1921), Russell (1980), Tompkins (1981), Izard (1979) and Plutchik (1980). Common to all of these classifications is the inclusion of fear as a basic and universal emotional experience.

Numerous theories have been proposed to explain emotions. Those of Plutchik (1980) and Soloman (1980) are among the most contemporary.

Some have attempted to link emotions and motivation. Certainly there is a relationship between the two since both terms are derived from *emovere*, meaning to move or stir up. There can be no doubt that emotions work as very strong motives and, conversely, hardly a motive exists without some accompanying emotion. Soloman and Corbit (1974) ponder the plight of a drug originally producing a state of pleasure: as the drug dissipates, a negative emotion follows and, with time, it is taken to escape the pain of withdrawal and not for obtaining pleasure.

But what about fear? In many ways fear is like every other emotion since all emotions are accompanied by profound physiological changes in the body. Fear, in fact, has been described by Levy (1975) as "a state of the neuro-endocrine system as well as a state of mind." Examining the physiological reactions accompanying emotions, Levy notes the following conclusions. During an emotional state, the entire body responds. The physiological response is controlled by the autonomic nervous system; thus, to tell a person to control an emotion is useless unless he can avoid or escape the stimulating event. Emotions are energy and act as motivating forces that push or pull behavior in certain directions or block it from going in another. Fear is an emotion of strong avoidance, a striving to get away or escape.

Using other terms and coming from another orientation, Senge (1991) describes behavior as driven by two visions. One vision is negative, the other positive. What one wants (aspiration) focuses on the positive and what one wants to avoid (fear) focuses on the negative. Senge believes that most individuals operate on a negative vision. Data supporting this belief were obtained recently by Teal (1991). A class of 29 undergraduates were asked to respond anonymously to the following question, "What is your primary reason for studying?" Only five responded that they study to learn (positive vision) while the remaining 24 indicated they study to avoid failing (negative vision). This trend must be reversed if teaching and learning are to be enhanced.

Recognizing the need to improve classroom instruction and having developed an interest in Quality Improvement, effort was made in the Spring of 1991 to apply the principles of QI in a classroom setting. Since quality improvement is based on customer satisfaction, and if students are indeed to be treated as customers, why not select a group of students and "open the box to their thinking" and look inside? With this in mind, the first attempt at Quality Improvement was begun.

A group of eight students were invited to form a quality team. They were selected based on their interest and major. The group consisted of three males and five females, and there were two freshmen, one sophomore, two juniors, and three seniors. All the students were psychology majors, and three of them had an interest in Industrial-Organizational Psychology.

Once formed, the team met on a weekly or biweekly basis depending on various schedules. The initial meetings were spent discussing the concepts of QI and the philosophy of Edwards Deming. Using the AT&T Process Quality Management and Improvement Guidelines as a reference, four Quality Improvement tools were described as follows:

Brainstorming: the technique used for tapping the creative think-
                                 ing of a group to generate, clarify, and evaluate
                                 ideas, problems, etc. In using this tool, the purpose
                                 is clearly stated with each person taking turns in
                                 sequence or expressing his ideas in a spontaneous
                                 fashion. There is no criticism or discussion until all
                                 ideas have been presented.

Pareto Diagram: a graph for rank-ordering causes from most to
                                 least significant. It displays the contribution of
                                 each cause to the total problem in decreasing or-
                                 der. The tool is based on the Pareto Principle which
                                 states that just a few causes account for most of the
                                 effect. By distinguishing the vital few from the less
                                 significant, one gets maximum quality improve-
                                 ment with the least effort.

Cause-Effect(Fishbone   a diagram that represents the relationship
or Ishikawa) Diagram: between a given effect and the potential causes.
                                 It is drawn to sort out and relate the interactions
                                 among the factors affecting a process. The
                                 problem is objectively defined and the major
                                 categories of possible sources are identified. A
                                 diagram in the shape of a fishbone is con-
                                 structed, defining the effect and positioning the
                                 sources into the effect box.

Flow Diagram:	a pictorial representation of the steps in a process. It gives a detailed understanding of how a process really works and allows an examination of how the various steps in a process relate to each other. It can be applied to any aspect of a process. The chart depicts the way things really happen instead of how they should happen.

After the initial orientation sessions, each team member explored the Deming principles in more depth, looking for ways they could be applied in the classroom. Follow-up meetings were brainstorming sessions where students identified features of the ideal classroom. By the end of these sessions, the team had agreed that the most ideal classroom setting would be free from threat and without fear. While the group admitted that fear is not totally undesirable, it was obvious that the negative attributes out-weighed the positive ones.

The quality team disbanded at the end of Spring Semester. It regrouped for the '91 Fall Semester, replacing three graduating seniors with three incoming freshmen.

In a summer class (Psychology of Adjustment, Psyc 302, May-July, 1991), the study of fear in the classroom was continued. Since the outline for this course always includes a unit on problem solving, it was decided that this particular unit would be devoted to the application of quality improvement tools with emphasis on the reduction of fear in the classroom. There were nine students in the class, ranging from sophomores to seniors. None of the students had been on the quality team during the previous semester and none of them had any significant exposure to the concepts of QI prior to the course.

The class agreed that fear in the classroom is a problem worthy of study and the first assignment in the unit on problem solving consisted of conducting informal interviews with fellow students to determine what evokes fear in the college classroom. Using a modified version of the brainstorming technique, each student transcribed on post-it note pads the causes of fear that had been reported to them. As each student completed the list of responses, the causes were placed randomly on a piece of poster board. Once all the responses had been placed on the board, the students categorized the causes of fear into major groups. It was determined that the sources of classroom fear fall into four major classes: tests, professors, personal, and peers. A Pareto Diagram showing these data is found in Figure 1.

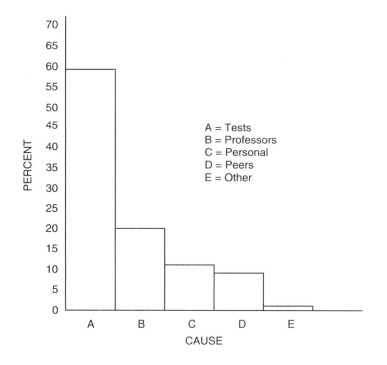

Figure 1 Pareto Diagram: Causes of Fear in the Classroom

Confirming the Pareto Principle, it appears that most fears in the class-room setting are generated from two sources: tests and professors. Relatively little fear was attributed to other sources. The reader should recognize that these data were collected on a very informal basis and from a relatively small sample and for demonstration purposes only. The specific cause-effect relationship is subject to change under different conditions.

A fishbone diagram was constructed showing how the effect (fear in the classroom) was influenced by the various causes (peers, tests, personal, and professors). Figures 2 and 3 depict this part of the process.

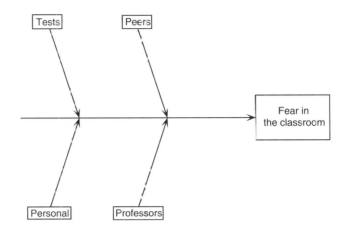

Figure 2 Fishbone Diagram: Major Causes of Fear in the Classroom

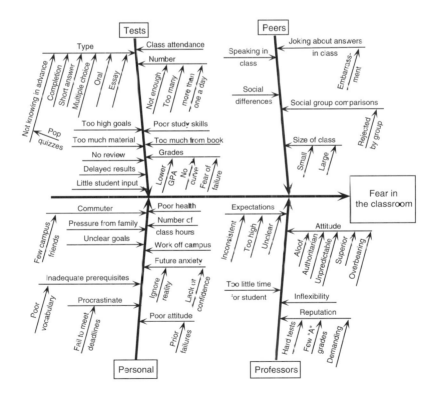

Figure 3 Fishbone Diagram: Specific Causes of Fear in the Classroom

Finally, a flowchart of the fear process was constructed based on the data that had been obtained from the interviews. Some liberty was taken in constructing the chart since no data had yet been collected to test the hypotheses. The flowchart is presented in Table l.

Table 1 Flowchart: Fear in the Classroom

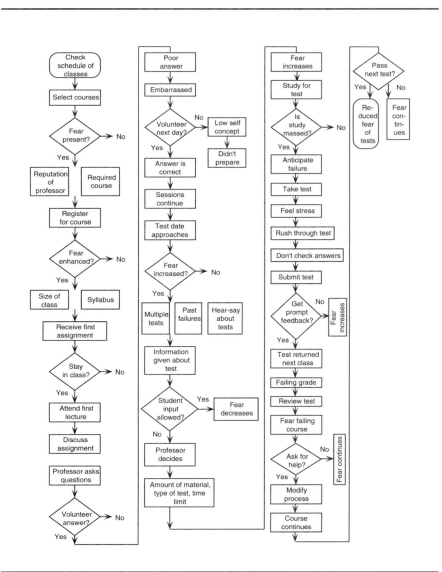

From the initial application of QI in the classroom, several conclusions became obvious. Students liked being treated as customers in the learning process. They appreciated the fact that their opinions were listened to and their input solicited. Some even indicated that this had already acted to reduce some of their fears. The admission was almost unanimous that the graphing of a subjective process such as fear removed some of the ambiguity and personal biases associated with the experience. They favored working as a team rather than on an individual basis and most expressed confidence that using QI tools could enhance the processes of teaching and learning.

Regarding the elimination of fear in the classroom, perhaps it is not possible to do this completely and it may not be altogether desirable to do so. Evidence indicates that no learning takes place without some sort of discomfort. However, it is also clear that fear is a very troublesome and chronic problem among many students. While some fear may have a positive effect, too much can be devastating and can lower the student's performance. It would be a grave mistake to attribute fear in the classroom as the result of a "natural occurrence" or to mere "human nature." The professor should be aware that much fault lies in the process. The purposes of education would be better served if both professor and student would seek to understand the processes involved in this emotion. Perhaps the continued application of QI techniques will make this more possible.

The student can be taught to analyze his fears. Many times, careful observation, objective assessment and graphing reveal situations far different from what one subjectively believes to be the case. Hopefully, if fear can be viewed as a process and solely to the human factor, attitudes toward it can be changed for the better.

The professor would be wise in not going overboard with the use of fear tactics. It is obvious from student input that the major cause of fear centers around test situations. Although it may be easy to use tests as threats to enhance the student's level of motivation, it appears that this is not the best method.

It is fortunate that testing situations, which create so much fear, are one part of the educational process that can be easily examined and modified. In enhancing classroom instruction, educators might wish to consider the use of QI to analyze their testing procedures.

References

AT&T Quality Steering Committee *Process Quality Management and Improvement Guidelines*. Issue 1.1. Bell Laboratories, 1989.

Ayers, J.T. "Let's Get to Work on Education." *The Wall Street Journal*. March 20, 1991, p. A-22.

Carr, J.B. *Communicating and Relating* (3rd ed.). Dubuque, IA: Wm. C. Brown, 1991.

Goode, E.E. "Where Emotions Come From. " *U.S. News and World Report*. June 24, 1991, pp. 54-62.

Juran, J.M. and Gryna, F.M. *Quality Planning and Analysis* (2nd ed.). New York, NY: McGraw-Hill, 1980.

Levy, R.B. *You and Your Behavior*. Boston, MA: Holbrook Press, 1975.

Lindgren, H.C. *The Psychology of College Success*. New York, NY: John Wiley and Sons, 1969.

Marks, E. "Students' Perceptions of College Persistence and Their Intellective, Personality, and Performance Correlates." *Journal of Educational Psychology, 58*, 1967, pp. 210-221.

Peters, T. S. and Waterman, R. H. *In Search of Excellence: Lessons from America's Best-Run Companies*. New York, NY: Harper and Row, 1982.

Pettijohn, T.F. *Psychology*. (2nd ed.). Guilford, CT: The Dushkin Publishing Group, 1989.

Russell, J.A. "A Circumplex Model of Affect." *Journal of Personality and Social Psychology, 39*, 1980, pp. 1161-1178.

Scherkenbach, W.M. *The Deming Route to Quality and Productivity: Road Maps and Roadblocks*. Washington, DC: CEEP Press, 1990.

Senge, P.M. *The Fifth Discipline: The Art and Practice of the Learning Organization*. New York, N.Y: Doubleday, 1990.

Skinner, B.F. *The Technology of Teaching*. Englewood Cliffs, NJ: Prentice-Hall, 1968.

Soloman, R.L. and Corbit, J.D. "An Opponent Process Theory of Motivation: Temporal Dynamics of Affect." *Psychological Review, 81,* 1974, pp. 119-145.

Teal, J.R. Unpublished data, 1991.

Janice R. Teal holds a Ph.D. in General Experimental Psychology from the University of Georgia. She is Professor of Psychology at Samford University.

Chapter 13

Writing: A Process that Can Be Improved[1]

David H. Roberts
Samford University
Birmingham, Alabama

Dr. W. Edwards Deming's revolutionary quality improvement process for industry can be applied to writing to improve the writing quality of students and the quality of learning in a writing classroom. Deming's 14 Points for quality improvement in industrial production (some slightly abbreviated from the original) are as follows (Deming, 1982):

1. Create constancy of purpose toward improvement.
2. Adopt the new philosophy.
3. Cease dependence on inspection to achieve quality.
4. End the practice of awarding business on the basis of price tag.
5. Improve constantly and forever the system of production.
6. Institute training.
7. Institute leadership.
8. Drive out fear.
9. Break down barriers between departments.
10. Eliminate slogans, exhortations, and targets for the workforce asking for zero defects and new levels of productivity.
11. Eliminate quotas . . . Substitute leadership.
12. Remove barriers . . . to pride of workmanship.
13. Institute a vigorous program of education and self-improvement.
14. Put everybody . . . to work to accomplish the transformation.

"What an odd way to begin a discussion of teaching and learning writing," you may be saying to yourself. "What has Deming's management methodology—or any industrial management philosophy—got to do with writing?" is an obvious question students and teachers may ask. The answer is simple: manufacturing a product requires a number of processes, and it is the quality and effectiveness of those processes that determine the quality and effectiveness of the product. Deming's philosophy of manufacturing-as-a-process is not unlike the pervading philosophy of writing-as-a-process.

For years, the industrialized world has focused its quality control methods on inspecting the final product. Inspect the final product and either fix the defect or reject the product altogether, with no thought of the underlying reason for poor quality production. Sound familiar? For years, the teaching of writing has been done in the same way: students write and teachers then inspect the final product. After inspection, the teacher suggests ways to fix the flawed essay or reject the essay altogether. In both systems, quality is a hit and miss, trial and error proposition.

Deming's Quality Improvement Process (QIP) focuses on the manufacturing and management processes, not only the finished products as they leave the assembly line; and contemporary writing pedagogies focus on the writing processes, not simply the end product, the finished essay turned in for evaluation. Deming's philosophy has revolutionized Japanese industry and is making significant improvements in the American automobile industry. One American car manufacturer currently brags, "Quality goes in before the nameplate goes on," indicating the shift in emphasis from product to process.

Rather than to recount the history of the paradigm shift in writing from product-centered teaching to process-centered teaching, I will simply refer you to the contemporary literature in the teaching of writing, and especially to the works of Donald M. Murray, who has influenced my thinking for more than a decade, and to the work of Peter Elbow, Patrick Hartwell, Janet Emig, and Mike Rose. I make the assumption that you will see the application of Deming's QIP to the teaching and learning of writing.

In the next few pages, I will attempt to relate, point by point, Deming's philosophy to learning to write in the context of a freshman English classroom. First, I will discuss a few necessary assumptions underlying the Deming method and how those assumptions apply, with modification, to writing. Then those of Deming's 14 Points will be explained and applied. Finally, what Deming refers to as "Seven Deadly Diseases" will be applied to problems that interfere with quality improvement in writing.

Assumptions Underlying Deming's Philosophy

First, writers need to understand a few assumptions underlying Deming's philosophy as applied to writing. (The five assumptions are listed in Mary Walton's *The Deming Management Method* (1986). I have reworded the five points and, in the discussion that follows each point, applied them to writing.)

1.   Variation is part of any process.

No one writes consistently well all of the time. Sometimes the muse is present and people write unusually well; at these times the writer exceeds her normal abilities to write effectively. Some people call it inspiration. One problem with developing writers is that they too often wait for inspiration to begin writing. If all writers waited for the muse to inspire them, few words would ever be written. Inspiration is a very small, even minuscule part of writing. Writing takes work, not just inspiration, and that work is often uneven because writing is a process and variation is part of any process.

The reality of variation in processes is one reason it is very important to give a writing task time. Begin a writing task well in advance of its due date so the writing processes—which will vary in quality and quantity—will have the time necessary to take advantage of the upswings in quality. If writers don't allow enough time, the emphasis is then on production, not on process, and the quality of the product always suffers when the emphasis is on production instead of process.

2. *Planning requires prediction of how things and people will perform. Tests and knowledge of past performance can be useful, but not definitive.*

Writers can predict how they will go about completing a writing assignment. Students have had years of experience in completing school assignments, and their experience gives them more information about their past performance than anyone else knows. Teachers may be able to predict a student writer's performance if the student's study and work habits don't change. If a student is an exceptionally good writer, for example, and he or she doesn't make radical changes in performance, the teacher may accurately predict that the student will do well on just about any assignment. Likewise, if a student's performance history is not exceptionally brilliant, the teacher may accurately predict the student's future performance.

Teachers and students plan the semester based on their predictions of how well assignments will work for their classes and how well the students will perform on the assignments. But the information that the teacher uses is different from the information that the student uses to predict performance. Teachers use their own performance data gathered from years of teaching; factors such as time of year, how well the football season is going, past success in the use of a particular textbook or assignment, entrance exam scores of students, and a number of other factors make up the teacher's knowledge base of past student performance. And that knowledge base helps the teacher predict how a particular class will perform. But the information is not definitive and does not necessarily enable the teacher to make accurate predictions about the performance of individual students or classes. Nevertheless, teachers use this accumulation of data in planning the course. Student writers have a similar reservoir of knowledge about their own past performances, and they can predict how they will perform in class. Even freshmen who have no experience with college life and college assignments can predict how they will approach assignments and how they will perform inside and outside class. They know how long they will wait after an assignment is given before they begin. They can predict how they will feel about the product, whatever it is, before they turn in the assignment. And they will predict the teacher's response to their work. The student writer may be right or wrong because data gathered from past performances is not definitive and does not necessarily enable a person to make accurate predictions about future performance or the teacher's response.

As the semester progresses, however, student writers will use informal data gathering procedures, analyze the data, and make new predictions about his or her performance and the performance of the teacher. Students and teachers must remember that variation is a vital part of any process, and for that reason, a person cannot always predict his or her behavior (performance) nor the behavior of others. A grade on a given paper or test, for example, is not an accurate prediction of future grades.

3. *Students work within a system that—try as they might—is beyond their control. To some extent, it is the system, not their individual skills, that determines how students perform.*

A great danger exists in point three. If students take this underlying assumption to its extreme, then they can easily shift responsibility for their poor work to the teacher, the course, the college, the textbook, the assignment, or some external factor unrelated to the individual's writing process. But the fact remains: sometimes a student's writing is not effective because the assignment failed. Sometimes a student fails to do her best work on a writing assignment because of the system: sorority rush; homecoming; the time of day the classes meet; the time allowed for the writing assignment; the topic assigned; fear of grading. Any number of factors determined by the system can hinder the student's writing. In such cases, the system must be changed.

When the system cannot be changed, writers must make changes in their approach to the work to be done, work within the system, do their best despite the system, and remember that variation is part of any process.

4. *Sometimes students can change the system.*

This point applies in a positive manner only in a student-centered classroom where the students have a great deal of input into the course of study and the writing assignments. In a classroom where the students have little to say, the system itself is probably unchangeable. But there is still hope if the student will imagine herself the manager of her own writing process and will make changes in the system that governs the way she works.

How a student writes, where a student writes, the student's attitude toward writing, and the writing assignment can be changed—must be changed if they are detriments to student writing—thereby freeing the student to write. It's not as simple as it sounds, though, because old habits die hard, as they say, and the student (under the guidance of a patient, caring teacher) will have to work hard to change her writing habits if they have not been successful in the past. So, if a student writer cannot change the system, she can change her attitude toward the system.

5. *Some students will be above average, some below.*

Grades and whether a particular student is the best writer in the class matter less than what the student learns. People are learning constantly, according to cognitive psychologists, and students can improve their writing process without the evidence showing up immediately in their grades. Students and teachers shouldn't be satisfied with short term improvement for the sake of a grade. Instead, they should concern themselves with long term improvement of their writing processes so the writing of both the student and the teacher will improve constantly throughout their lives.

Deming's Fourteen Points[2] as Applied to Writing

Point One: Create constancy of purpose toward improvement.

Innovation is necessary. Businesses capturing new markets find new, cost-efficient, and better ways to do business; results are worth the risks of innovation. It is a necessary ingredient to the improvement of any process.

Trying new things in writing is important to the growth and development of writing abilities. A student who has done much writing in school is likely to have practiced one or two kinds of writing over and over. Sometimes students have relied on a tried and tested writing form and style to get them through an assignment such as an in-class theme, a book report, or a term paper. Many students are more interested in completing the assignment with a decent grade than in improving their information-gathering, writing, or critical thinking skills. While they may eventually perfect certain writing forms, those students will not learn innovative and creative writing processes that will allow them to solve the rhetorical problem in interesting, challenging, and effective ways. So, innovation is necessary for writing growth. Writers who experiment with different ways to write, different circumstances, and new techniques find new ways to write that help them develop effective and efficient ways to write. Innovation will help any writer improve her writing processes so she can meet the expectations of a variety of audiences for a variety of purposes, so she can employ a number of rhetorical techniques to individual writing tasks.

Put resources into research and education. Businesses that grow and experience greater success invest in research on what will make their business successful and educate and train their employees. It's worth the investment of time and other resources because of improved productivity and efficiency.

Students are in college because they have decided to put resources into their own education. Even if a student's parents are paying the bills, the student is still committing time and efforts to education, so it is in the student's better interest to take advantage of that commitment to the fullest. If the instructor will help the student keep in mind that the purpose of writing class is to improve everyone's writing and to help all involved learn new ways to write, everyone will increase his or her writing repertoire. As more time and energy—more resources—are put into writing efforts, all should remember that the constant purpose is to improve the writing processes of every individual.

The status quo will not do. Business organizations that maintain operations and procedures as they always have will stagnate. Whatever the status quo is, it will not do unless the organization's purpose is to hang on, never grow, never become more competitive, and never improve its service, product, or process.

Applied to writing, the understanding that the status quo will not do implies that a person's writing skills, no matter how effective, no matter whether they receive straight A's in writing, and no matter how effective their writing is, their writing processes, and thus their writing, can be improved. If teachers and students were interested in simply maintaining the status quo, neither would probably be involved in education. Students and teachers alike must keep before them at all times that they have a clear and constant purpose: to improve their intellectual, problem-solving, and communication abilities.

Invest in the maintenance of equipment. Businesses that purchase expensive manufacturing equipment but fail to see the wisdom of investing in the maintenance of that equipment soon find themselves operating less efficiently, turning out defective products, and losing business. Business must maintain their equipment in order to stay in business.

People and their minds are the most important equipment on earth. Students should understand that they need to take time during their college career to maintain that equipment. They (and faculty) should exercise, eat right, and take time for relaxation. As psychologists say, "Take time for yourself." Educators and students should invest in their futures by maintaining good physical and mental condition.

People are concerned about the future, but there is no future; there is only the present. In business, there is no future. What counts is what happens today: quality production, sales, efficient operations, and attending to the tasks for today are sufficient. Businesses and people that spend excessive energy thinking about and planning for the future get too little done today, when it counts. A healthy concern for the future is important, but dwelling on the future is counterproductive.

Applying this idea to writing means, basically, student and professional writers shouldn't put off until later what they can write now; don't habitually procrastinate. Students shouldn't be pressured by worries about the final exam or the final term paper until it's time to start working on them because such worrying will hinder their ability to focus on the writing they need to do today.

Point Two: Adopt the new philosophy.

Ronald Reagan popularized a slogan for General Electric: "Progress is our most important product." But that's not enough; we must now believe in quality, not simply progress.

Certainly, progress toward a goal is important, but progress without clearly defined and attainable goals is hopeless. Writers need to seek quality in their work, and that quality happens only by adopting the attitude that writing is a process that continues until the quality is of sufficient level to be evident in an effective, audience-centered piece of public writing.

Point Three: Cease dependence on inspection to achieve quality.

The old way, in manufacturing, was inspect the product and discard or repair the defective product, but the new way, according to Deming and his followers, is to build good quality in during the manufacturing process. With the new way, inspection becomes a way of finding out what is going on in the process.

What is the old way of writing evaluation? A teacher or other evaluator inspected the final product and marked the defects or rejected the product. A better way, based on what researchers and teachers know about how writers really write, is to use the evaluation to find out what is going on in the writing process and to make changes in the process to improve the product: the paper. Spelling errors, for example, can be analyzed, studied, and classified. Then the teacher or the writer can look at the underlying psycholinguistic cause of the spelling error, understand why the error was made, and make appropriate changes in the writing process. That is a much better way than to simply try to memorize the spelling of words writers have difficulty with, because they understand the causes of the errors and can eliminate the errors at their root cause.

Point Four: End the practice of awarding business on price tag.

In manufacturing, price has no meaning without a measure of the quality being purchased. Furthermore, active involvement in never-ending improvement of processes will bring quality improvement regardless of price.

Price, in improving writing, is time. Writers who rush through an assignment are sacrificing quality for a lower cost. A focus on improving writing processes will pay off in greater quality regardless of the cost in time and effort.

Point Five: Improve constantly and forever the system of production.

Zero defects, according to Deming, is a misguided notion. The goal should not be to manufacture a product with no defects, but to improve the manufacturing processes. No organization, no product, no process, no person, is entirely perfect. Therefore, it is equally unrealistic to expect writing to have no flaws whatsoever; so, the constant task is to improve the writing processes, not to produce flawless writing. Improvement in effective communication, not perfection in communication, is the goal of a writing class.

Points Six and Seven: Institute Training and Leadership.

A person learns to ride a bicycle by riding a bicycle, learns to play a piano by playing a piano, and learns to write by writing. Writing classes have, by their nature, already put into effect point six, institute training. Additionally, each person in the class—student and teacher—becomes a leader in taking responsibility for learning.

Point Eight: Drive out fear.

Many people suffer from writing anxiety, or fear of writing. They just stare at a blank page or write a few words and stop. The more people write, the more comfortable they become with their own writing processes, and if they remember that their writing doesn't have to be perfect the first time, that their goals are to improve their writing processes rather than to produce perfect writings, then a lot of any fear they may have will diminish.

Point Nine: Break down barriers between departments.

In a writing classroom, this means to work together instead of competing with each other for better grades or longer essays. An effective writing classroom exhibits a strong sense of community; writers struggling together to improve the writing processes of all the people involved. Teachers and students in a classroom who share their writing with one another create a community of writers. Such a community provides support for developing writers in an atmosphere of tolerance and acceptance, regardless of varying skill levels, and provides opportunities for growth not found in other writing atmospheres.

Writing improves quickly when a community of writers develops, and many techniques can be used to create a community of writers. Whatever the technique, teachers and students must all write. Writing teachers who write with their students show the students that writing in the classroom is as important to her as it is to the them, that she struggles with her writing, and that she can learn through her writing as well. Teachers of all disciplines who write with their students and share their writing with their students show the importance of writing as part of the learning process and help foster learning in a writing community. And teachers who share their writing with each other and with their students make significant headway toward breaking down barriers.

Point Ten: Eliminate slogans, exhortations, and targets for the workforce.

Slogans suggest that workers could do better if exhorted to do so. Workers do better because of a sense of pride. The same is true of writers, even beginning writers. They improve because they want to, not because some teacher or other person in authority preaches at them. If a writer wants to improve her writing she will, just as long as she remembers that the goal is to improve constantly and forever her writing process.

Point Eleven: Eliminate quotas.

In manufacturing, quotas impede quality perhaps more than any other single working condition. An airline clerk's job, for example, is to satisfy customers, not to handle a certain number of calls an hour. My son, who just finished his freshman year in college, works in a large department store. During training for his sales job, he was told over and over that his job is to satisfy customers, even if it means refunding money for an item the customer has no sales receipt for. But at the same time, his pay is based on commissions. The store's philosophy is that both the clerk and the company will make more money if the customer is satisfied and returns to make additional purchases; the clerk is taking the chance on refunding money on an item bought at a competitor's store, just to ensure that every customer is satisfied.

In writing, the audience is the customer for public writing. If the needs of the audience are satisfied, the writing is successful, no matter what other factors are involved. Furthermore, some attempts at writing will be better than other attempts. No matter what a writer does, some writings will be better than others, some will fall below average and some will fall above average. Therefore, rather than to impose certain quality-oriented quotas on writing, if the writing processes are improved then writing ability will improve overall.

Point Twelve: Remove barriers to pride of workmanship.

The greatest barrier in pride of workmanship in writing is for the writer to set his or her standards too high. Excessively high standards also create writing anxiety and prevent writers from writing. Some writers start out by lowering their standards and just write. Then, as their writing progresses, they take many opportunities to improve the final product as they write draft after draft. In other words, many professional writers don't start out trying to write a finished product; they start out trying to write. Students and others should start out writing a first draft and leave themselves plenty of time to revise and rewrite the text as many times as necessary to achieve their purpose in writing.

Point Thirteen: Institute a vigorous program of education and self-improvement.

By looking at their own writing processes and studying them, writers are involved in a program of writing improvement.

Point Fourteen: Put everybody to work to accomplish the transformation.

Total transformation in one's writing processes and one's view of writing is often necessary for improvement. Writers seeking improvement often know what might improve their writing. They know at least one thing that can be improved. When I ask my students, "How can you improve this piece of writing?", their answers vary from, "Spend more time on it," to "Revise it again," to more specific answers like, "Rearrange the information so the reader isn't confused by the arrangement," and "Add more information so the reader will understand the circumstances behind the main action," and "Soften the tone so I don't offend the reader."

Every writer has some ideas about how to improve a specific piece of writing. Once some of those ideas have been revealed, the next step is to make the changes. The writer then looks at the new version and asks what improved and what didn't improve. The never-ending quality improvement cycle is then back to the first question, "What can be improved?"

Seven Deadly Diseases

Finally, according to Dr. Deming, there are seven deadly diseases that hinder progress in an organization (Deming, 97-98) and the first two can be applied to writing:

1. Lack of constancy of purpose.
2. Emphasis on short-term profits: short-term thinking.

University administrators, writing teachers, and student writers who understand that lack of constancy of purpose and emphasis on short-term goals both stand in the way of successful and effective writing are well on their way to improving the writing abilities of everyone on campus.

References

Deming, W. E. (1982). *Out of the Crisis*. Cambridge: MIT Center for Advanced Engineering Study.

Walton, M. (1986). *The Deming Management Method*. New York: Dodd, Mead, and Company.

Endnotes

1 A version of this paper is scheduled to appear in 1993 as the opening chapter of a book by the same title to be published by McGraw-Hill, Inc.

2 Mary Walton, *The Deming Management Method*. New York: Dodd, Mead, and Company, 1989, pp. 55-118, passim.

David H. Roberts is the Director of the University Writing Program and Professor of English at Samford University.

Chapter 14

What Can QI Contribute to Teacher Education?

Julian D. Prince
Public Education Forum of Mississippi
Jackson, Mississippi

A Carnegie Foundation report, *A Nation Prepared: Teachers for the New Century*, published in the mid-1980s (Carnegie, 1986) set the tone for a time of increasing pressure on American teacher education institutions to produce a better quality teacher. The 1986 report concluded that past ways of training teachers do not suffice for the future. Pressure or not, teacher education's response to the Carnegie report has not produced much change (Harris, 1988; Goodlad, 1989); past practices seem hard to discard. The crux of the problem appears to be with the institutional paradigms which guide thinking about the training of teachers.

The nature of the teacher education paradigm problem is linked both to an understanding of *what kind of* quality is needed, and *where* quality improvement in teacher education needs to take effect. As with American industry when first confronted by superior automobiles and electronic products from Japan, the first reaction has been, "Certainly the problem cannot be with the way *I* do business." The initial efforts at change have been to tinker with a system which seemed to be working fine in the past. A paradigm shift is needed to convince teacher educators that better academic training in the university, while remaining isolated from *the developments which need to happen in public schools,* will not solve the problem outlined in the 1986 Carnegie report. The real problem is to produce teachers and a public school education program suited for turbulent times!

Ron Harris (1991) maintains that the American national culture is changing: the changes often affect children and youth negatively; the changes are dramatic, and transformations in the national character occur almost daily. These changes impact the effectiveness of teachers trained in the ways of the past. As evidence that cultural changes do impact upon the quality of the academic atmosphere of a school, Carl Grant (1989) stated, "Working professionally with urban students means that a teacher must teach an entire class of urban students for at least several months under the guidance of a senior teacher who knows how to teach urban students." In Grant's statement is the gist of a new paradigm for teacher training—beginning teachers must enter the profession able to adapt to many different circumstances, they will do this by possessing different entry skill levels than their predecessors. Joel Barker stated the problem succinctly (1989, p. 7), ". . . the most important managerial skills during the times of high turbulence is *anticipation."* Being equipped to properly *anticipate* is the rationality which must be established in the teacher character. This required character is defined as the ability to be a reflective decision maker—the teacher skill to plan, present, and assess in a way to help each student learn.

Turbulence describes the current cultural backdrop for most of American society (Harris, 1991). This turbulent background influences the academic atmosphere in any public school. The urban student characterizes but one aspect of the ways in which a changing culture affects public school classrooms. As Grant suggested above, thoughtfully directed hands-on experience under a successful master teacher is one necessary element of productive training. This hands-on training becomes more powerful as practical experience in the classroom is linked with the academic training given in the institution. The two can come together to produce the quality of training needed in schools of education if master teachers and university professors are provided channels to give each other feedback about the *system of academic training in which the intern is imbedded.* Each of these partners in the education of teachers could give good advice to the other based on accumulated experience with interns from the institution. Such conditions can never exist, however, if the mind-set guiding teacher education institutions remains as it is today.

There are several paradigm problems to be overcome to change ineffective programs; however, Quality Improvement Procedures (QIP), if properly applied, could assure that any changes made in teacher education in the name of progress would improve the caliber of entry level teachers.

Before developing a rationale for using Deming style QIP to improve teacher education, a brief reminder of recent and past history is essential to establish a basis for the argument that new paradigms are needed to guide thought about how teachers should be educated. The next generation of teachers will be adequately trained only to the extent that universities, professional teacher groups, and the public schools join together to produce a coordinated system to educate the cadre of new teachers.

There is an error in current university thinking which seems to be repeated frequently[1]—more and better academic rigor as we knew in the past will suffice to prepare a teacher for teaching. This error is compounded by a related paradigm, a way of life much honored within the university setting, that of collegial isolation. Nested within this concept is that hallowed university icon, academic freedom. The paradigm of academic isolation is a cultural standard of university life. This cultural pattern's manifestation in practical operation is distilled into two parts: a reluctance to operate in concert with other faculty members; and an unwillingness to undergo evaluation which would determine if a faculty member's teaching procedures are adequate. Under current practice there are very few ways to determine if any part of a university teacher training program represents the quality needed to produce a high quality teacher.

Dealing With the Old Paradigms

The first historic paradigm affecting teacher education programs is an attitude which ignores the impact of cultural forces on school success. During the nineteenth century, and through most of the current one, grass-roots opinion about public education was different from that which developed during the decade of the 1980s. Then the public (including teacher educators) believed American schools were *the* factor adding value to the worker, unifying the immigrant population, and transmitting the ideals of American society to a diverse population. In this era of good feeling, schools received more credit than was due for a growing American national power. Few realized that formal schooling was only one of many educational processes shaping the nation. Lawrence A. Cremin (1976) explained that what was really occurring hid a fundamental weakness in the system. This weakness would become critical and obvious only when a high percentage of students in a school are of a background culturally different from the standards of training of the system (teacher training, code of conduct, curriculum) in which they were enmeshed. Cremin used mid-western schools in the last century to illustrate what problems differing school culture and home culture could create:

> [W]hat we have traditionally thought of as the influence of the nineteenth century common school…derived…from a configuration in which the common school was only one element. Ordinarily including the white Protestant family, the white Protestant Sunday school along with the common school, it was a configuration in which the values and pedagogies of the several component institutions happened to be mutually supportive. Other contemporary configurations were fraught with internal conflict. Thus, if one considers the Indian reservation as a configuration of education, one is immediately impressed by the tensions between familial instruction and missionary instruction, between Indian values and white values, between the virtues or resistance and accommodation. (p.36)

More than ever the realization of the new paradigm is that cultural factors cause tensions which overwhelm attempts of weak teachers to manage the classroom. The difference today is that the entire substance of the tension in today's classrooms can be laid at the feet of some cultural disparity between what exists in society at large and what the teacher believes he/she must accomplish in the classroom.

Beginning teachers must be fortified with training to help youth who are increasingly less prepared by home and society to deal with academic matters. The youth's academic preparation must be laminated with a number of other skills if he/she is to be prepared to compete in a world in which rapid societal change is the norm. Fortunately, the lamination of vital human skills which are needed in the 21st century can be acquired by the student and teacher being immersed in a setting which daily reflects Deming style QIP. Tragically, many university educators seem not to be aware that their own fund of experiences do not contain the elements which are necessary. What teacher educators know, by and large, is not sufficient to prepare the next generation of teachers.

A second historic paradigm compounding the problem of improving teacher education is found in the concept of how teacher education is to operate. The details of educating prospective teachers are as varied as are institutions certified to train teachers. National accrediting agency and state departments of education impose standards on teacher education institutions through accreditation guidelines. These guidelines reflect the historic paradigm mentioned above. Yet, even if the regulations were not there, university cultural paradigms still would guide the training, philosophy, and personal standards of behavior of individuals who teach, and deeply believe in the concept of collegial isolation. What the accreditation and collegial isolation paradigms lack are exactly those behaviors which can provide quality assurance to improve teacher education.

Putting the Right Program in Place

There are no general solutions to the improvement of teacher education. A quality teacher can be produced only if every phase of the education of the teacher represents a portion of the process which, at the outset, is of sufficient quality to get that part of the job done properly. There are seven phases of teacher education which must be in operation to produce a quality teacher:

1. Development of a philosophy of teacher education to which all members of the department adhere.
2. A curriculum is developed which is true to the chosen philosophical principles.
3. All faculty members teach the curriculum as adopted.
4. Teacher education candidates are selected who can successfully complete the program.
5. Field experiences which allow appropriate practice give feedback to university faculty to allow corrective action for the trainee where problems are found.

6. Testing, surveys, and other evidence allow students to exhibit mastery of academic content and quality of on-the-job performance.
7. Follow-up of graduates determine individual success.

Most schools of education achieve the seven tasks with varying degrees of success. Many do none of these tasks well. What is disturbing is that the literature indicates no evidence of comprehensive systematic plans in place in schools of education to monitor the quality of any or all of the seven elements. Most evaluation activities deal with individuals who have completed teacher education programs, what Deming would call "mass inspection" activity.

The purpose of this article is to integrate each of the seven functions with Deming's principles to illustrate how a practical system of QIP can be put in place in schools of education.

In this section, Deming's 14 principles (Deming, 1982) are translated into teacher education terminology. Many who hold to the collegial isolation paradigm insist that only a few of Deming's principles apply to academia. At first glance, academicians are put off by "business" terminology (Deming's business language appears in italics below). However, when the language is softened into that of the educational service industry one can see that all of the principles apply to schools of education. The 14 principles translated are:

1. *Create constancy of purpose for the improvement of production and services.*

   All people involved in the training of candidates for teaching certificates must be continually involved as members of a team of colleagues who seek consistent and reliable ways to improve undergraduate teacher education.

2. *Adopt a new "Quality Consciousness" philosophy.*

   The system of training teachers (the university and its allied institutions) must embrace a philosophy in which each of the seven phases of teacher education is constantly evaluated to assure that the desired training effect is being achieved.

3. *End dependence on mass inspection.*

   End-of-the-program testing of graduates is not a sufficient measure of quality; activity which meets stated program goals in each of the seven phases of a teacher education program is the assurance of quality.

4. *End the practice of awarding business on the basis of price alone.*

The practice of placing student teachers and students receiving field service experiences where there is an available slot must be stopped; instead, student teachers must be placed with a cooperating teacher who has proven effective in the classroom and agreed to be a partner in the total training philosophy adopted by the school of education.

5. *Improve constantly every process.*

Every phase of the system must be judged by one or more of seven statistical tools[2] (Using the Plan-Do-Check-Act cycle the tools are histograms, process flowcharts, cause and effect diagrams, pareto charts, control charts, scatter diagrams, and measures of quality improvement.) to determine if there are variances which must be adjusted to gain quality.

6. *Institute training on the job.*

Individuals working in every phase of the system of education of beginning teachers must be involved in training of how best to operate in their area of responsibility.

7. *Adopt and institute leadership.*

Each team member must be willing to accept a role in which he/she makes suggestions, and at the appropriate time, takes the lead in improving teacher training in one of the seven areas she/he knows best.

8. *Drive out fear.*

All team members must feel confidence that when his/her performance is evaluated the evaluation is for the purpose of improving the system.

9. *Break down barriers between staff areas.*

Every person in each portion of the system must feel the sense of team membership, that her/his contributions to the training of teachers is vital to the process.

10. *Eliminate slogans, exhortations, and targets for the staff.*

   Exhortation to "do the job right" is a thing of the past. Every person, including the leader, is a part of the solution as a team member. "We" not "you" solve problems and contribute to any quality effort.

11. *Eliminate numerical quotas for staff and numerical goals for management.*

   There are no quotas to be met to measure success. Every part of the teacher training process must be determined to be on target with the quality of training which is planned. The ultimate judgment to be made is the success of the beginning teacher on the job.

12. *Remove barriers that rob people of professional pride and self-esteem.*

   Everyone within the system of training teachers should feel a part of the team no matter how large or small the role.

13. *Institute a vigorous program of education and self-improvement.*

   All staff and faculty are involved in an education program related to what QIP is, how it relates to the teacher education program, how it relates to the long term success of teacher education graduates.

14. *Organize for quality: Put everybody in the organization to work to accomplish the transformation for quality improvement.*

   Eliminate collegial isolation. Everyone in the organization has a role to play within the total scheme.

To achieve the above circumstances, all participants in the training process must have a common philosophy and body of knowledge about what constitutes quality teaching. Theory must be put into practice in a sensible way. The teachers and supervisors of beginners must model the appropriate teaching skills in their own practice: one philosophy of teacher education drives a systematic teacher education department; all members of the department buy into the system; the curriculum is true to the chosen philosophical principles; faculty members teach the curriculum; teacher education candidates can successfully complete the program; field experiences fit the philosophy of the training system; the seven statistical tools produce evidence of quality performance; follow-up of graduates shows individual success.

Given that the current practices in teacher training should undergo substantial change in the next decade, what model might hold the greatest promise to achieve this? We believe it should be a model with these traits:[3]

- Public school units would be invited to associate with a university for the purpose of training teachers within existing classroom activity;
- Teachers selected for team activity would have quality teaching skills and commitment to the QIP teacher education system. They would be employed for at least 11 months of the year to compensate for times spent on university/public school planning teams;
- Trainers of teachers at the university would be chosen for a strong record of public school teaching and extensive graduate academic training; they too would be employed for eleven months of the year;
- University and public school teachers would form QIP teams to develop the seven phases of the teacher training program;
- All participants at the university would follow the guidelines the program has outlined, all members of each team would be taught the seven QIP statistical tools;
- All pre-service training would be accomplished within the context of a carefully chosen setting, where each team member works to improve the quality of the public school and the university educational setting.

This QIP model would build teaching skills under close supervision of well-qualified professionals within and without the bounds of the university. As can be noted, this would require an interchange of faculty between the two types of institutions. The QIP process would involve use of virtually every one of Deming's 14 principles through QI teams.[4] University and public school paradigms about the education of teachers would have to be merged. This would benefit both parties.

Current practice provides students limited opportunity to participate in a teacher training system where all professionals team to develop the teacher training model. Student teachers often draw experienced teachers who are poor teachers, or who do not understand or appreciate the theoretical training given by the university. The beauty of the proposed QIP model is the conversion of academic content into practical procedures.

The teacher training described above defines clinical teacher education training. The teacher training system (when the term system is used it includes the working partnership between the university and its related public school districts) melds theory and practice into a working unit. Training takes place through duplicated practice under effective mentors. This clinical training would become a blend of the theoretical taught in the university classroom and technical training in the public school.

Clinical training of the type described would give the student a better chance to become the desired reflective decision maker. A particular plus to such a QIP teacher training model would be that public school teachers and university teachers would understand their profession better. Mentor teachers known to be successful at the process of teaching youth from a different culture would be in a position to transmit this skill to many others. Achieving this level of competency on the part of a teacher training system could be accomplished if a Deming style QIP was in place.

To meet societal demands, the teacher training experience should afford the student the opportunity to work in many school settings—not just those schools that provide convenient or "acceptable" student teaching surroundings. The clinical school settings should be carefully selected effective schools. In these surroundings the faculty members of the university and participating schools would train each other as to support to be provided beginners. Cooperation involving planning, leadership, policy support, and adequate financial support would be necessary. Most importantly, all team members would know how to give feedback as to corrective measures necessary to improve the QIP system's effectiveness.

Deming style QIP could have great impact on teacher education. It could take a program which has come in for much national criticism and turn it into an effective way to prepare American youth for the 21st century.

References

Barker, J. A., (1989). *Discovering the Future: The Business of Paradigms*. St. Paul, MN: ILI Press.

Carnegie Forum on Education and the Economy. *A Nation Prepared: Teachers for the 21st Century*. Report of the Carnegie Task Force on Teaching as a Profession. Washington, D.C.: Carnegie Forum, May 1986.

Cremin, L. A. (1976). *Public Education*. New York: Basic Books. p. 36.

Deming, W. E. (1982). *Quality, Productivity, and Competitive Position*. Cambridge, MA: Massachusetts Institute of Technology, Center for Advanced Engineering Study.

Goodlad, J. I. (1989, April). *Some Thoughts on the State of American Education.* Paper presented at the Alabama Council on Teacher Education. Montgomery, AL.

Grant, C. A. (1989, June). "Urban Teachers: Their New Colleagues and Curriculum." *Phi Delta Kappan. 70*(10). pp 764-770.

Harris, L. (1988, November 3). "2001: The World our Students will Enter." *Educating the Class of 2001: An Agenda for Education.* Addresses to the College Board Forum. New York: The College Board, pp. 3-6

Harris, R. (1991, May 12). "Youth Isn't Kid Stuff These Days." *The Los Angeles Times*, p. 14.

Endnotes

1 Refer to the polemics of Alan Bloom (1987). *The Closing of the American Mind.* New York: Simon and Schuster. Bloom's belief was that the academic setting he found in the late 1980s was very difficult for university teachers. He was not satisfied with the cultural attitudes of his students. If university life could return to the academic standards of the past where he was allowed to teach the best and shoot the rest, all would be well.

2 For more details on these processes see virtually any book on Quality Improvement Procedures. A suggested source of information is found in Peter R. Scholtes, *The Team Handbook*, Madison, WI: Joiner Associates Inc., 1990.

3 For an expansion of this theme see Prince, J. D. Buckley, M. R. Gargiulo. (1991, March). Rethinking the laboratory school: Teacher training through a mainstream academic partnership. Robert C. Hymer, Ed. *National Association of Laboratory Schools Journal.*

4 The Scholtes' *Team Handbook* (Joiner, 1990) is again recommended for substantive details on team operations.

Julian D. Prince is Executive Director of the Public Education Forum of Mississippi, located in Jackson, Mississippi.

Chapter 15

Quality Legal Education By Design: Institutionalizing the Process of Change in a Law School

Alexander J. Bolla, Jr.
Samford University
Birmingham, Alabama

The heralds of change in legal education, today, reveal an underlying consumer unhappiness with the *processes* used to fashion competent lawyers for the twenty-first century—a reflection of perennial tension between actualizing the goals of the practicing Bar and those generally of the legal-training academies.[1] During recent American Bar Association discussions focused on "models for law school action" to ensure competency, the well-meaning advanced various stratagems for pulling down resistance and barriers to decanal agendas for program improvements. Ultimately, the notion of institutionalizing-the-process-of-change was dismissed as fancy of the wistful and visions of the hopeful in face of organizational reality. This article examines a paradigm shift for actualizing the goals of legal education through a renascence of defined *quality* in the work we do—teaching to competency—educating the lawyer for a changing world tomorrow.

Classical Legal Education, Change and Folly

At some pubescent point in the emerging dominance of a professional association, those responsible for the training processes of new admittees tire of "indulgences" fostered by the absence of acceptable educational standards. By 1893, the American Bar Association (ABA) moved to promote improvement in "legal education" which suffered from a decline in competency standards. In fact, the very ideals of a democratic society worked against lawyer training and competency. For example, in Indiana and Maine, one was eligible to practice law solely on qualifications of citizenship and moral character.[2] The first section created by the ABA was the Section of Legal Education and Admissions to the Bar. "Law school[s] . . . were now provided with an organization in which they could contribute to raising the standards of legal education. . . . [T]he acceptance by the Association of education in schools and the rejection of training by apprenticeship was made clear."[3] The centenary of the first officially recognized ABA section will be reached with mixed opinion of the ability of legal education to supply the profession with competent lawyers. Notwithstanding, "[t]he progress has been encouraging. However, further emphasis should be placed in the future on the *quality* of legal education and somewhat less emphasis on the purely quantitative results [italics added]."[4]

While pejorative cries for reform abound within and around organized legal education, the leadership warns of little hope for lasting change unless the present paradigm for achieving the goals of legal education shifts dramatically. Of the two professional organizations that guard entry to the legal profession, the ABA suggests its needs are not served by legal education and, the American Association of Law Schools (AALS) offers change methodologies without surmounting the issues of pedagogy. In sum, most reform plans are too-little-too-late tokens for change in an unworkable environment.

Coping with the traditional law school environment is more a variable of reorientation of *collaboration* and *group consensus* than it is opening a canon of pedagogy for a populist movement. There is some merit in forcing colloquia on the law school professorate about the discipline of pedagogy, but lasting improvement should not be sacrificed for the expedient. "We talk about having to keep ourselves intellectually alive through doing research in our disciplines, while the most fascinating intellectual challenge of all sits before us every day. . . . The more we know about learning, the more intellectually challenging teaching will become."[5] And the more we are able to close the gap between Bar and academy.

Yet, the chasm separating the responsibilities between Bar and school is widened through politicization of legal education goals which focus on "collective individualism" more than lawyer competency. The issue, however, is complicated by the difficulty of defining "the education." I hear the customer group (represented by the organized Bar) of legal education institutions express dissatisfaction with the product; the producers (represented by organized legal education) often reply using answers from 1950s American manufacturing standards. Consequently, *quality* represented by the value of "satisfaction to the consumer," comes behind the "processes" of production. Using the manufacturing analogy then, quality control in legal education means end-of-line inspection! A quality control approach that is, once again, too-little-too-late.

The majority of legal educators are not formally schooled in pedagogy and come to use a "process" over which they had no contribution to the original design. Still, each is responsible for "added-value" to the student; relying on end-of-line inspection (such as bar examinations, course grading, etc.), faculty cannot measure the effectiveness of the processes of education and cannot be certain of the quality it produces. By ignoring the pedagogy of legal education, those educators more closely align law school training with the guildhall, the very opposite goals of scholarly pursuits. There is much good in the processes of legal education, but it can be improved. Not every one needs formal training in the "art of pedagogy" to qualify for the professorate. Yet, there is a void in most institutions of *any* training, guidance, help, review, or constructive development of faculty members. Peer review, class audits, student evaluations, and the like abound in most institutions for end-of-line inspections—rank and tenure or goal assessments. If one innately scores well on such measurements, then there is customer satisfaction and personal advancement. (The notion of customer-service is foreign to universities and schools. Yet, each teaching institution is a "service" organization.)

Quality is frequently defined as the outcome of the education-process [production] presently used. Who defined it, what's in or what's out? Whoever the legal education establishment is says what it ought to be. An incorporeal consensus, then, drives the design of legal education processes. It is no wonder that most program change, while possible, is unworkable. Those with agendas for change know "what" but not "how." Following, it seems rational to approach improvement-in-quality by redesigning the processes and make change by design rather than to tangle with the will-of-the-wistful.

Forcing change through an institutional exercise of power is subject to the same frailties that mark many historical disasters of government. Barbara Tuchman, *The March of Folly*, suggests that when feasible alternatives are available people commit folly by yielding to fear. Even when the exercise of institutional power is considered negatively, it carries veneration. According to Tuchman, people "fail to see it as sometimes a matter of ordinary men walking into water over their heads, acting unwisely or foolishly or perversely as people in ordinary circumstances frequently do."[6] A more particular warning to legal educators from her historical perspective is that folly is "contrary to self-interest" and results from a "perverse persistence in a policy demonstrably unworkable or counter-productive."[7]

Many major research universities are presently struggling with the needs of reform. The president of Stanford University, Donald Kennedy, states he, among others, is searching for the "new paradigm in the purposes and organization of the university."[8]

Universities are searching for dramatic changes in management and teaching; ". . . a portrait emerges of a group convinced that while their universities are basically sound, major transformations are needed if they are to thrive."[9] Although futurists like John Naisbitt and Alvin Toffler suggest that the United States will lead in industrial knowledge during *The Third Wave*, "the major raw material of such an industry comes from strong

minds, the sort not being matriculated from American schools. Consequently, the country has two alternatives: completely restructure its current
means of education or import knowledgeable workers from other countries
... [I]t seems unlikely that importing the by-products of foreign educational
systems will appeal to the American psyche."[10] Therefore, change is inevitable and obligatory. How do we accomplish purposeful change and
particularly apply it to legal education?

What is it that the Japanese did to change and continue to do so well to
position themselves today with commerce that they could not do yesterday
with war? In fact, this people relied on American leadership and know-how.
What part of "yankee ingenuity" did the Japanese use to rebuild themselves
so formidably? Can we now, in this time of educational crisis we call "the
condition," get the same help and results?

Unhappily, learned journals are filled with pejorative calls for reform, yet
the response by the academy is still to practice unfulfilled wishing, and
worse, exacerbating goal-setting; goals are worthy, but only when a part of
the process of designing quality. Some examples from the dismayed include
deans, professors, and students:

> Those of us in legal education would do well to heed these voices
> demanding change in our approach to training lawyers[11]

> I think there are serious flaws in how we train lawyers today and
> so I have some wishes I would like to actualize.[12]

> Legal education is neither sufficiently legal nor sufficiently educa-
> tional.[13]

> Legal education is predicated upon unexamined assumptions that
> survive only through the loving conservatorship of the institution
> that depends upon those assumptions for its survival.[14]

> Along with its traditions and myths, the school honors its dead by
> teaching its living in a manner that is ultimately unfair. The school
> and the profession remain closed systems, blind to the possibilities
> of change, locked in congratulatory and exclusive self-perpetua-
> tion.[15]

> The reason the law school does not include new approaches in the
> core curriculum is a combination of belief in its own tautology—if
> [by definition] it ain't broke, don't fix it—and the unreflective
> assertion that "thinking like a lawyer" is beyond the range of
> normal experience.[16]

Not all parts of Dr. Deming's methodology can be easily adapted to education until some reforms occur; those usable parts that can be quickly adapted are highly significant and so uniquely different that change must follow application. Change for itself is not a goal; *the purpose of change is improvement*. There is no perfect process or product—least of all education!

Education is a behavior, a commodity, and a process. Each state of its being is improved or diminished in value by choices from its possessor, designer, or process regulator. "For years, the educational debate in America has raged over the issue of value. What do Americans get for their educational dollar? How much is a good teacher worth? While Wall Street bankers and lawyers pull in millions per year, school teachers . . . take home an annual wage that totals less than the annual tax payment of senior corporate executives."[17] Professional educators, at all levels, have some control over quality in the roles they serve, the processes they regulate, or the commodity its institution "sells." Education as a service industry is composed of complex organizations each fulfilling its self-defined mission; each is subject to consumer demand, whether or not that is the driving force behind the mission. Does education, as a commodity, have customers? Does education, as a process, have scrap and rework? Can the customer be satisfied without always being right? What images of learning, literacy, or scholarship are conjured by using "manufacturing" terminology to assess "the condition"?

The tower-minded most likely shun the economic reality of the "education" marketplace and narrow their self-role and importance to their pedagogy. The realist, meanwhile, is aware of the current crisis in American education, public and private, and will improve himself and dominion by changing the *quality* of the nature, character, and process of education. "Every activity is a process that can be improved."[18] We can evaluate "the condition" of legal education as a process. We can change "the condition" using methodologies and theories designed distinctively American by Dr. Deming while perfected cross-culturally by the Japanese.

A market example of an organization repositioning itself under the influence of Deming is The Ford Motor Company—"Quality is job 1" (for everyone). Florida Power and Light (FP&L) won the coveted Deming Prize from the Union of Japanese Scientists and Engineers (JUCE) in 1988; the first American company to achieve the exacting standards required for the honor.[19] The Malcolm Baldrige Award was created in the image of the Deming Prize in the United States to honor those who achieve quality with highest distinction.[20] FP&L is a service company, not unlike a university, a school, or an academy. Quality improvement in education is everyone's job, as it is for all providers of goods or services.

More responsibility rests with faculty than with the administrators to achieve quality where teaching is the nucleus activity of the academy. The teacher stands in the classroom as principal obligor of quality for the classroom experience as a part of the "learning process." But many well intentioned administrators ignore modern *quality* design procedures because of the tyranny of perceived fear and "control" that flows indiscriminately between faculty and administration. Without cooperation and commitment to remove fear, uncertainty and doubt in the workplace, thereby freeing *everyone* in the organization to cooperatively design quality, there can be little value using Deming-type methods, and the pursuit of quality will not go far. If present barriers to teamwork and the narrow definition of its concept are not removed from a law school environment, then the effect of making a commitment to quality and change is diluted and improvement unlikely.

It is no virtue for anyone associated with an educational organization to remain ignorant of theories that enable improvement. It is even less virtuous for those in positions of authority to remain uninfluenced by the value possible from using a systematic approach to the "professional practice of administration." The theories of management, human behavior, learning, and group dynamics, naming a few, are as essential to the teacher for conducting class as doctrinal theories are to research and scholarship. After all, there is a dearth of those formally trained in law school management as there is of law professors formally trained to teach. The use of theory by seasoned administrators to manage the organization, while not new, often is taken for granted and becomes the unstated assumption for the reason "why" a particular action is taken or a policy adopted. The educator should welcome any tool that will help him understand the "process" he creates and the "product" the process builds. Law school management is a shared divination and deans will always quit prematurely unless they have successful role interaction with the phenomenon known as *primary group affiliation.*

Present Reality In Historical Perspective

Perhaps the most important aspect in applying Deming methodology to legal education is to recognize that *organizational behavior* is the central activity *process* that needs change. Three distinct theory periods have passed whereby we assess the working processes of an educational organization.

> Sound theory, which is to say, theory that gives us an accurate picture or model of how the organization actually functions, is useful in that it enables us to better understand, predict, and ultimately control what is happening in the busy "confusion" of a school.[21]

The early 1900s ushered in the "principles of scientific management" formulated by Frederick W. Taylor. His goal was to reduce overhead production costs by (1) "distributing minute, specialized tasks, which when taken together would get a job done," and by (2) coordinating or ordering these numerous small tasks to accomplish the entire job."[22] He viewed labor as a commodity, a buyable resource, that managers could manipulate to control the costs of production to achieve *efficiency*—meaning the lowest dollar cost per unit of production. His ideas had universal appeal and application apart from industry; educators adopted the "new school" of management. Administrators and managers, however, often misread Taylor's principles about line and staff—the former they believed indispensable while the latter were expendable. Yet, Taylor held that worker dignity would increase under his influence and that management could not expect workers to "bloom" with devotion to duty since it was management's job to use labor efficiently and correctly.[23]

According to Taylor, if adjustment was necessary, then workers had to adjust to the physical processes of the organization. If they could not adjust, their only recourse was termination. Today's schools, for example, that continually "turn over" entry-level faculty and treat line and staff personnel with indifference, unwittingly practice Taylorism to their detriment. Interpersonal worker relations and "groupness" were not value traits acceptable to Taylor and the scientific theorists who followed him. But, they are valuable to later theorists and extremely important to the Deming methodology. Groupness should not be viewed as a cultural quality very peculiar to the Japanese without replication in America. It is a dynamic that American industry and behavioral science "officially" recognized in our culture before 1929; Dr. Deming's philosophy was originally "designed" to appeal to that same quality in the American business culture.

The denouement of 20th century management theory appeared to be the development of *bureaucracy*. Max Weber brilliantly posited an apparatus to manage a large, complex organization that would be rational (that is, less subject to claim of whimsy or caprice), fair, predictable, and give results efficiently. Efficiency was expressed in "expert, impartial, and unbiased *service* to the organization's *clients* [emphasis added]." Weber's bureaucracy characteristics were an attempt to reduce human frustration in the workplace of a complex structure where employee relationships had to be included as a "reality" factor in a theory of management. The *well-run* bureaucracy would come from "highly trained, technical specialists" who would "be very impersonal, minimizing irrational personal and emotional factors. . . ."[24] Unwittingly, many seasoned administrators are Weber bureaucrats; they awoke one day in their professional lives and found the mantle of "power" resting on them. Some sought it, others fought it, many succumbed to it, but only few trained for it. In their organizational management role they subliminally "bureaucratized" holding to:[25]

1. A functionally specialized division of labor
2. A strict hierarchy of authority
3. A rule system for rights and duties of employees
4. A work situation procedures manual
5. Maintenance of impersonal worker relations
6. A technical competence-based reward structure

These basic characteristics envisioned by Weber are not necessarily causes of workplace evil; there is danger, however, in managerial application. I refer not to an administrative abuse of "power" or a preference for "disorder," but rather to one holding a restricted view or understanding of the architectonics of *quality*. Weber-lings can only function *linearly*. That is by Weber's design! In it, there is only room for human obeisance to the *process*. But, what of the nature of man and his desire to associate self-actualization with work? Yesterday's theorists saw only through the large end of a funnel; they saw that mankind had a need to work because he had a need to eat. This was reality to the classicist who believed that man increased his productivity in ratio to his economic need. Pay by piece-work was classical management activity when an increase in productivity was set as a goal; again, a response to the assumed reason for why people function in an organization.

The "economic man" myth crumbled somewhere within the ephemeral boundaries of the Great Depression. Academic acceptance of behavioral science as a legitimate discipline would eventually have its influence on classicism. The behaviorists established, through credible methods, that people do not function in organizations solely for economic fulfillment. Rather, man responds to a keenly felt need for group belonging and satisfaction from "adhering to its standards and expectations; thus, the concept of *morale* was born. . . . Managers and administrators in industry, business, the military—all kinds of organizations, including schools—were admonished to pay attention to 'the human side of the enterprise.'"[26]

A. H. Maslow suggests a hierarchy of needs is what motivates and keeps one in an organization. The highest order is self-actualization and the lowest is physiological. The insightful administrator recognizes Maslow's principle that "higher needs emerge in an orderly and predictable manner as lower needs are satisfied and only after they are satisfied."[27] Her adoption of a management theory now determines her "motivation" technique when developing human participation in the mission of a behavior-oriented organization. She would use "motivational stimuli" that reflect a faculty member's placement in Maslow's hierarchy. This is certainly a more developed and refined management philosophy than the linear functions of Taylor's "scientific management" principles. Reckoning with the stages of worker needs is a "loop or feedback" process that is an integral part of process design and quality output. The same notion applies to legal education. The Socratic teaching method is a familiar example in the law classroom of a process that can be designed and managed by applied Deming methodology. The usual repartee between instructor and student is action—response (rejoinder)—check response—new action. Viewing law classroom activity in this way is not inconsistent with the way the law develops.

> The law does not assign rights out of process of divine revelation. It assigns rights, sees how they work, checks to see how a different set of rights worked in another jurisdiction and modifies the assignment of rights accordingly. At common law this was a judicial *process*, one court adopting one rule, another court adopting another.[28] [Emphasis added].

Refrain: *Every activity is a process.* As such, it can be managed and become a component of *quality* for the mission of the organization.

The human relations movement introduced democratic administration into the organizational fabric of education as well as industry. Four tested sociological discoveries by Elton Mayo between 1927 and 1932 foster managerial emphasis on worker groupness in learning institutions:

1. The "output" of a worker—hence, the output of the organization—is determined more by his social capacity than his physical capacity.
2. Money is only one motivation for working in an organization; there are other, and perhaps more important, rewards that the worker seeks.
3. Highly specialized division of labor is not the most likely way of maximizing efficiency of an organization.
4. Individual workers react to the organization—its hierarchy, its rules and its reward-system—not as individuals, but as members of *groups*. [Emphasis added].[29]

The mandate[30] for shared governance and "management" in law schools cannot remedy human distrust of "power." Often faculty feel their positions are insecure under a dean who still follows his own agenda while outwardly subscribing to "democratic" administration. The cure is not in exposing a hidden agenda, but rather in the group identifying with the *mission* of the organization, a necessary prerequisite to organizational "harmony" that the Japanese call *wa* and the first of 14 Points in Deming methodology, *infra*.

Personal identification with the group is often explained in systems theory terms by focusing upon the complex organization (such as a law school) having a dual structure, namely, the formal and the informal. The *formal functions* of the school are performed by those incumbents of pre-defined roles; they frequently are represented in a pyramidal organization chart describing the authority one role has over another. Unfortunately, the concept of *role interaction* in the formal organization is sterile and does not account for the more invasive activity by the social system phenomenon called *primary group affiliation*. Since people interact with other persons and not solely with "roles," it is impossible to explain the functioning processes of a group without regarding the needs of the person. Groupness, then, becomes the link between the formal and informal structure of the complex organization and principally drives its activity. Of course, "[t]he power of the informal organization is of great practical concern to the administrator . . . because he is always interested in getting things done . . . [and] unless the informal organization is dealt with realistically, it can react in a variety of ways such as lowering work norms and reducing cooperation with the legal authority of the administrative hierarchy."[31]

In a real sense the organization is "controlled" by the informal structure which articulates its behavioral norms. It is a fair characterization to view management and administration of the law school as a shared activity among faculty despite the representations of the formal structure in the "chain-of-command." Legal educators can use systems theory to analyze the ways in which a law school is managed and thus determine the way to manage for *quality*. The "reality" of the law school character, structure, and organizational behavior, reflected in another useful theory, is that individual expectations and perceptions exist simultaneously with institutional expectations and perceptions of role, mission, success, and *quality*. Often the interaction is expressed in theory by B=f(RxP). The behavior (B) is a function (f) of the interplay between the institutional role (R), and the personality of the role incumbent(P).[32]

The ABA mandate, *supra*, to share law school governance with the faculty belies the "image of alums who believe the dean is the captain of the ship calling commands to an eager crew. . . . Many faculties, whatever they say, have . . . the stablehand theory [of management]: someone to clean up the messes and provide first-rate hay to a thoroughbred faculty."[33] At the same time, their perceived position is that of a freeman in the agora of Athens during the Golden Age of Greece; they also liken their "role" to membership in the pantheon of gods over whom Zeus (the dean) is only first among equals. Any ensuing conflict among the gods has the certainty of outcome as would Conan meeting Godzilla. Without effective leadership directing the "groupness" of such a cast of characters, their combined output efforts are, predictably, a function of serendipity. In rewriting systems theory to reflect that "reality" the formula for group behavior would be $B = f(R) \times f(P^n)$. In this situation, leadership demands or pressures from management for *quality* would result in nothing measurable or lasting! Leadership in this context is more than establishing goals and reckoning with recalcitrant faculty or staff members. It begs for confrontation, by everyone in the group, with a mission; one that reflects *unifying goals* of the organization.

Goals, Mission and a Philosophy

"Each new dean begins with a set of goals and objectives for the institution and begins to build a consensus base for the achievement of those goals. Many deans step down prior to fulfillment of their goals, the demands and the frustrations of the position persuading the dean to return to teaching and scholarship."[34] If James P. White, Consultant on Legal Education to the ABA, is correct in saying that most deans quit before their goals are realized, then they do so rationally believing their goals unattainable. And perhaps the simplicity found in "rewriting" the goals begs the greater question—how well did the worker "group" respond and perform according to the stated goals? Defeated decanal goal expectations may be a result of group resistance shrouded in the echoes from the unified voice of the "informal organization structure" chanting "his ways are not our ways." The outcome, nonetheless, is a demoralized role-incumbent awaiting the dean-elect.

Goals are best defined for this inquiry as "planned positions"—training competent lawyers is one—or results that we want to achieve where the overall purposes are defined by objectives of the *organization*. While goal setting is a worthwhile activity for every constituency of an institution, the task is usually liveried in *negativism* because the organization is frequently *evaluated or assessed* in terms of the goals established; the measure of a successful organization, and its dean, continually is a variable of meeting the stated goals. Assessment tools have become synonymous with goal measurement. And this type of "evaluation tends to become either criticism for not doing better or a long discussion of the reasons for lack of success. . . . The *system model* [however] for evaluating organizational effectiveness, rather than dealing directly with goals, is concerned with the operating relationships that must exist for the organization to function."[35] This system-model is preferable to the goal-model since it openly recognizes the existence of groupness in the institution and can be acknowledged, not only by those in hierarchical authority, but by everyone associated with the organization.

The culture of a law school, caught in any managerial "theory" outlined above, is a ready target for *morale* deflation and, at the same time, for a change. The type of change needed is not merely in leadership or direction but in "cultural view," where the organization works towards self-fulfillment or self-actualization of the individual and collectively of the "group." Management theorists demonstrate repeatedly that the highest rung of Maslow's needs ladder, *supra*, can only be reached by adopting a new philosophy—one that radically repositions the totality and essence of organizational (group) life in a *"supportive environment."* There is a demonstrable need in legal education to break-out from the endless search for decanal candidates and to change reality from that which we would expect reflected in a management theory designed by Charles Darwin. "There are currently 175 law schools approved by the American Bar Association. Over a four-year period, at least 109 law schools will have a new dean. The number is undoubtedly even greater than 109."[36] Annually, at least one-third of the nations approved law schools search for a dean whose average "role" tenure will be 3.4 years. Adopting Deming's philosophy or one like it will not be a "quick fix" for the fruitbasket turnover in law school management. What it will do over time, however, is provide a philosophical perspective of the organization as an "integrated entity"; one where the "driving" force behind management is the quest for *quality* and the focus is "on the never-ending improvement of all processes [including the classroom] to improve quality."[37]

Quality Types and Systems Variation

There is a variety of classifications in *quality* typology (e.g., good, better, best, first, irregular, etc.). Most are unusable in the "service" sector because they classify a "goods" value to the consumer using a rating system designed by the manufacturer. For example, most Sears products are labeled as "Sears Best Quality" or "Sears Good Quality" to help the consumer distinguish pricing schema and make purchase decisions. There are three notable types of *quality* that best apply in Deming methodology. "These are: (1) quality of design/redesign, (2) quality of conformance, and (3) quality of performance."[38] Transferring the concepts of *quality* to education is deceptively easy.

The first focuses on the consumer's needs; a required core curriculum, after all, is a statement by the professional faculty telling the consuming student what she needs. " . . . [I]t is critical that [schools] look years ahead to determine what will help [students] in the future."[39] The driving force behind "redesign" is continuous anticipation of the student-consumer needs even though what they presently receive *ain't broke and don't need fixing*. Conformance quality is the measure of the institution's performance to exceed its quality of design which is necessary to first meet the student needs. Performance quality is actualization of how the students perform in the marketplace, life, or other activities the *process* equips students to do.

"Quality of performance leads to quality of redesign, and so the cycle of never-ending improvement continues."[40] I believe most law school faculty are keenly interested in the bar-examination "passing percentages" of its students, yet openly disclaim this as indicia of quality of performance; somehow, without acknowledging its concern publicly, it protects against outsider claims that the "mission" of the institution does not differ from a "trade school."

Poor bar-pass rates are frequently dismissed as a variable of the "quality" of the raw materials (students) a faculty had to fashion into its product. Yet, good pass rates for a class the faculty perceives as lower quality raw material, often is viewed by it to confirm the quality of performance in the original design of the instruction process—again, *if it ain't broke, don't fix it* is the likely response to a call for change. Quality of performance by a particular class may be due to lesser admission qualifications, but may be ultimately due to a faculty indifference, misunderstanding, or non-exposure to *process variation.* If every *activity is a process,* every process has *variation.*

Variation in a process directly affects the quality of performance and conformance. Therefore, educators need to understand the critical differences of *variation* and adjust their methods accordingly. Law classroom activity, usually Socratic-method learning, is widely used by law professors—when the professor has skill using the methodology—but varies somewhat from day to day. Classroom objectives are nonetheless actualized. This is an example of *common variation* (assuming the professor used the method with a given caliber of student—that caliber determined by the admissions *process*). Imagine using the same instruction method with a lesser caliber student—the results will not predictably be equal. Introducing the new raw material (lesser qualified student) is now a *special variation* in the process. Unless a definite (and usually substantial) change is made in the system of instruction, "the system's process capability will remain the same," and the results are usually poor quality. The assumption is made, in arguendo, that the "process" is designed to yield uniform results and hence lesser qualified students should not be expected to perform well. In reply, if the process gives a certain result, rework through the same process will not improve the "quality." If the student is cast as a "value added product" of the institution, concerns of adjusting the processes to give quality results are mandatory. The cure cannot realistically be "scrap and rework (repeating a failed course is rework)" but lies in the redesign of the *processes* of instruction to account for the variation. *Common* and *special variation* must be controlled to eventually achieve total quality.[41]

Fourteen Points and Warnings of Deadly Diseases

How to improve quality and productivity? 'By everyone doing his best.' Five words—and it is *wrong*.... *The* system is such that almost nobody can do his best. You have to know what to do, *then* do your best ... with a system of improvement. The system of improvement consists of the Fourteen Points and removal of Deadly Diseases and Obstacles.[42]

The philosophy of Dr. Deming is found in his 14 Points from which "the methodology" is actualized. There are many excellent primers that outline these points apart from his own work *Out of the Crisis*. The following synopsis is to only acquaint you with the system of points. "No one sentence or even chapter can really capture the full intent of one point. It takes reading and rereading and pondering and doing to understand his philosophy. There is no instant pudding."[43] The points[44], comments and application[45], and diseases[46] are principally from the sources footnoted. They are presented, however, in my order of preference; there is nothing magical or predestined about the ordering of each point.

Point One: *Put everybody in the organization to work to accomplish the transformation. The transformation is everybody's job.*

While this may seem self-evident for teamwork, it is the capstone of the philosophy. "Its major thrust is that top management has to accept the responsibility for never-ending improvement of quality in organizations and has to create a structure conducive to the implementation of this philosophy."[47] In any complex organization there is a wall of resistance to change. Bottom-up efforts to improve can rise no higher than the first conflict with immovable resistance. It is human nature to interpret bottom-up requests for improvement as admitting to "a problem" while openly confessing that it represents a weakness. Middle management fears that it will be blamed; this is usually where the first wall occurs blocking an organization-wide pursuit of "quality." Top-down management commitment to improvement and quality signals to everyone that teamwork is expected and that "messengers" with problems are not blamed nor sacrificed.

A very popular term in Japanese TQC [total quality control] activities is *warusa-kagen*, which refers to things that are not really problems but are somehow not quite right. Left unattended, *warusa-kagen* may eventually develop into serious trouble and may cause substantial damage. In the [system], it is usually the worker, not the supervisor, who notices *warusa-kagen*.[48]

Soichiro Honda rejects the notion that his countrymen must submit to group goals; he believes that "first, each individual should work for himself—that's important. . . . People will not sacrifice for the company. . . ."[49] In fact he lauds the thinking worker, one who is responsive to *warusa-kagen*: "A thinking work force must be given the freedom to take risks. When people are afraid to make mistakes, they will continually repeat the same *processes* [emphasis added]."[50]

Point Two: *Create constancy of purpose toward improvement of service, with a plan to improve competitive position and stay in business.*

The fundamental purpose of the organization is best expressed as survival while its priority is in its reason(s) for existence. In base terms, "[t]he most fundamental purpose [priority] of an . . . institution is to produce graduates employers need and hire."[51] Continuing and constant purpose requires activity other than preserving the status-quo-ante; a true commitment to quality demands ongoing innovation:

> Search for and fund instructional methods that facilitate more learning while also making efficient use of student/teacher time and energy as well as materials and equipment costs. Identify and use recruiting and admitting techniques that place students in programs which they have a high probability of completing. Don't keep doing the same thing over and over again just because no disasters have occurred. Assume that if what you are now doing in placement works well then there is probable some way it can be made to work even better. Plan to spend time, energy, and money training faculty in new methods of teaching, acquiring better instructional equipment, and changing the way instructional space is arranged. Dare to be as different as you need to be to improve.

It is difficult for any organization to pursue never-ending improvement without adopting a long-term perspective. "Managers under the Deming philosophy are concerned with the problems of today and tomorrow and inspire confidence with their long-term view of the [institution] and its commitment to quality."[52] The deplorable roll-over rate of law deans works directly against such a commitment to quality. This point is not an argument for decanal "tenure" but emphasizes that "short-term" management introduces constancy—not of purpose, but of *variation!* Perhaps the "informal structure" of the organization which endures long after a gaggle of deans come and go, can give an institution its focus for constancy of purpose; this is unlikely given the nature of man. The Japanese wrestled with the fabric of its informal structure in a similar way and found that the concept of "leadership" needed redefinition. It seems that the dominance of the informal power structure strengthened and perpetuated *gakbatsu*–what we would call "the good old boys club" system of management.

When Dr. Deming writes of "knowing" to do one's best, *supra*, he speaks "... of knowing what to do—establishing the constancy of purpose and then doing your best—maintaining consistency of purpose."[53] The mission statement of the organization is the likely starting point to examine "consistency of purpose." Generally, it is the expressed mission of generally all law schools to provide high-quality legal education (a random sampling of law school catalogs and bulletins illustrates this point). Just exactly what *is* quality legal education? Which cartel of schools set the standard apart from guidance given by the ABA or AALS accreditation standards? There is too much platitude and not enough measurement in legal education; to state that students "receive a quality legal education" sets the purpose—to do one's best—without knowing how to do it or when it is done defeats *that* purpose. Certainly the process of legal education works—there is good result for the most part—but it is unknown quality, and that can be improved.

Point Three: *Adopt the new philosophy. We are in a new economic age. Western management must awaken to the challenge, must learn their responsibilities, and take on leadership for change.*

Like Bilbo Bagins in *The Hobbit* we are comfortable in our habit because it is known. The Deming philosophy and methodology is a call for major change and the adoption of something new.

> Adopting [a] new philosophy requires changing attitudes. ... This creates mistrust, fear, and anxiety, particularly for people who are satisfied with the status quo ... [M]anagers probably have the most to fear. They have succeeded in the current systems and know how to negotiate them. They don't know what life in an organization that uses Dr. Deming's methods will be like and how they will fare. So, naturally they resist change.[54]

The "newness" in the philosophy for education is to directly change the quality of it by improving what we call the "programs" that come from examining (assessment) the observable, and measurable results of those programs.

> This contrasts to running a school by conventional methods. That is, we teach in a given way because that is the way most schools teach a subject. This new philosophy is to commit to finding out what works at a particular place and continuing to improve it constantly.[55]

Often faculty are stymied in making decisions until they "sample" what is done in other schools, as if "the frontier" has already been crossed and they must follow others. The danger in a deferential approach is that it permits others to define and create "quality" standards. Adopting a new philosophy frees a faculty to define what it means by *quality.*

Point Four: *Institute modern methods of training on the job.*

Formal preparation and training is often not required for the actual doing of a job in postsecondary education. Professionals are recruited on the basis of their practice abilities and someone's prediction about a successful "competency transference"—from competent doer to competent teacher (from competent teacher to competent administrator). But, the heralds of caution dangle the *Peter Principle* before the wistful recruiter. Yet, the unguided accomplishments from "new" faculty repeatedly performing in the same manner most likely introduces *special variation* into the teaching/ learning process and, if left unchanged, eventually affects total quality.

Where do law professors learn to use the Socratic method? What training do they take? Answers range from "experiences on the job" (mostly infor- mal—learning from "hard knocks") to acquired skills from a successful professional practice. How many among the professorate know, by design, that examinations are "reliable" or "valid"? This is the principal measuring devise used to determine the "performance quality" of students and, yet, there is uncertainty about the *conformance quality* of the processes. How is it possible to determine that we meet "student needs" if our measuring devise is wanting?

The AALS annually offers three days of "training" for new law teachers[56]; it is mandatory that law schools provide ongoing "training" to their faculty. Formal training "makes a difference only if inadequate performance is due to a knowledge or skill deficiency. If the inadequacy is due to lack of motivation or opportunity to practice the skill, training will not be worth the cost. That is, if someone is capable of performing up to expectation but for some reason chooses not to do so, that person does not have a training problem. To change such behavior, something will have to be changed in the person's work environment."[57]

Point Five: *Drive out fear so that everyone may work effectively.*

Consider the parable of the *Tares Among Wheat.*[58] It seems that a certain man sowed good seed in his field, but while he slept, an enemy came to his field and sowed tares among his wheat and left. Immediate damage to the crop was undetected. When the wheat grew and bore grain, the tares were revealed. The servants of the field owner were told not to uproot the tares because they were so intertwined with the wheat that the good grain would be destroyed as well. Fear is a tare in any organization. Its presence, usually unapparent, is a negative value and must be eliminated when a new philosophy is adopted. Obviously, it is best to guard the institution, at all times, against fears that rob people of their ability "to do their best." Since few are fortunate enough to design an institution's programs from the beginning, we must look for every occasion within to drive it out when it is found. Unlike the wheat parable, removing the tare will improve the quality of the grain. Fear was often a management technique to leverage more performance from workers (which it quantitatively measured). Few will agree that fear is the best motivational stimulus. Perhaps quantity may increase with its use, but quality will never result from it. Simply consider the "fear" factor present in the average law classroom. Fears cannot be totally removed from the learner, but they can be reduced by a caring faculty reducing it from the learning processes. The same can be said for employees (faculty and staff) when they face promotion, retention, and merit possibilities. Simply stated, fear affects quality.

Point Six: *Break down barriers between departments [people].*

This point is consistent with the preceding one and deserves separate focus because of our particular American culture. "Generally, Americans intellectually believe in teamwork and cooperation; but when confronted with giving up some individual control to a group, our emotions resist. Despite the fact that it was groups—families, clans and religious communities—that really pioneered and settled the West, we persist in our myths of the lonely pioneer. Gary Cooper by himself at *High Noon* is still a powerful image with us."[59]

Point Seven: *Remove barriers that rob people of pride of workmanship.*

Some reformers suggest that law schools borrow from law practice management and use those people specifically trained to "manage" and who are not necessarily trained in the calling of those they manage viz., this is a call for Weber's "trained bureaucrats." Certainly, not everyone in the formal management structure of a law school need be an "academic lawyer," but the top post role-incumbent should be. It is central to Deming's philosophy that workers, if given a chance, want to excel at their jobs but they are often stopped from achieving excellence because of the management policies they work under. "The barriers to a teacher being effective may be particularly unnoticeable to administrators without direct experience in teaching under similar circumstances. Job-hopping is very common in postsecondary education. It's considered by some to be the quickest way to advancement. . . . Among its many problems, it communicates a lack of long-term commitment to the school."[60] Pride in one's work is above the baseline needs in Maslow's hierarchy discussed earlier. Law faculty seek fulfilling results from their work, and they enter teaching with high expec-

tations of their need closer to "self-actualization" than to physiological
necessities. An example often cited from Deming's work is that there is
"such an emphasis on individual performance that teamwork is discour-
aged. Managers who move frequently . . . creates prima donnas for quick
results."[61] I like to believe that faculty invest their work efforts in a particular
institution because they experience self-actualization, not simply comfort
derived from a sinecure. Even so, factors in an organization that foster
mobility of deans, faculty, and staff "annihilates teamwork, so vital for
continued existence."[62]

Point Eight: *Implement modern methods of management—institute*
                   leadership.

Modern methodology in leadership recognizes that achieving success in
the pursuit of quality requires managing for *that* success. What directions
that leadership take, and the results desired are planned for:

> . . . [A] positive atmosphere [where] supervisors are not policing
> workers and blaming them for the handicaps of the system. The
> worker is treated with dignity trained, supervised properly, and
> knows what the job is so that performance can improve. . . . It is a
> cycle of positives that is set in motion by the new supervision and
> attitude.[63]

Point Nine: *Improve constantly and forever the system of . . . service to*
                  improve quality and productivity.

Line personnel (faculty) are quick disclaimers of responsibility for *common variation* in a system (of instruction). Management is traditionally
regarded as the owner of the system and hence workers cannot change
variation without conflict or resistance from the hierarchy. Law faculty bear
an incredible responsibility under the ABA Standards to "design and
manage" legal education; if common variation is a part of a system, it stays
there from institutional inertia nourished by malfeasance, misfeasance, or
nonfeasance of the informal power structure and the dynamics of *primary
group affiliation*, noted <u>supra</u>.

Point Ten: *Institute a vigorous program of education and self-improvement.*

Individual betterment is necessary for self-actualization and concomitant
with pursuing the "human side of enterprise." The notions of *morale* that
became a part of twentieth century management methodology are directly
related to the "quality" health of an organization. This positive action by an
institution requires a commitment of resources that are invested with the
long-term view of return. Professorial sabbaticals, leaves-of-absence, re-

lease time, funding travel, are as necessary to meeting the mission of the organization as meeting the student's needs in the classroom. Also, formal training in the methods used for quality improvement gives "an organization [a] road map to achieve its goals [and foster] a positive attitude and a sense that all can work together, under a management that knows what to do to succeed."[64]

Point Eleven: *Cease dependence on mass inspection. Require, instead, statistical evidence that quality is built in to eliminate the need for inspection on a mass basis.*

American industry standards accepted defects (poor quality) and chose during postwar growth to overcome them by production-volume which was quality inspected at the end-of-the-line. Lower standard output was directed by quality inspectors to scrap or to rework. Of course, the main problem with rework is that it uses the same *processes* that created the defect from the beginning. Whimsy reigns. The Japanese approach to "systems engineering" is noted in the "zero defect" approach—alter the systems of production or service so the process ensures quality.

Education does not build products per se, and cannot separate good widgets from bad widgets. As a service provider, however, educational organizations can "observe how the process works through observing a representative sample of cases. . . . The current response to declining quality is to demand more inspection—testing of students at certain points."[65] Law schools, by accreditation standards cannot give academic credit for "bar review" type courses; these teaching-to-the-test experiences, while useful, may improve performance on a target test, but the question of actual competency is never addressed, therefore averting the true questions raised by applying "quality control."

> A better use of outcomes assessment is to collect valid and reliable information about how an educational system is working. Given that information, programs with consistently poor results become the object of intense analysis to identify causes of the poor results.[66]

Reichheld and Sasser posit that service institutions have their own peculiar junk pile—*customers (students) who will not come back.*[67] Worse yet, those that will not come back (educators speak in "retention rate" jargon) stop others who would otherwise come initially. Like zero defects, managing to minimize zero defections is a quality control approach. These authors claim that the service industry revolution in quality is just beginning. Institutions "are beginning to understand what their manufacturing counterparts learned in the 1980s—*that quality doesn't improve unless you measure it.*"[68] An organization that measures quality will act on that information and adjust its processes accordingly. Managing for "zero defections" as a measure of quality pays long-term dividends that show up, for example, during the annual capital fund drive or pursuits for endowment. We need to create mechanisms to deal with students who are about to conclude an institutional relationship so they leave campus without a N.O.P.E. bumper-sticker (Not One Penny Ever). This idea is not to adhere slavishly to the customer "always being right" nor that he must be kept at any cost; rather, "[t]he idea is to use defections as an early warning signal—to learn from defectors why they left... and to use that information to improve...."[69] Since "defection" is part of a process, it can be measured, managed, and improved by reducing the rate.

Points Twelve and Thirteen: *Eliminate slogans, exhortations, and targets for the work force asking for zero defects ... the bulk of the causes of low quality belong to the system; replace managing by numbers with never-ending improvement.*

Since Deming's philosophy is an attitudinal focus on an organizational goal of pursuing never-ending quality, "... the emphasis should be on the progress that management [administration and law faculty governance committees] is making in never-ending improvement."[70] No amount of "talking" or exhorting for improvement changes the quality of a service or product—leadership is required. Frequently leadership and administration are interchangeable terms used to describe the process of "guidance" in goal-actualization within an organization. Plainly stated, an administrator is a bureaucratic leader—a role-incumbent in a bureaucratic office that "practices" leadership. "Not infrequently, school administrators oversee administrative responsibilities almost exclusively, to the detriment of their effectiveness as leaders."[71]

Using work standards and quotas is managing for failure. They offer no road map for improvement of quality, and they encourage ... [defect]. Workers' pride is diminished because they know they are not turning out quality . . . and the general atmosphere is clouded with negativity and failure. Workers are either under-worked or overworked but certainly not happy and fulfilled.[72]

Point Fourteen: End the practice of awarding business on the basis of the price tag. Move towards a single supplier ... on a long-term relationship of loyalty and trust.

This point is one of the most difficult to manage in legal education apart from the mundane of material procurement. A recurring comment among law school recruiters indicates the admissions "process" must be managed similar to every other activity. "We blithely accept students from University X, Y, or Z, but College W, Q, and R graduates have not been so successful in our program." Graduate school organizations do not see themselves as "customers" of undergraduate schools despite the law admissions requirement that an applicant has an undergraduate degree. Individual applicant merit is largely the focus for admissions decisions. Yet, an admittee with training from a "weak" program introduces *special variation* into the graduate learning processes. If no other quality control measures are used in screening applicants from undergraduate programs, schools can

> . . . identify those sending schools and agencies that account for most of the incoming students. A relationship can be developed with those schools to build a long-term partnership. The purpose of the partnership is the development of a student stream that has a high probability of completing the program.[73]

Of course admissions administrators hide behind a red-herring of quality if they advance, in arguendo, compliance with ABA Standard 304 as its organizations' assurance of "quality supply." Under that standard a law school shall not admit or retain one who manifests inability to do satisfactory work. Recall the Russian TVs; they work the same as ones made by the Japanese—the consumer just doesn't know when one will explode!

Conclusion

Futurist Joel Barker[74] warns organizations that their futures are only extensions of the past unless they shift from established rules and regulations that are presently used. He calls the impact of those sets of rules the "paradigm effect." In essence, our paradigm establishes activity boundaries and sets requirements within those boundaries for success. Everyone in an institution then filters incoming data and experiences to select that which fits the current paradigm; the rest is rejected—the new idea, procedure, method, program, etc. Any effect of a paradigm influences one's perceptions, hence its effects are directly related to decisions and judgements—we see a problem, solution, design, etc., the way we are "supposed to see it" from the paradigm in force at the time. When change is necessary it will meet resistance from the old "paradigm effect" of the organization; many will try to look to the future (or the change) by looking through the established paradigm. How is the process of legal education supposed to be designed and function? We essentially all "look alike"—i.e., the established paradigm. "Taking the run of national and regional full-time, university-connected law schools as a unit, a visitor could sit blind-folded in, say, a first-year torts class in any one of them with some assurance that he would not be able to tell whether he was at Harvard, Yale, Columbia, Chicago, Stanford, or East Cupcake."[75] Dr. Deming offers a "new" paradigm to achieve quality in "process" activity. Much of what the Japanese have used successfully is due to their willingness to shift paradigms even though the "transaction cost" risk in doing so was uncertain. The wonderful revelation this idea adds to education "systems engineering" is that "when a paradigm shifts, everyone goes back to zero, i.e., past successes guarantee nothing for the future" thereby freeing personnel creativity and advancing INNOVA-TION.

Applying the Deming philosophy and methodology to education is indeed a "paradigm shift" itself for legal educators, but deeper understanding and application of the 14 Points gives meaning to the worn phrase—"quality legal education"—that before was unascertainable under the old paradigm. The administration and management of law school functions, apart from classroom activities, are easier targets for change using Deming methods. Copy machines, libraries, typing pools, etc., are readily changed. But, the classroom experience is a process too. As such, it can be measured, managed, and improved using the same principles. [76]

Endnotes

1   Speech by Robert Macrate, Chair, ABA Task Force on Law Schools and the Profession, to the conference *Making the Competent Lawyer: Models for Law School Action.* Sponsored by the Standing Committee on Lawyer Competence in cooperation with the Section of Legal Education and Admissions to the Bar, November 1-3, 1990, St. Louis, Missouri.

2   For a discussion of the early history of the ABA and AALS and its control of lawyer education, see generally, Sullivan, *The Professional Associations and Legal Education,* 4 J. Leg. Ed. 401 (1952).

3   Ibid. at 408.

4   Ibid. at 426.

5   To Enhance Prestige of Teaching, Faculty Members Urged to Make Pedagogy Focus of Scholarly Debate, The Chronicle of Higher Education, Oct. 31, 1990.

6   Barbara W. Tuchman, The March of Folly at 23 (New York, 1984).

7   Ibid. at 33.

8   Some Research Universities Contemplate Sweeping Changes, Ranging From Management and Tenure to Teaching Methods, The Chronicle of Higher Education, Sept. 12, 1990, at A29, col. 4.

9   See Ibid. at col. 1.

10 Silva & Sjogren, *supra* note 3, at 114.

11 Kay, What is Legal Education? and Should We Permit It to Continue in Its Present Form? 6 Ga. St. U. L. Rev. 367 (1990).

12 Fasan, If Wishes Were Horses: Reflections Without Footnotes On Legal Education, 9 N. Ill. U. L. Rev. 123 (1988).

13 Matthews, Sketches For A New Law School, 40 Hastings L.J. 1095 (1989).

14 Ibid.

15 Ibid.

16 See Ibid. at 1103.

17 M. Silva & B. Sjogren, *supra* note 3, at 114.

18 M. Walton, *supra* note 10, at 88.

19 See M. Walton, *supra* note 10, ch. 21, for general background on the Deming Prize, its creation and award process.

20 Malcolm Baldrige National Quality Improvement Act of 1987, Pub. L. No. 100-107.

21 Robert G. Owens, Organizational Behavior in Schools at 38 (Englewood Cliffs, N.J., 1970).

22 See Ibid. at 5-6.

23 Frederick Herzberg, Work and the Nature of Man at 36 (New York, 1966).

24 R. Owens, *supra* note 21, at 7.

25 Ibid.

26 See Ibid. at 17.

27 See Ibid. at 31.

28 Gibbons, The Relationship Between Law and Science, 22 Idea 51 (1981).

29 R. Owens, *supra* note 21, at 48.

30 American Bar Association Standards For Approval of Law Schools and Interpretations, Standard 205 (Chicago, 1989).

31 R.Owens, *supra* note 21, at 50-51.

32 See Ibid. 54.

33 A Look at the Long Haul, Syllabus, Dec. 1988, at 2, col. 2.

34 Why Do Deans Quit?, Syllabus, Dec., 1988, at 1, col. 1.

35 R. Owens, *supra* note 21, at 55.

36 Syllabus, *supra* note 34.

37 Howard S. Gitlow & Shelly J. Gitlow, The Deming Guide to Quality and Competitive Position at 6 (Englewood Cliffs, N. J., 1987).

38 See Ibid. at 8.

39 Ibid.

40 Ibid.

41 See Ibid. at 9.

42 M. Walton, *supra* note 10, at 32.

43 William W. Scherkenback, Introduction to The Deming Route to Quality and Productivity, (Milwaukee, Wisc., 1986).

44 Ibid.

45 John Harris, Susan Hillenmeyer, James V. Foran, Quality Assurance for Private Career Schools (Washington, D.C., 1989).
46 M. Walton, *supra* note 10.
47 H. Gitlow & S. Gitlow, *supra* note 37, at 194.
48 Masaaki Imai, KAIZEN The Key to Japan's Competitive Success at 164-5 (New York, 1986).
49 Robert L. Shook, HONDA An American Success Story at 13 (New York, 1988).
50 See Ibid. at 127.
51 J. Harris, et al., *supra* note 45, at 6.
52 H. Gitlow & S. Gitlow, *supra* note 37, at 17.
53 W. Scherkenback, *supra* note 43, at 13.
54 H. Gitlow & S. Gitlow, *supra* note 37, at 33.
55 J. Harris, et al., *supra* note 45, at 8.
56 The AALS workshop description for 1991 is: "This workshop is designed to help the new law teacher learn how to function effectively in the law school environment and to introduce the new law professors to classroom methodologies and techniques, as well as philosophies of teaching. Particular attention will be devoted to demonstration and explanation of different teaching styles and the process of evaluating student work. Topics include: Introduction to Teaching; Teaching Strategies; Colleagues and Community; Scholarship (Nuts and Bolts, Trends and Types); Students."
57 J. Harris, et al., *supra* note 45, at 13.
58 Matt. 13:24
59 J. Harris, et al., *supra* note 45, at 16.
60 See Ibid. at 19.
61 J. Harris, et al., *supra* note 45, at 19 citing *Out Of the Crisis* (107-09).
62 See Ibid. at 19.
63 H. Gitlow & S. Gitlow, *supra* note 37, at 117.
64 See Ibid. at 184.
65 Harris p. 8
66 See Ibid. at 9.
67 Reichheld & Sasser, "Zero Defections: Quality Comes to Services", *Harvard Business Review*, Sept/Oct 1990 p. 105.
68 Ibid.
69 See Ibid. at 109.
70 H. Gitlow & S. Gitlow, *supra* note 37, at 157.
71 R. Owens, *supra* note 21, at 136.
72 H. Gitlow & S. Gitlow, *supra* note 37, at 167.
73 J. Harris, et al., *supra* note 45, at 11.
74 Discovering the Future: The Business Paradigm, (Joel Barker & Associates, Videotape, 1990).
75 H. Packer & T. Ehrlich, *New Dimensions in Legal Education* 29 (1972).

76   For a bibliography of works designed to familiarize the reader with detail on the methodology, contact the author: Cumberland School of Law, Samford University, Birmingham, AL, 35229; or BITNET ajbolla@samford; or FAX 205-870-2673.

Alexander J. Bolla is Associate Dean and Professor of Law at the Cumberland School of Law, Samford University. He received B.A., B.S., and J.D. degrees from Ohio State University.

Chapter 16

QI from a Health Professions School Perspective

Lucinda L. Maine, Ph.D.
Samford University
Birmingham, Alabama

Introduction

Health Care, Education, and Quality Improvement

Health care, like education in America, finds itself increasingly under fire. Consumers and policy-makers are not convinced that they are getting the optimal outcomes from their health care or education expenditures. But unlike education, where consumers as taxpayers and as law-makers have at least some say over the amount of tax dollars allocated to support public education, seemingly no one has control over medical expenditures. In spite of a decade of strenuous cost controlling measures which cut across all practice environments, health care cost increases continue to outpace the rate of inflation for other consumer goods and services.

While bothersome to all, no one seems to be able to get a handle on the root cause of the problem. The increased expenditures simply do not translate into improved health outcomes for the people of the United States. Structure and process approaches to the accreditation of health care organizations have not improved either the efficiency or effectiveness of medical care. Attention is now being directed, as it is in educational assessment, to outcome measures of performance by physicians, hospitals, and other players in the health care system.

Conceptual Introduction to Quality Improvement Principles

Given this scenario, it is not surprising that the introduction of total quality management (TQM) principles in higher education coincides with their introduction in the health care industry. The School of Pharmacy at Samford University first heard of W.E. Deming and the 14 Points in a postgraduate seminar sponsored by the School in April 1988. Dr. Paul B. Batalden, Vice President for Medical Care at the Hospital Corporation of America (HCA), was the seminar leader. When he joined HCA in 1986, Dr. Batalden's responsibilities included the initiation of a company-wide TQM program for this complex hospital corporation. His seminar focused upon the use of TQM principles as effective tools for identifying patient and provider needs and for improving the outcomes of health care in the populations served.

The Dean of the Samford University School of Pharmacy immediately recognized the potential for applying the same principles to pharmacy education. He was extremely enthusiastic when Dr. John Harris, a guest lecturer at Samford in the fall of 1988, introduced the Deming Principles as tools for assessment and quality improvement in higher education.

This chapter will review the earliest steps taken by the Samford University School of Pharmacy to equip its leaders and faculty to operate the academic programs and administrative processes using TQM principles. Initial attempts to apply the tools are described. Additional evidence is also provided of the increasing use of these quality improvement methods by providers of health care services in the United States.

Earliest Learning Steps

The American Association of Colleges of Pharmacy (AACP), in cooperation with the SmithKline Beckman Foundation, coordinates an annual grant funding program "to support programs and projects in pharmacy education that are innovative, unique and that have potential benefit to all pharmacy education." The 1988-89 Grant Awards for Pharmacy Schools (GAPS) funding priorities included the area of performance evaluation in the curriculum. Specifically, the association (1989) sought proposals for projects that would provide models for more accurate and effective evaluation of student performance in all environments of pharmacy education.

Dr. Timothy Burelle, then Dean of the Samford University School of Pharmacy, and Dr. Lucinda Maine, Associate Dean for Student/Alumni Affairs, applied for funding under this GAPS priority. Their original proposal, entitled "Use of Performance Assessment Techniques and Deming's Management Principles to Systematically and Continuously Improve Pharmacy Education," targeted the teaching of communication skills in the pharmacy curriculum as the process to be improved using TQM techniques.

Although AACP did not fund the original proposal at the amount requested, GAPS support was made available to the investigators to facilitate their understanding of TQM and its application to pharmacy education. The funding allowed for several levels of activity, including: (1) the acquisition of resource materials on TQM, (2) travel to observe the application of TQM principles in the corporate setting, and (3) sponsorship of a conference on Quality Improvement in Higher Education.

As the end of the two-year GAPS funding period approaches, one of the investigators has begun outlining a model for the use of TQM in assessing and improving pharmacy students' communication skills. A more detailed discussion of this is provided later in this chapter.

Quality Improvement in Higher Education Conference

With the external support provided by AACP, Samford University was able to host a conference on "Managing for Improved Quality in Higher Education" in November 1989. The meeting agenda and list of speakers can be found in Appendix A. Conference participants included the University's administrators, deans, department heads, several faculty, and a small number of other invited guests.

The objective for the meeting was to bring together those individuals who had begun to draw upon the lessons of TQM either to improve administrative processes or as tools for assessment in higher education. One community college president was able to relate the first-hand experience of a top administrator who had championed the cause of TQM in his institution.

The speakers and audience members walked away from the November conference with several impressions. The first was that all had much more to learn about the rudiments of TQM. The more pervasive attitude, however, was that continuous improvement of quality did hold substantial promise for higher education. Although none underestimated the task at hand, there was a significant amount of excitement about the important journey those committed to total quality in higher education had embarked upon.

Samford University's Training Process

The Schools of Pharmacy and Nursing, the only health science schools at Samford, began sending members of the schools' administration, staff, and faculty to the QIP training program developed by Samford's Office for Assessment and Quality Improvement in the fall of 1990. Each participant completed the 20-plus hours of coursework, and several traveled to see TQM at work in the manufacturing environment. A few individuals traveled to West Paces Ferry Hospital in Georgia to learn how TQM principles were working in a health care system.

Training of faculty and staff in pharmacy and nursing continues at this time. In addition, individual reading and studying goes on constantly, and the principles of TQM are being introduced into the daily activities of the schools.

Using the Tools — Administrative Activities

Training in quality improvement has altered the mindset of the School of Pharmacy administrators in several key ways. "How do you know?" is a question that promotes the acquisition of *data* in an effort to assess and improve many of the recurring activities in the educational program. Efforts to identify and reach the School's many customers to determine their satisfaction and improve the exchange of information are also the direct result of training.

The examples of QI in health professions schools that are provided in this chapter are tentative first steps to systematically examine our administrative and academic processes. They do not always employ TQM principles and tools in their "purest" form. They do represent efforts to continuously improve upon what is done in the School of Pharmacy.

Three examples of the School's efforts to employ TQM principles in its administrative arena include: (1) an advisor network questionnaire, (2) an employer's roundtable, and (3) an advising survey. Each is described in this section.

Advisor Network Questionnaire

The School of Pharmacy admits 110 new students each year. Only a small percentage of the entering class has completed their pre-professional coursework at Samford University. Pre-pharmacy courses may be taken at any accredited college or university. A network of feeder schools has matured over the years, each with someone designated as a health professions, or more specifically pre-pharmacy, advisor. A series of on-campus visits by the Director of Recruiting and Admissions for the School of Pharmacy and periodic mailings provide the primary vehicles for communication between our "customers" — the feeder schools and their students — and the School.

A questionnaire was developed in 1990 and distributed to the 75 colleges and universities in the Samford University School of Pharmacy advising network. Thirty-one usable responses were received (41% response rate). The survey asked 18 questions in three general areas of inquiry: (1) general perceptions of our academic program; (2) communication assessment; and (3) advisor information.

While a detailed discussion of the results of the survey are beyond the scope of this chapter, we learned that, on balance, our style of communication met the needs of the respondents. There were, however, opportunities for improvement. Increased visits by our representative, improved timeliness of information dissemination, and feedback on the outcome of the admissions decisions for each advisor's students are examples of process enhancements already incorporated into the School's ongoing activities. These and other improvements will increase the likelihood that advisors will encourage their students to consider Samford University and will help to maintain the high quality of the School's applicant pool.

Employer's Roundtable

The pharmacy profession is enjoying a period of high demand for its services. There are expanding opportunities for pharmacists in traditional practice primarily because of corporate growth in the chain pharmacy sector. An increasing number of nontraditional practice positions are available to graduates of the Bachelor of Science in Pharmacy and Doctor of Pharmacy programs in a variety of institutional and noninstitutional settings. The School of Pharmacy assists its graduates in placement by sponsoring an interview day in the final semester of the program. An average of 30 employers from the chain, hospital, governmental, and industrial sectors participate.

The School of Pharmacy recognizes employers of its graduates as one group of customers. In 1990 the School decided to employ a focus group format with employers to seek two basic types of information: (1) how our graduates were viewed in terms of preparedness to practice after completing our undergraduate program, and (2) how the structure and management of our interview day met the needs of our "customers," the employers who participated.

The Dean of the School of Pharmacy conducted the discussion session with representatives of approximately 10 companies. Most were from the chain pharmacy sector. The employers were enthusiastic about the Samford pharmacy graduates they had employed in the past. They noted that most had a true affinity for practice in the community setting. Opportunities for improvement included more emphasis on appropriate communication skills and attention to a growing problem (not just for Samford graduates) of chemical impairment among pharmacy and other health care professionals. Employers' sensitivity to the need to improve the communication outcomes of our graduates served to underscore this area as the focus of academic QI initiatives.

The feedback on the conduct of our interview day was also very positive. Employers cited their encouragement to other schools to adopt an interview structure similar to ours as convincing evidence of their satisfaction with the level of organization and service provided. The one recommendation for improvement, that employers receive the profiles of the students scheduled to interview with them the evening before the interviews, was implemented the following year.

Advising Survey (PDCA)

The adequacy of academic, career, and personal advising is an issue of considerable concern to the School of Pharmacy. In 1989-90, the Student

Affairs Committee began to seriously examine the existing structure of advising for pharmacy majors. At that time each student was randomly assigned to a faculty member who served as an individual advisor for the student. Each faculty member maintained an approximately equivalent number of students and served as the advisor throughout the time the student was enrolled in the professional program. Little training of advisors, new or old, occurred and considerable variation in the quality of advising was apparent.

In its preliminary discussions, the Student Affairs Committee noted that historically students had entered the School of Pharmacy during three different academic terms (fall, winter, and summer). Courses were offered several times during the year. While the advisors tried to provide guidance and oversight, it was sometimes true that a student enrolled in courses without completing prerequisites. Without computerized transcript support, and with such a large number of possible sequences for completing courses, it was difficult for advisors to monitor students' progress accurately. This had changed when the School adopted a single, fall admissions cycle and a lock-step curriculum.

The Committee examined the current experience of students relative to academic, career, and personal advising and discussed the resources for each available in the School and on campus. A *PLAN* was formulated to change the advising system from individual to class advising. Two faculty members would volunteer to serve as the advisors for a class of 110 students. It would be the responsibility of the advisors, in conjunction with the Office of the Associate Dean for Student/Alumni Affairs, to oversee students' registration, to work closely with class leaders on problems and projects, and to consult with individual students on academic, career, and personal problems/issues. Centralization of student records and the progression of students through the curriculum in a lock-step fashion made the class advising system a practical alternative to the decentralized advising system of the past.

The new advising system was introduced in the fall of 1989 *(DO)* and was implemented for all classes in the B.S. and Pharm. D. curricula. This meant that one class of B.S. students, the Class of 1991, was enrolled under two different systems of advising, having been originally assigned individual advisors for their first year and making the transition to class advisors for their final two years.

After two academic years using the class advising system, the decision was made by the Student Affairs Committee to evaluate the impact of the changes *(CHECK)*. The preliminary initiative used to assess the effectiveness of the advising system employed a survey instrument administered to the Class of 1991 as they were completing their final requirements for graduation. A copy of the survey and the results obtained are found in Appendix B.

The School of Pharmacy Student Affairs Committee will use the results of this survey and additional input from students and faculty during the 1991-92 year to make recommendations for changes in the advising system. With appropriate administrative approval these changes will be implemented in a timely fashion (*ACT*).

Using the Tools — Academic Applications

There have been three academic projects which represent the first attempts by the School of Pharmacy to employ TQM in the assessment and improvement of its academic programs. These are described in this section and include: (1) an examination of national board examination scores for a four-year period, (2) an assessment of the academic outcomes of interviewed vs. non-interviewed pharmacy students, and (3) a project designed to assess and improve the terminal communication skills of pharmacy graduates.

National Board Exam Assessment

The School of Pharmacy first employed a QI statistical tool, the control chart, in an analysis of Samford graduates' rate of passage on the pharmacy licensure examination. Figure 1 provides the results of this study for nine administrations of the exam between June 1986 and June 1989.

Part of the motivation for examining the board scores, and more specifically the rate of failures on the national exam, was the fact that in 1985 a substantial percentage of Samford pharmacy graduates failed the exam on the first attempt. Two things had occurred however since 1985: (1) the national exam had changed to an integrated format to more closely reflect both the content of contemporary pharmacy curricula and the patient-oriented style of data presentation that students had become familiar with during their degree programs, and (2) Samford's curriculum was revised substantially in both content and structure.

SU CONTROL CHART

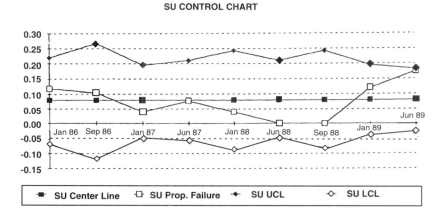

Figure 1 Rate of Passage on Pharmacy Licensure Examination

The control chart in Figure 1 suggests that our students' performance on the national exam was "in control" over the period covered by the study. There are no apparent special causes of variation in passage rates that warrant closer scrutiny for this time period. The other message is that the content and delivery of information in the educational program during this period were sufficient for fairly consistent, and generally successful, performance on this important licensure examination.

Samford students have participated in six additional administrations of the exam since this statistical exercise was completed. To continue to examine the impact of curricular refinements on the outcome performance of our students, the School should refine its use of this statistical tool and learn more about the applications of QI tools in the process.

Evaluation of Interview Outcomes

Nowhere is the issue of continuous improvement as important to the School of Pharmacy as in the admissions process. A highly competitive applicant pool is attractive as it allows for more careful selection for the limited positions available. As is true in many professional schools, however, the Pharmacy Admissions Committee was forced to make admissions decisions based on transcripts, essays, and letters of recommendation for students from 75 to 100 different colleges and universities.

Interviews had not been employed in the admissions process prior to 1990. During that admissions cycle, the committee formalized the criteria for selecting and evaluating those interviewed. Not all students were interviewed. Those with clearly superior academic records were admitted without interview. Applicants whose academic record was marginal were excluded from the interview process. The philosophy in interviewing was that every attempt should be made to identify those candidates whose insight into pharmacy, maturity, and communication abilities reinforced their academic record sufficiently to warrant admissions consideration.

The class admitted in the fall of 1990 included 35 people admitted after interviewing. The balance, 73 students after two withdrew from the program, entered on their academic record alone. Following the first semester, and again after a full year in the professional curriculum, comparisons of the academic outcomes of these students were completed. Figures 2 and 3 provide a graphic representation of the academic outcomes for the two groups of students (Interviewed vs. Not Interviewed). The first reflects academic standing of students that were interviewed. Figure 3 shows the same information for students not interviewed.

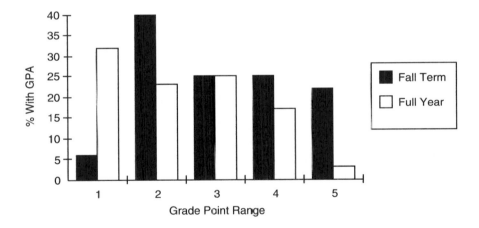

Figure 2 Interviewed Students' Performance

There are interesting differences in the data. At the end of one semester there were approximately the same percentage of students in the "less than 2.0," "2.5 - 2.99," and "3.0 - 3.49" groups. Substantially more of the interviewed students clustered between 2.0 and 2.49. The highest percentage of students in the other group achieved a grade point average greater than or equal to 3.5. These were not surprising findings given the difference in academic profile of the two groups on admission. The Committee was primarily interested in determining whether substantially more students in the interviewed group were in academic jeopardy (GPA < 2.0) after the fall semester.

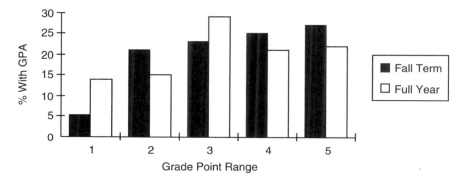

Figure 3 Not Interviewed Students' Performance

The notable disparity after the second semester was the substantial increase (from 5.7 to 31.4 percent) in interviewed students whose GPA was below 2.0 by year end. While both groups experienced increases in the number of students in academic jeopardy, there was a 5-fold increase for interviewed students. The factor was 2.5 for those not interviewed.

The data will now be analyzed by the School of Pharmacy Admissions Committee. That committee continued to use interviews for the fall 1991 admission cycle but will need to determine its value for 1992 and beyond. Initial impressions of the committee following fall semester were quite positive given the small percentage of students in both categories who fell below the 2.0 grade point criterion for good academic standing. The committee has not seen the data for the full year at the time this manuscript was prepared. The greater disparity in outcomes may influence their future admissions procedures. Certainly, additional data will be collected to assist them in refining the processes used for making admissions decisions.

Communication Competencies of Pharmacy Externs

The pharmacy literature is replete with citations which call on the profession and its schools to better prepare pharmacists to educate patients and other health professionals. To accomplish these educational goals the communication skills of pharmacy graduates must be enhanced. The original AACP/GAPS proposal called for the development of a model for applying QI principles to the assessment and improvement of pharmacy students' communication skills.

Initial work on the development of such a model began in earnest in the spring of 1991. The steps which might be undertaken in a QI initiative aimed at improving pharmacy graduates' communication skills are outlined in Figure 4. Thus far the process has been completed through Step 2. Step 3 began in summer 1991. Although the overall Communications Quality Improvement Project is still in its infancy, a brief description of the effort is provided.

Communication Skills Assessment in Spring 1991 Graduates A Case Study

Step 1: Survey preceptors to identify communication skill strengths and weaknesses

Step 2: Analyze responses using histogram

Step 3: Form QI team to identify issue (greatest deficiency)

Step 4: Team diagrams teaching of pertinent skills in current curriculum

Step 5: Plan for improvement (course or curriculum modification)

Step 6: Implement recommendations

Step 7: Assess performance of Spring 1992 graduates

Step 8: Standardize changes or modify approach based on findings in Step 7

Figure 4 Quality Improvement in Pharmacy Education

Bachelor in Pharmacy graduates spend the final 20 weeks of their program in supervised externships and clerkships. Each spends a minimum of five weeks in community practice, five weeks in institutional practice, and five weeks with a Samford faculty member in a clinical clerkship. The final five weeks is a selective rotation which may involve any number of practice settings. Several hundred community and hospital pharmacists serve as adjunct faculty and precept these students, closely observing their practice abilities and communication skills.

It was determined that this group of adjunct faculty was the best source of information about the communications competencies of new Samford graduates. A survey was developed by the primary investigator who first called upon the School's Advisory Board to identify those specific communication skills (e.g., "ability to communicate at the patient's knowledge level") which *should* be present in a pharmacist about to enter professional practice. This exercise produced nine patient communication competencies and six professional communication competencies to include in the survey.

The survey was distributed within one month of the end of the spring externship semester to all pharmacists who had served as preceptor that term. Each was asked to identify the number of students supervised and the number of those who demonstrated mastery of the 15 specific communications competencies. The results of the survey are shown in Figures 5 and 6.

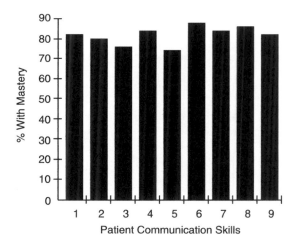

Figure 5 Patient Communication Skills

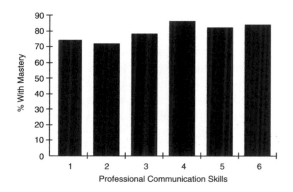

Figure 6 Professional Communication Skills

The results of the survey are now being examined by a small QI team of faculty whose courses include objectives related to the building of communication skills. They will identify the specific skills to be targeted for improvement, diagram how those skills are currently being taught, and plan and implement changes to improve those skills in the 1992 graduates.

The final steps of the process (Steps 7 and 8) include the assessment of the impact of the changes by resurveying the pharmacy preceptors and continuing the process of analyzing mastery of communication skills on an annual basis. Curricular adjustments based on the findings will be managed by the faculty with appropriate course responsibility and the School's Curriculum Committee if more substantial changes appear necessary.

Quality Improvement In the Health Services Industry

This chapter opened by drawing a parallel between the forces introducing QI to the health care industry and higher education. A discussion of the application of QI in health professions schools would not be complete without a small digression which will serve to demonstrate how these principles are being embraced by at least some corporate providers of health care. Some comments relative to the implications of these corporate initiatives in health professions' education will serve to close this chapter.

Hospital Corporation of America (HCA)

As previously mentioned, Paul B. Batalden, M.D., joined the Hospital Corporation of America management team as Vice President of Medical Care in 1986. This outstanding pediatrician had long championed the cause of systematic process improvement in health care as a quality assurance mechanism.

Mary Walton (1990) includes HCA in her book, *Deming Management at Work*, which profiles six companies that are using Deming's principles. "Crisis" was the appropriate word to use in describing health care and hospital funding when HCA turned to this radical new approach to managing quality and productivity. HCA's chief executive hired Dr. Batalden, who agreed to first introduce TQM on a pilot basis in a small number of hospitals.

In the HCA case, according to the Walton review, the CEO, Tom Frist, and his new quality advisor did not initially agree on some of the underlying theories of quality management "Deming-style." However, increased productivity and profitability of quality managed units, in contrast to the traditionally-managed HCA hospitals, helped make Tom Frist a believer.

Readers are referred to this reference for a more in-depth and fascinating discussion of exactly how HCA is applying Deming's principles to the management of such complex organizations as modern hospitals and to the improvement of patient care. At this writing, TQM is spreading throughout this multi-hospital chain. As it spreads, doctors, nurses, pharmacists, orderlies, business managers, and health care employees of every variety are becoming involved in its implementation. The implications for health professions education become more obvious.

"Quality in Healthcare Management"

Another indication of the emerging interest in TQM among providers and managers of health care is the introduction of a new publication entitled "Wellcome Focus on Quality in Healthcare Management" (1991). It is edited by the chairperson of the Department of Quality Improvement at Group Health, Inc. in Minneapolis, MN and is distributed as a free service by Burroughs Wellcome Co.

The first issue of the publication includes two well-written articles on implementation of TQM in healthcare organizations. The first is a theoretical guide to the process of transforming an organization through the application of the TQM principles. A step-by-step approach is outlined. The second article is a case study of a health maintenance organization, Group Health Northwest, which is using the Juran process to introduce continuous quality improvement to the corporation.

The Walton chapter and these articles, in addition to several other pieces which have appeared recently in the literature, document the growing interest in a new approach to managing quality in health care delivery. Certainly the promise of higher productivity and lower cost could be "just what the doctor ordered" to bring some rationality back to America's expenditures for medical care.

Conclusion

Where does a health professions school like the School of Pharmacy go now in its efforts to become a "total quality" institution? There are several answers to the question. First and foremost, the upper management must remain committed to the implementation of TQM throughout the academic and administrative activities of the school. This must include a continued emphasis on training of all faculty, staff, and administrators such that everyone in the school begins to approach their daily worklife with the attitude of continuously improving what they do.

Such training could be internalized by demonstrating, with trained facilitators and coaches, how committee activities can be conducted using QI principles. Several examples of QI activities at the committee level were included in this chapter—the advising quality project for the Student Affairs Committee and the interview assessment for the Admissions Committee. Much of the Curriculum Committee's work would be enhanced by the direct application of QI tools.

A question which has not been addressed by the School of Pharmacy is the extent to which students should be educated about the application of TQM in the industry they are about to enter. It would seem logical that HCA and other corporations committed to continuous quality improvement would be interested in hiring health professionals already exposed through formal training to TQM. Elective classes in TQM could be conducted, either in the school or as a general university elective. The principles could also be introduced in management courses that are currently required in both the B.S. and Pharm.D. curricula.

It is a happy coincidence that health professions schools and the providers that they have educated are learning of and implementing TQM at this same point in history. It can be taken as a good omen, perhaps, for the future viability of both. Management of the crises that confront education and health care today will require significantly more advanced administrative skills than either industry has employed in the past.

But perhaps that is why we are at this point. Educators are taught to teach; health care providers to diagnose and treat disease. Neither have historically emphasized good management practices. There is no better time than the present to change that. Continuous Quality Improvement offers the tools to help.

References

American Association of Colleges of Pharmacy (1988). Grant Awards for Pharmacy Schools (GAPS).

Walton, M. *Deming Management at Work.* New York: G. P. Putnam's Sons, 1990.

Wheeler, J. W. *Wellcome Focus on Quality in Healthcare Management* Vol. 1, no. 1, 1991.

Lucinda Maine, formerly Associate Dean of Students at the Samford University School of Pharmacy, is now Senior Director at the American Pharmaceutical Association in Washington, D.C.

Appendix A

Managing for Improved Quality in Higher Education
Robert I. Ingalls Hall
November 11, 1989

8:15 A.M.	Welcome/Conference Introduction	Dr. Burelle
8:30 A.M.	Is There a Better Way to Manage Higher Education	Dr. Sherr
10:00 A.M.	Break	
10:15 A.M.	Key Organizational Issues That Affect the Pursuit and Assessment of Quality	Dr. Chaffee
11:15 A.M.	Managing Quality in Academic Programs	Dr. Seymour
12:15 P.M.	Lunch	
1:30 P.M.	The Relationship Between Assessment and Quality Improvement	Dr. Banta Mr. Fisher
2:45 P.M.	The Delaware County Experience: This is What Works for Us	Dr. Decosmo
3:30 P.M.	Break	
3:45 P.M.	Panel Discussion with Audience	Dr. Harris
5:00 P.M.	Summary and Conclusions	Dr. Hull
5:15 P.M.	Adjournment	
6:30 P.M.	Banquet - Flag Colonnade Dining Room -Welcome/Introduction of Speakers	Dr. Corts

-Speakers: Dr. Curt Reimann
                  Dr. Charles Karelis
-Reaction for Samford University

Appendix A (con't)

Faculty
Managing for Improved Quality in Higher Education

Dr. Lawrence Sherr
Chancellor's Club
Teaching Professor
School of Business
University of Kansas

Dr. Ellen Chaffee
Associate Commissioner for
Academic Affairs
North Dakota State Board of
Higher Education

Dr. Daniel Seymour
Visiting Scholar
Higher Education Research Institute
University of California at
Los Angeles

Dr. Trudy Banta
Director
Assessment Resource Center
University of Tennessee

Mr. Homer S. Fisher
Senior Vice President
University of Tennessee

Dr. Richard Decosmo
President
Delaware County Community College

Dr. Curt Reimann
National Institute of Technology and Standards
Department of Commerce
Associate Director for Quality Program
Malcolm Baldrige National Quality Award

Dr. Charles Karelis
Director
Fund for Improvement of Post
Secondary Education
U. S. Department of Education

Dr. Timothy N. Burelle
Professor and Dean
Samford University
School of Pharmacy

Dr. John Harris
Assistant to Provost
Samford University

Dr. William Hull
Provost
Samford University

Dr. Thomas Corts
President
Samford University

Appendix B

Advising Feedback
Survey Response

1. Overall I think the changes in the advising system have been positive.

SA	A	NO	D	SD
8	33	12	15	4

2. The process of registering for classes has been improved with the new advising system.

SA	A	NO	D	SD
18	43	2	8	2

3. When I had a concern about academic issues it was easier to discuss with:

A	B	C	D
41	18	12	0

4. When I had a personal problem for which I wished to seek advice I could seek it with:

A	B	C	D
33	12	16	11

5. When I had a question about completion of prepharmacy courses I sought advice from:

A	B	C	D
36	14	18	4

6. When I had a question about careers in pharmacy I sought advice from:

A	B	C	D
14	13	23	16

Questions 1 & 2
SA = Strongly Agree
A = Agree
NO = No opinion
D = Disagree
SD = Strongly disagree

Questions 3 - 6
A = My individual advisor
B = My class advisor
C = Others
D = No one

Chapter 17

The Quality Quest in Academia

William E. Hull
Samford University
Birmingham, Alabama

A handful of colleges and universities have embarked upon the quest for a new corporate culture characterized preeminently by a commitment to quality. In so doing, they are consciously aligning themselves with a movement whose methodology is often described as the Quality Improvement Process. As an organized discipline, the QIP approach first surfaced in the Japanese business world at mid-century under the leadership of W. Edwards Deming.[1] Since then it has spread to this country and been adapted to an increasingly wide variety of settings. My university intends to build upon the application of this system to the non-profit service sector because we believe that its contribution is consistent with our mission, expressive of our values, and relevant to the needs of our constituency.

Part I: The Quality Mood

My task is to explore QIP's potential for achieving academic quality. In Part I, I shall first identify its basic presuppositions, then isolate what is generic in those principles for any field of human endeavor, and finally apply these emphases to our task as educators. I shall limit my explorations to the relevance of QIP for academics, leaving for Part II a closer analysis of its method as applied to the educational endeavor. We may begin by reflecting on the three words "Quality Improvement Process" which suggest that the dominant spirit of this approach is (1) competitive, (2) creative, and (3) collaborative.

A. Quality

After World War II, Japanese industry found itself in shambles, its products widely regarded as inferior "junk." But in 1950, Ichiro Ishikawa arranged for the American statistician W. E. Deming to lecture on quality control to the top 45 industrialists in Japan, and a revolution was launched that, in one generation, carried their goods to the pinnacle of worldwide acceptance. At first, not even the Japanese believed that Deming's radical proposals would work, but they had nothing to lose by doing what they were told — and the rest is history. The same kind of turnaround did not occur in the United States until our business elite realized, in the late seventies and early eighties, that America was being hopelessly outclassed by its Pacific Rim competitors. QIP is animated by a survival imperative. Nothing short of that urgency will motivate human nature to meet its rigorous demands.

The first key to the success of the Deming method lies in its extraordinary emphasis on the achievement of "quality." The concept is universal in scope and, therefore, in application. Anything can have quality, whether it be automobiles or apple pie, sermons or survey courses. Further, quality is inexhaustible: no matter how much quality I achieve, it is never at the expense of the quality available to others. We can all pursue quality to the limit of our abilities. We do not compete against one another in a win/lose fashion but against what golfers call "par," i.e., against an extrinsic norm where we are all equal. Quality is not something which I can capture and compel to serve me, but is something which I am compelled to serve that challenges me to the depths of my being.

The limitless character of quality must claim our total commitment. QIP has such an intense focus on quality, it produces a transforming effect on corporate culture. Dedication to quality must pervade every level of organization, from the CEO to part-time hourly workers. Nor are there any limits to this open-ended quest. As David Kearns of the Xerox Corporation put it, "In the race for quality, there is no finish line."[2] Lurking in QIP testimonials is the evangelical paradigm where those who embrace the movement experience something akin to a "conversion." To borrow categories made famous by William James,[3] the quality quest is for the "twice-born" rather than for the "once-born," whether they be executives, entrepreneurs, or educators.

Which brings us to the academic arena. Deming's manifesto of the QIP movement is entitled *Out of the Crisis* because he is convinced that most businesses are in a competitive race which they are bound to lose unless their whole way of doing things is radically altered. But is American higher education in general, and Samford University in particular, in a similar crisis of survival? Such alarmist rhetoric is distasteful to the traditional academic mind. "Truth is not something for which one competes," goes the reply, "but is sought for its own sake. The desire to know, which is inherent in human nature, guarantees that young men and women will always seek out institutions of higher learning for study, and will do so in ever greater numbers as they are increasingly able to afford the cost. Which explains why the educational establishment has never been larger, wealthier, or more influential in American life."

Over against that widespread mood of complacency, which is fatal to the success of any quality quest, we must set the rising tempo of reform proposals associated with critics as different as William Bennett, Allan Bloom, Ernest Boyer, Dinesh D'Souza, Chester Finn, E. D. Hirsch, Roger Kimball, John Silber, Page Smith, and Charles Sykes.[4] It is relatively easy to dismiss some of these devastating critiques as manifestations of a political pendulum swing to the New Right, but, even after due allowance has been made for ideological gamesmanship, this facile explanation fails to cover all of the evidence. Our own measures of achievement by standardized test scores *do* continue to sag. There *is* a massive loss of confidence by business leaders in the ability of the educational establishment to produce a competitive work force. Parents and politicians alike *are* beginning to revolt against an escalation of tuition costs that far exceeds the value added to the curriculum. The Japanese and others *have* outpaced us in the academic achievements of their graduates.

It is extremely important to monitor the emotional tone in which we respond to this crisis of credibility. It is so easy to become defensive, especially in a ponderous academic jargon that only obfuscates the issues. It is equally easy to become defeatist, complaining that education has no business being drawn out onto a competitive playing field. I suggest that a better response is to summon a healthy sense of urgency, mobilizing our intellectual, moral and spiritual energies in a crusade to lift the quality of our academic enterprise to a level worthy of the challenges of a new millennium. If that rhetoric sounds a bit inspirational, even "evangelical," I can only say that you have heard me correctly. The posture of detached, bemused indifference long preferred by many academicians is no longer adequate to the survival imperatives of our time!

Academic life in America today exists in a world with too many schools and too few students, too many fixed costs and too few discretionary dollars, too many competitors and too few supporters. In such a world, survival *does* belong to the fittest, which will be those institutions imbued with a passion for quality that extends to every member of the community, faculty included. Some may prefer a more sedate, less demanding academic lifestyle, but this will no longer fill our classrooms, build our buildings, and pay our salaries. Accepting a quality quest means, first and foremost, a willingness — yea, an eagerness! — to be truly competitive in the educational arena.

B. *Improvement*

To pursue the evangelical paradigm further, Deming is unsparing in his judgment of the organizational status quo. A paraphrase of his indictment of the traditional business culture might read, "For all have sinned and fallen short of the quality that they could have achieved" (cf. Romans 3:23). To this crusty prophet of a new order, the standard way of doing things is not just wrong, it is wrong-headed! His famous Fourteen Points are not improvements, or even modifications, but in most cases are contradictions of the received wisdom. What Deming is calling for is *metanoia*, a repentance that results in a whole new mind-set, an about-face that permits movement in a totally new direction, a root-and-branch reform that leaves nothing the same ever again. Talk to those who take QIP seriously and you will find them convinced that they are participating in nothing less than a revolution of rising expectations.

Just as Jesus announced the coming Kingdom of God before asking his followers to repent (e.g., Mark 1:15), so the quality quest asks its adherents to reinvent the future, to envision a better way of doing things, to imagine what their institution might become before they abandon what it has always been. Such catalytic thinking is based on the faith that there really will be a future and that it really can be better than the past. This approach shifts the whole incentive structure from the privilege of living off the accumulated capital of the past to the opportunity of participating in breakthroughs that will produce something new. The impelling force that drives the institution forward is no longer based on the claim, "Look how long we have been doing it this way" but on the claim, "It doth not yet appear what we shall be." (cf. I John 3:2)

Central to that middle word "improvement" in the QIP formula is a profound understanding of the potentialities of the creative act. Creativity may be defined as the capacity to originate, to bring into being something new, to give expression to that which did not exist before. As Doris Grumbach has described it: "Creativity is the synapse between what is known and common and accepted, and what is unknown until now, uncommon and unexpected. It is the leap between the surmise and the conviction, the conjecture and the inevitable. It is the guess made certain."[5] Creativity is not cleverness that merely manipulates the familiar in order to give an illusion of originality, nor is it novelty masquerading as newness. It is participation in that ongoing genesis by which the darkness becomes light, the chaos becomes order, and the void becomes spirit (cf. Genesis 1:1-3).

Academics may have more difficulty accepting QIP's creative aspect, as opposed to its competitive aspect. Many educators see the nature of their task as drawing out of the past those riches accumulated through centuries of ceaseless study. Until an idea or discovery stands "the test of time" it is deemed unworthy of mention. A great deal is made of *"critical* thinking" by which we learn to evaluate "objective" evidence, but little attention is given to *"creative* thinking" by which we develop the capacity for intuition and liberate the imagination to explore the frontiers of the not-yet-known. We are forever talking about "what *is*" rather than about "what *if*." Not many teachers embrace the credo attributed to Robert Kennedy by his brother, Edward: "Some men see things as they are and say, `Why?' I dream things that never were and say, `Why not?'"[6]

What is the role of teachers who imbue in their students the possibility of continuous improvement for a lifetime? It is to deepen the discontent between things as they are and as they ought to be, planting seeds of permanent dissatisfaction with the status quo. To struggle against the vestiges of chaos that distort the original design of creation, fracture its intended unity, and frustrate its highest potential. To search for new symbols adequate to express reality as it is being reshaped by the onrushing future. Rollo May well described creative teachers at work on the never-ending task of naming the not-yet: "They do not run away from non-being, but by encountering and wrestling with it, force it to produce being. They knock on silence for an answering music; they pursue meaninglessness until they can force it to mean."[7] In so doing, they teach their students to live out of the future just as surely as they teach them to live out of the past.

Most crucial of all, and most difficult to implement, is the claim which QIP lays on our courage to become catalysts of change: the courage to look at reality through the bifocals of the now-but-not-yet, the courage to rage against the forces of disintegration that would return the ordered universe to its primeval chaos, the courage to speak and live "as if" the future were already becoming present, the courage to challenge the tyranny of a positivism that leaves no room for serendipity or surprise. Such courage is not an easy confidence that "some day everything will work out fine." It is not the absence of doubt and despair but the capacity to commit oneself to act in spite of doubt and despair. As James Lord said of the artist Giacometti, creative teachers are forever "tormented by the hopeless dichotomy of their ideals yet condemned by that helplessness to struggle as long as they live to try to overcome it."[8]

C. Process

The strong element of futurity in QIP produces a creative tension between the "now" and the "not yet" which is one source of its internal dynamic. Deming proposes to bridge this catalytic gap with a clearly defined set of activities which he calls "process." Because he operated primarily in the industrial arena, we may most readily grasp his point about process by considering the assembly line. Standard operating procedure had long called for mass inspections of the final product to ferret out defective merchandise which would need to be reworked. No, said Deming, don't spend time and effort on endless checking; instead, redirect that energy to studying every step in the manufacturing continuum which produced those goods in the first place. If the system itself is continuously improved, the results will take care of themselves. Quality is maintained, not by the costly policy of redoing or discarding mistakes, but by carefully training every participant in the process to avoid mistakes.

Behind this deceptively simple shift in focus lay an even deeper indictment by Deming of prevailing managerial styles. Basically two approaches were in vogue: (1) "Strategic planning," which tended to emphasize the beginning of the process, a fresh start to "get something going," the launching of bold new initiatives to carry out a grand design. (2) "Management by objectives (MBO)," which tended to emphasize the end of the process, "judgment day" when everything is evaluated in terms of final results. No, Deming insisted, focus not on a point, whether it be the alpha-point or the omega-point, but focus instead on the total process. Forget the desire to make a big splash with some grandiose plan which will soon lose momentum because no thought has been given to sustaining it with constancy of purpose. Forget quotas and numerical goals buttressed by slogans on posters that put all of the blame on the workers for failures that may be the fault of management for not adequately strengthening the system itself. In short, don't be primarily proactive (strategic planning) or reactive (MBO) but interactive (QIP).

Process, at its deeper level, is about collaboration, about teamwork, about partnership. Its underlying interdependence is neatly captured by the Greek preposition *sun*, meaning "with" or "together." To select but three illustrations of this etymology: (1) Process is symbiotic, meaning that we live (*bios*) together (*sun*) in an interlocking unity despite our enormous diversity. (2) Process is synergistic, meaning that we work (*ergon*) together (*sun*), combining dissimilar contributions in a concerted effort that increases the effectiveness of each component. (3) Process results in synthesis, meaning that we put (*tithemi*) together (*sun*) disparate elements in such a way that they form "one coherent or consistent complex." Process means that quality is developmental rather than transactional, that it seeks reciprocity rather than autonomy, that it flourishes best in solidarity rather than in isolation. Quality is constructed out of a passionate incrementalism that seeks a consensus empowering all who participate.

The implications of this philosophy for academicians are enormous. How many times have we "reworked" our student failures simply by insisting that the student repeat the course — when the way the course was taught may have been the problem in the first place? How often have administrators, desiring a place in the sun, concocted some clever new program, secured a one or two year grant to get it launched, and then moved on to something else, leaving their offspring to "sink or swim" without further support? How frequently have we concentrated only on how many applicants we admitted rather than on whether we admitted the right ones? Or on how many students we taught rather than on whether they learned the right things? Or on how many graduates we placed rather than on whether they know how to do a better job? We have paid far more attention to surface statistics which count results than to the ways in which learning actually takes place throughout one's educational pilgrimage.

Obviously QIP speaks profoundly to the central issue of disciplinary specialization. For a full century now the dominant dynamic in higher education has been the proliferation of disciplines, with a corresponding increase in the number of departments sponsoring each specialty. While this lush growth of the curriculum has greatly expanded our fund of knowledge, it has also left faculty completely mystified about what many of their colleagues teach and has left students with a deep sense of fragmentation at the heart of their learning experience. This is why calls are now coming with increased urgency to restore structure, integrity, and coherence to the curriculum. As Ernest Boyer has so eloquently argued, the great need of our day is to search for "connections" that knit up the seamless robe of truth.[9]

The emphasis on process also defines both faculty teaching and student learning primarily in terms of teamwork rather than individual achievement. Most faculty approach professional development in light of their personal needs, desiring to be evaluated for promotion, tenure, and other forms of advancement only on the basis of personal performance. But QIP would stress the importance of working well in groups and would suggest that a professor can hardly succeed individually if his or her department fails collectively. A shift from competition to cooperation among faculty would, hopefully, model a similar shift among students in their quest for recognition and reward. Traditionally students have been taught to work in isolation against their classmates for the best grades, being severely penalized for attempting any form of collaborative learning, as if this were cheating. Not only is such an approach to problem solving almost unknown in the work place, increasing evidence suggests that it is also pedagogically unsound. One of the clearest findings of the Harvard Assessment Seminars is that learning in small groups is much more effective than learning alone.[10]

Part II: The Quality Method

The quality movement is both a mood and a method. First the mood must become both intensive and pervasive if there is to be a culture change so fundamental that a scientist might call it a "paradigm shift"[11] and a saint might call it a "conversion." It requires a radical revolution in the corporate mindset to support a reform movement with a futuristic (i.e., post-modern) agenda which seeks nothing less than the holistic integration of reality through a shift from ideology to praxis, from authority to service, and from competition to cooperation.[12]

In Part I above, I sought to suggest the relevance of the Quality Improvement Process for the spirit in which we approach the challenge of higher education. Now I want to discuss how the method developed by Dr. Deming might be applied to our academic task. The heart of the QIP technique is called Statistical

Process Control (SPC)[13] and its primary purpose is to achieve consistency at every stage of production. Quality is synonymous with product reliability, and product reliability is the result of systemic dependability, and systemic dependability is sustained by maintaining a high degree of planned predictability as to how the process will function. Building a bedrock for such stability is the task of management, whose preeminent challenge is to create constancy of purpose and infuse it throughout the organization. A key function of SPC is to identify and reduce variation in the system. That is, an entire process should be monitored so carefully that the workers themselves will immediately spot those atypical fluctuations which suggest that some part of the system is out of control. An essential characteristic of quality is conformity to expectations, what the prophet Amos called being judged by a plumb line that does not deceive (Amos 7:7-9).

Before he became a guru and an icon, W. E. Deming was a mathematical physicist and an industrial statistician. While there is no opportunity here to expound the techniques which he used to analyze problems, let me identify the Seven Tools which must be mastered to practice SPC[14]: (1) Flowcharts that diagram the systemic nature of some activity by tracing the path of a key process in its various relationships. (2) Pareto charts that display the frequency of causes so as to indicate their relative importance. (3) Cause-and-effect ("fishbone") diagrams that delineate causes in relation to their effect on outcomes. (4) Scatter plots that identify how one variable affects another, such as in a relation of cause and effect. (5) Run charts that trace selected trends within a defined period, thereby suggesting the changing value of a variable over time. (6) Histograms that measure the extent of variation in a process so as to locate patterns in random occurrences. (7) Control charts that plot variation in a process so as to distinguish special causes from systemic causes.

Although SPC has been utilized as a management tool in the administration of higher education, and has been taught in a few schools as a discipline for use in the business world, very little has been done thus far in adapting it as a guide to the way in which our academic work is done.[15] Here I would like to encourage such experimentation by examining the importance which the Deming Method attributes to criteria, to contributors, and to clients. I should warn you that there is a reductionism in the tripartite structure of my analysis. Deming himself sought to summarize his operational principles in Fourteen Points[16], and it is always dangerous to single out only three of them for emphasis. But we must remember that Deming was offering a list of correctives for industrial management, whereas we are concerned here with those aspects of his method which are most applicable to higher education, hence my selectivity.

A. Criteria

At first it may seem that SPC is only a preliminary technical procedure to be carried out by a handful of specialists before the real work of leadership begins, but we quickly learn that it is closely linked to the pervasive concern of the QIP philosophy for reliable criteria. There are two primary reasons why Deming insists on this complicated approach. First and foremost is his desire to banish fear from the climate of the workplace. A common practice in hierarchical organizations is for persons in authority to use their power coercively to blame subordinates for performance failures. This judgmentalism succeeds only in creating insecurity, anxiety, powerlessness, and hostility, which in turn increases stress, reduces motivation, damages relationships, and threatens health. The only way to overcome the resulting fear is to demonstrate conclusively that results will be evaluated by using the most objective data available in order to analyze the workings of the system rather than to expose the shortcomings of individuals. Once workers see that everyone is trying to improve the process rather than trying to find a convenient scapegoat, they become much more open and helpful in contributing to a solution.

Campus lore abounds with stories of presidents who tyrannize deans, of deans who tyrannize faculty, and of faculty who tyrannize students! The promotion and tenure system as applied to faculty, and the grading system as applied to students, have traditionally aroused fear because they tend to judge individual performance without evaluating the adequacy of the support systems that produce such results. When a professor fails to teach creatively or to publish regularly, do we simply withhold recognition or do we carefully analyze the faculty development process to determine whether it offers specific opportunities for continuous training to help overcome these deficiencies? When students do poorly in a course, do we simply pass out D's and F's or do we, together with the students, examine needed prerequisites, syllabi materials, teaching approaches, tutorial options, and testing methods to see if the pedagogical process might have been deficient? To the chagrin of academic traditionalists, Deming is an implacable foe of numerical quotas (e.g., the use of a grading "curve" to determine the distribution of rewards), of mass inspections (e.g., final examinations designed to weed out the unfit), of performance reviews (e.g., basing rank on individual achievement without regard to effective teamwork), and of periodic layoffs (e.g., "up-or-out" tenure policies) — and he takes all of these heretical positions in the name of quality!

A second reason for concentrating on objective statistical data is the enormous capacity of any organization for self-deception. When something goes wrong, there is a tendency to camouflage the problem by talking in vague generalities or in ponderous jargon, by becoming selective in reporting results so as to please a supervisor, by concentrating only on an assigned area of responsibility when the problem is one of coordination between separate areas, or by looking inward at how well the status quo is being maintained rather than outward at the new demands of the marketplace.

What Deming is trying to do with his data-driven approach is to force organizations to face all of the facts, in all of their relatedness, in a form that resists subjective manipulation. He wants them to spot trends that still lie beneath the surface of accepted perceptions and to assign these emerging patterns a priority based on their intrinsic significance. He teaches them to translate reality into numbers, the most neutral symbols available, so that even the most adverse developments can be evaluated rationally rather than shooting the messenger who delivers bad tidings.

Academic life in this century has been dominated by three "A-words." The first was Accreditation, which measured quality in terms of inputs such as faculty degrees, academic budgets, and campus facilities in order to determine legitimacy. Then came Assessment, which shifted the focus on quality from inputs to outcomes in measuring the extent to which educational programs produce intended results. Both of these emphases now support the call for Accountability, which demands that the total educational process, from beginning to end, be responsive to the needs of its users. It is no longer enough for schools to determine their quality by comparing themselves to themselves (i.e., how much better we are now than we were ten years ago), or by comparing themselves to each other (i.e., how much better we are than our rivals). Society is insisting that we now estimate quality by comparing our measured achievements to the magnitude of the challenge facing our world in the twenty-first century. Furthermore, it is convinced that many schools have buried their heads in the sand, that they have unintentionally squandered resources by allocating them to outdated priorities, and that they need a strong dose of realism infused into an inbred academic mindset. The way Deming uses hard data to awaken complacent manufacturers to their competitive peril is exactly what many of our most thoughtful critics want to happen in higher education today!

B. Contributors

One of the important ways suggested by Deming for controlling quality is to adopt a radically new relation to suppliers. Instead of awarding business to the lowest bidder in a highly competitive arm's-length relationship with vendors, Deming insists that quality is promoted by fostering collaborative relationships of loyalty and trust with a few suppliers who consistently provide items statistically proven to meet desired specifications. Multiple sourcing leads to short-term, expedient, unpredictable results while single sourcing encourages long-term investments in quality needed to develop dependable goods and services. Commitments both by the producer and by the purchaser sufficient to ensure such a partnership are worth the price, according to Deming, because the quality of a final product is never better than the quality of the components that went into its manufacture.

In practice, what this means is that quality is not self-contained but is profoundly interdependent. It cannot be achieved in isolation, no matter how large the operation may be. "Others have labored" and we enter into their labor (John 4:38) — for good or for bad! That is why quality companies such as Ford, 3M, and Xerox are going to such great lengths to identify trustworthy suppliers of every component needed to produce their products. This involves the development of elaborate vendor manuals specifying the quality standards which must be met. It requires a new breed of purchasing agents skilled in measuring value rather than in calculating price. It includes extensive training sessions for suppliers so that they will know exactly how their goods and services fit into the total process. It climaxes with highly visible celebrations emphasizing the indispensable contribution of key suppliers to the achievement of quality in the finished product.

The applicability of this assumption to higher education is immediately apparent. Nothing shapes the character of the academic process more than the makeup of the faculty. And yet we do precious little to collaborate creatively with those who preside over the graduate programs that supply us with potential faculty. At the moment, our university is working on a new general education curriculum that is a beauty to behold. It seeks to integrate the essential knowledge needed by undergraduate students in ways that are not even being attempted in most core curricula. It seeks to relate Christianity to all aspects of the learning process, something that the great host of tax-supported institutions are forbidden even to attempt. Thus, we are developing a distinctive academic product, expressive of our distinctive institutional purpose, found in no more than a few hundred of the 3500 colleges and universities in America.

This means that we need an equally distinctive faculty of 250 drawn from the 350,000 teaching in higher education. We know a good bit about the kinds of goals we want our students to be pursuing; the personal and social agendas about which we want them to be concerned; the attitudes, values, and commitments which we want them to bring to their studies; and the kinds of competencies which we want them to develop in order to derive maximum benefit from our course of study. But what we do not know is whether the present suppliers of our future faculty are equipped to teach this kind of curriculum with effectiveness. The reason we do not know this is because we are not in a meaningful dialogue with those who are determining what the professorate of tomorrow will be like.

C. Clients

Central to the QIP methodology is the insistence that every process designed to produce quality must recognize the critical importance both of the suppliers with which it begins and of the customers with which it ends.

Within these external limits, all internal work is also done as links in an endless supplier-customer chain. Such marketplace vocabulary is offensive to some educators because it suggests that professors somehow "sell" their knowledge to students for the "price" of tuition. Deming would reply that every service activity is a transaction between the server and the served in which there is an exchange of value whether it can be measured in dollars or not. Not only must the consumers of such services feel that their needs are being met, they must also perceive that the value of the services rendered is commensurate with the investment required in time, energy, and money.

Clearly, schools do not exist as ends in themselves but for the benefit of those whom they serve. The beneficiaries of this contribution may be called "customers" or "clients" or "constituency," but it must never be forgotten that, in our voluntaristic system of higher education, an institution either satisfies the expectations of its various clienteles or it loses them to others. Deming is keenly aware that organizations can get so large or so successful or so prestigious that they become complacent about the needs of those whom they seek to serve. After all, who should be telling General Motors how to build cars, or the Swiss how to make watches, or the Harvard faculty how to teach courses? Answer: their customers! — as all of these venerable dynasties have recently learned to their dismay.

Since Deming finds customers everywhere, it is especially important for colleges and universities to decide just who they are really trying to serve. In the for-profit sector this question is not as difficult, since customers are usually the purchasers of a product at a defined price. But in the non-profit sector the question of constituency is complicated by the crucial role of volunteers who contribute time and money to the enterprise.[17] It is clear that Samford serves students, which is why we call our QIP emphasis the Student First Quality Quest (SFQQ). But we also serve their parents, who pay many of the bills. We serve their potential employers, as well as the professional and governmental agencies that expect us to certify their credentials. More broadly, we serve the churches of the Baptist denomination that control and support our enterprise. In a general sense we serve the city of Birmingham, the state of Alabama, and the ever-expanding region beyond that looks to us for a steady stream of intelligent, capable citizens.

Amid these many claims, how shall we sort our priorities regarding our primary audience? I suggest that two historic paradigm shifts define three stages in our understanding of this important issue. (1) The pre-modern position was that an institution exists for those authorities whose expertise qualifies them to make the best use of its resources. Thus colleges exist for faculty, as hospitals exist for doctors and churches exist for clergy. (2) The modern position, created by the democratic inversion of the power pyramid, is that an institution exists for those individuals in greatest need of its services. Thus colleges exist for students, as hospitals exist for patients and churches exist for members. (3) But now a post-modern position is emerging, according to which an institution exists for the organic whole of which it is a part. Thus colleges exist for those who will benefit from the lifetime contributions of their graduates, just as hospitals exist for those health care providers who seek wellness in society, and churches exist for those parishes who depend upon them to combat the forces of evil.

I am not prepared to choose among these three ideas of elitism, individualism, and organicism as if they were mutually exclusive. There is a sense in which those who have dedicated themselves to a lifetime of intellectual leadership in higher education, often at great sacrifice, deserve to receive rich fulfillment for their efforts. There is another sense in which students who choose to invest four of the most pivotal years of their life in a particular school, also at great sacrifice, deserve to receive the kind of preparation which will enable them to maximize every opportunity that comes their way. But there is yet a third sense in which Derek Bok is right in his contention that higher education must learn to fulfill its public stewardship by contributing to the common good.[13] Therefore, I suggest that we define our customers in a dialogue about academic responsibility in which all three of these claimants have equal say.

At the moment, the Deming Method seems to favor the student as the prime customer of schools, but a closer look at the exchange of value in the learning transaction suggests a better balance. To be sure, current tuition is critical to cash flow and eventually to institutional survival, thus we must satisfy that source of value received. But the faculty and administration who conduct the instructional program bring to their task a lifetime of learning which cannot be purchased in full by a tuition-supported salary. Unlike energy, knowledge is not consumed but is rather compounded by time; thus we pay for a year of work but get 40 years of accumulated wisdom—and that surplus is as valuable as all of the tuition dollars which students pay. It buys an educator the right to a meaningful payoff from the learning process. Finally, remember that, even at the dollar level, approximately half the cost of a college education is borne by the wider public in the form of endowment earnings, current gifts from donors, allocations from the denomination, awards from foundations, as well as a variety of governmental grants and loans. In one sense, "private" colleges and universities are more dependent on the wider public than are tax-supported institutions!

In highlighting a few of the main features of the Deming Method, I hope I have shown that this approach is not just an organizational style or a management tool but is also a philosophy of life. There is a totalism about QIP which rebuffs any efforts to utilize it half-heartedly or in piecemeal fashion. Ultimately, this approach insists that what students learn in the classroom be reinforced by the way in which they see the university being operated. If, as Dr. Deming would say, we can get the administrative and the academic processes in alignment, then we will have enhanced the learning environment in ways that more effectively prepare our students for the challenges of life.

Endnotes

1. The story has been told many times. For recent examples in a popular style see Mary Walton, *The Deming Management Method* (New York: Putnam, 1986); *Deming Management at Work* (New York: Putnam, 1990); Andrea Gabor, *The Man Who Discovered Quality* (New York: Times Books, 1990); Rafael Aguayo, *Dr. Deming: The American Who Taught the Japanese About Quality*, (New York: Lyle Stuart, 1990).

2. Cited in "Quotable Quotes," *The Reader's Digest*, May, 1990, p. 152.

3. William James, *The Varieties of Religious Experience* (New York: Modern Library, 1902), pp. 78-82, 163-168, 477-478, note 1.

4. Representative literature includes: "A Nation at Risk: The Imperative for Educational Reform," *The Chronicle of Higher Education*, May 4, 1983, pp. 11-16; Allan Bloom, *The Closing of the American Mind* (New York: Simon and Schuster, 1987); Ernest Boyer, *College: The Undergraduate Experience in America* (New York: Harper & Row, 1987); Dinesh D'Souza, *Illiberal Education* (New York: Free Press, 1991); Chester E. Finn, Jr., "A Nation Still at Risk," *Commentary*, May, 1989, pp. 17-23; E. D. Hirsch, Jr., *Cultural Literacy* (Boston: Houghton Mifflin, 1987); Roger Kimball, *Tenured Radicals* (New York: Harper & Row, 1990); Page Smith, *Killing the Spirit* (New York: Viking, 1990); Charles J. Sykes, *ProfScam* (Washington: Regnery Gateway, 1988).

5. Doris Grumbach, "Creativity: Flights of Fancy and Leaps of Faith," *The Chronicle of Higher Education*, September 17, 1979, p. 64.

6. Adapted from George Bernard Shaw, *Back to Methuselah*, Act I, in *Bernard Shaw Complete Plays with Prefaces* (New York: Dodd, Mead, 1962), vol. II, p. 7, and spoken by Edward M. Kennedy at the funeral service for Robert F. Kennedy in St. Patrick's Cathedral, New York City, June 8, 1968.

7. Rollo May, *The Courage to Create* (New York: W. W. Norton, 1975), p. 93.

8. Adapted from James Lord, *A Giacometti Portrait*, p. 38, cited by May, *op. cit.*, pp. 83-84.

9. Ernest L. Boyer, "Making the Connections: The Search for Our Common Humanity," *Rethinking the Curriculum*, edited by Mary E. Clark and Sandra A. Wawrytko (New York: Greenwood Press, 1990), pp. 13-21.

10. Richard J. Light, *The Harvard Assessment Seminars: First Report, 1990* (Cambridge: Harvard University, 1990), pp. 70-79.

11. On the meaning of paradigm shift see Thomas S. Kuhn, *The Structure of Scientific Revolutions*, second edition (Chicago: University of Chicago Press, 1970). For a popular application see Joel Arthur Barker, *Discovering the Future: The Business of Paradigms* (St. Paul: ILI Press, 1989).

12. On this shift in modern culture see Stephen Toulmin, *Cosmopolis: The Hidden Agenda of Modernity* (New York: Free Press, 1990).

13. Kaoru Ishikawa, *Guide to Quality Control* (Tokyo: Asian Productivity Organization, 1982).

14. The seven traditional tools are discussed in all of the literature on Statistical Process Control. For more recent advances, see Shigeru Mizuno, editor, *Management for Quality Improvement: The Seven New QC Tools* (Cambridge: Productivity Press, 1988). The New Seven tools are: (1) relations diagram, (2) affinity diagram, (3) tree diagram, (4) matrix diagram, (5) matrix data-analysis diagram, (6) process decision program chart, and (7) arrow diagram.

15. For a recent progress report on QIP/SPC in higher education see *The Chronicle of Higher Education,* February 6, 1991, pp. A27-28.

16. W. Edwards Deming, *Quality, Productivity, and Competitive Position* (Cambridge: Massachusetts Institute of Technology, Center for Advanced Engineering Study, 1982). Virtually all secondary studies of Deming discuss his Fourteen Points. For representative expositions see William W. Scherkenbach, *The Deming Route to Quality and Productivity* (Washington: CEE Press, 1986); Howard S. Gitlow and Shelly J. Gitlow, *The Deming Guide to Quality and Competitive Position* (Englewood Cliffs, NJ: Prentice-Hall, 1987).

17. Larry W. Kennedy, *Quality Management in the Nonprofit World* (San Francisco: Jossey-Bass, 1991), pp. 21-41.

18. Derek Bok, *Beyond the Ivory Tower: Social Responsibilities of the Modern University* (Cambridge: Harvard University Press, 1982); *Higher Learning* (Cambridge: Harvard University Press, 1986); *Universities and the Future of America* (Durham: Duke University Press, 1990).